W9-BWG-803
Journalism After Snowden
9/26/2017
RNF DISCARDED

JOURNALISM AFTER SNOWDEN

COLUMBIA JOURNALISM REVIEW BOOKS

COLUMBIA JOURNALISM REVIEW BOOKS

For more than fifty years, the *Columbia Journalism Review* has been the gold standard for media criticism, holding the profession to the highest standards and exploring where journalism is headed, for good and for ill.

Columbia Journalism Review Books expands upon this mission, seeking to publish titles that allow for greater depth in exploring key issues confronting journalism, both past and present, and pointing to new ways of thinking about the field's impact and potential.

Drawing on the expertise of the editorial staff at the *Columbia Journalism Review* as well as the Columbia Journalism School, the series of books will seek out innovative voices and reclaim important works, traditions, and standards. In doing this, the series will also incorporate new ways of publishing made available by the Web and e-books.

Second Read: Writers Look Back at Classic Works of Reportage, edited by
James Marcus and the Staff of the *Columbia Journalism Review*

The Story So Far: What We Know About the Business of Digital Journalism,
Bill Grueskin, Ava Seave, and Lucas Graves

The Best Business Writing 2012, edited by Dean Starkman, Martha M. Hamilton,
Ryan Chittum, and Felix Salmon

The Art of Making Magazines: On Being an Editor and Other Views from the Industry,
edited by Victor S. Navasky and Evan Cornog

The Best Business Writing 2013, edited by Dean Starkman, Martha M. Hamilton,
Ryan Chittum, and Felix Salmon

*The Watchdog That Didn't Bark: The Financial Crisis and the Disappearance
of Investigative Journalism*, Dean Starkman

Beyond News: The Future of Journalism, Mitchell Stephens

The New Censorship: Inside the Global Battle for Media Freedom, Joel Simon

The Best Business Writing 2014, edited by Dean Starkman, Martha M. Hamilton,
and Ryan Chittum

Engaged Journalism: Connecting with Digitally Empowered News Audiences, Jake Batsell

The Best Business Writing 2015, edited by Dean Starkman, Martha M. Hamilton,
and Ryan Chittum

JOURNALISM AFTER SNOWDEN

THE FUTURE OF THE FREE PRESS

in the

SURVEILLANCE STATE

EDITED BY
EMILY BELL AND TAYLOR OWEN,
WITH SMITHA KHORANA
AND JENNIFER R. HENRICHSEN

Seymour Public Library
176-178 Genesee Street
Auburn, NY 13021

Columbia University Press
New York

Columbia University Press
Publishers Since 1893
New York   Chichester, West Sussex
cup.columbia.edu

Copyright © 2017 *Columbia Journalism Review*
All rights reserved

Library of Congress Cataloging-in-Publication Data
Names: Bell, Emily, 1965– editor. | Owen, Taylor editor. | Khorana,
Smitha editor. | Henrichsen, Jennifer editor.
Title: Journalism after Snowden : the future of the free press in the
surveillance state / edited by Emily Bell and Taylor Owen,
with Smitha Khorana and Jennifer R. Henrichsen.
Description: New York : Columbia University Press, 2017. | Series: Columbia
journalism review books | Includes bibliographical references and index.
Identifiers: LCCN 2016040217 (print) | LCCN 2016056966 (ebook) |
ISBN 9780231176125 (cloth : alk. paper) | ISBN 9780231176132 (pbk. : alk. paper) |
ISBN 9780231540674 (e-book)
Subjects: LCSH: Freedom of the press—United States—History—21st century. |
Journalism—Political aspects—United States—History—21st century. |
Confidential communications—Press—United States. | Snowden, Edward J.,
1983– | Government and the press—United States. | Electronic surveillance—
Government policy—United States. | Leaks (Disclosure of information)—
United States.
Classification: LCC PN4888.P6 J68 2017 (print) | LCC PN4888.P6 (ebook) |
DDC 070.4/3—dc23
LC record available at https://lccn.loc.gov/2016040217

♾

Columbia University Press books are printed on permanent
and durable acid-free paper.
Printed in the United States of America

COVER DESIGN: Lisa Hamm

CONTENTS

INTRODUCTION

EMILY BELL, TAYLOR OWEN,
AND SMITHA KHORANA

I. THE STORY AND THE SOURCE

1. JOURNALISM AFTER SNOWDEN

ALAN RUSBRIDGER

2. IN DEFENSE OF LEAKS

JILL ABRAMSON

POSTSCRIPT: JOURNALISM AFTER SNOWDEN

JONATHAN ZITTRAIN

291

FOREWORD

LEE C. BOLLINGER

Every society that accepts the principle that government must operate under some degree of legitimacy in the eyes of its citizens faces this difficult question: How should it balance the government's need to conduct its business with privacy, even secrecy, against the public's need to have access to government information in order to exercise, meaningfully and intelligently, its responsibilities of oversight and ultimate sovereignty?

The problem becomes more complex when, in practice and over time, it becomes clear that every government will vastly overuse its powers to operate out of public view and, most worrisome of all, will do its very utmost to hide from its citizens any evidence indicative of its mistakes, errors, or outright misconduct. Meanwhile, there are always some individuals inside the system ready and willing, for good and bad reasons and with good or bad judgment, to act as the conduit of information to those outside. These are the leakers. And, finally, there are those who engage with the leakers, perhaps even persuading them to don that role, who then make their own decisions, again for good and bad motives, about what to publish and what to withhold from publication.

This scene can be observed day after day and poses a host of vexing issues: What degree of secrecy does an effective government really need? What means does it possess to protect itself against unwarranted disclosures? What motivates leakers, and what should be done with them?

What harms to the nation have resulted from leaks? When people or institutions—notably, the press—receive improperly released information, how should they proceed? Consult with the government? Presume that the government will be right in its estimation of the harms that will ensue from publication? Or presume the opposite? What should happen to those who choose to publish the information in the public domain? This list reflects only the beginning of the dilemmas to be faced.

In the United States, the First Amendment has spoken on some of these fundamental issues. In a series of decisions beginning in the mid-1960s and spanning roughly a decade, most significantly in a landmark case involving the Pentagon Papers, the U.S. Supreme Court established a seemingly messy, but highly practical, arrangement. Its essence, oversimplified to be sure, is this: neither the press nor the public has a constitutional right to information in the government's possession; therefore, the government is free to hide what it can. We can be sure that more will be hidden than should be the case. Leakers will also always exist, and some will convey information the public should know about. Whether the disclosure is good or bad from the public's point of view will not matter: leakers are not protected by the First Amendment and can be prosecuted and punished. The press, though, stands as a nearly coequal adversary of the government, and, absent a showing of immense harm to society from publication, it is free to publish with constitutional protection.

This summary of where we are in our constitutional jurisprudence overlooks the many lacunae and ambiguities in the decisions that add a significant measure of uncertainty at every level, which in turn have tangible effects on behavior in real life. But the larger point is that this system of sorts, as chaotic as it might seem, is one that has worked reasonably well over the past half century to reach the right balance in the tension between the government's need for secrecy and the public's need to know.

The essential question we face today, highlighted by the Snowden leaks, is whether this system still has merit in principle in a world that has changed dramatically in recent years. Internet access and new technologies vastly increase the amount of government information that can be disclosed, making possible the release of millions of documents at a stroke. Moreover, the likely recipients of leaked information are no longer major press institutions such as the *New York Times* and the *Washington Post* (as was the case with the Pentagon Papers) but organizations like

WikiLeaks with very different agendas. Meanwhile, the ability of the government to gather vast amounts of private information using surveillance techniques made possible by these very same technologies has raised the specter of unchecked, centralized power. It is a new era presenting myriad threats to transparency, privacy, the integrity of sensitive government operations, and freedom of expression, each and every issue requiring the most careful attention and consideration.

No one could serve as better guide through this labyrinth of questions than Emily Bell, director of the Tow Center for Digital Journalism at the Columbia School of Journalism and editor of this indispensable volume. Here, in a series of thoughtful and provocative essays, the leading journalists, scholars, and practitioners of our time confront us with the full complexity of these issues and show us what we need to be thinking about to address these challenges today and in the years ahead.

The Snowden revelations of 2013 have had a profound impact on our ideas about the balancing of secrecy and openness and on what will always be an imperfect accommodation of the interests of the government, the press, and the public. There is work to be done to sort out these essential elements of our democracy and to reassemble them in a manner that achieves a sustainable and productive tension. It is a project that will never go away and one that must be persistently addressed.

This book begins the next round of that process.

ACKNOWLEDGMENTS

T he majority of the chapters in *Journalism After Snowden* are the result of a body of research and associated events supported by the Tow Foundation and the John S. and James L. Knight Foundation. We would not have been able to perform this work without their support.

We are grateful to all the contributing authors in the book who gave up their time to write on this subject, and whose insight and suggestions formed a core part of the entire program. In addition, we are particularly grateful to participants who appeared at "Journalism After Snowden" events throughout the year: Jill Abramson, former editor of the *New York Times*; Julia Angwin of ProPublica; James Bamford; Dean Baquet, executive editor of the *New York Times*; Marty Baron, executive editor of the *Washington Post*; Janine Gibson, former editor of the *Guardian*-U.S.; Susan Glasser, editor of *Politico*; Morgan Marquis-Boire of First Look Media; Jesselyn Radack of the Government Accountability Project; David Sanger of the *New York Times*; David Schulz of Yale Law School; Cass Sunstein of Harvard Law School; and Trevor Timm of the Freedom of the Press Foundation.

As part of the Journalism After Snowden project, the Tow Center organized a series of lectures with the Information Society Project at Yale Law School in the fall of 2014. Special thanks to Valerie Belair-Gagnon at Yale Law School for helping to organize and host these events. In helping to facilitate access and publishing we owe special thanks to Ben Wizner at the ACLU, Andy Fishman at the *Intercept,* and Liz Spayd at the *Columbia Journalism Review.*

Not represented in this book, but a very important part of the Journalism After Snowden program was research conducted by Susan McGregor, assistant director of the Tow Center, who wrote the Tow Center report *Digital Security and Source Protection for Journalists.* Harlo Holmes created educational videos about digital security. We would also like to thank Amy Mitchell and Jesse Holcomb of the Pew Research Center for their help and research partnership. In the fall of 2014, the Tow Center hosted two fellows, Chris Walker and Carol Waters, who taught the first digital-security classes at a journalism school in the United States and also coauthored the Tow report *Learning Security: Information Security Education for Journalists.*

The small but dedicated team of staff and fellows at the Tow Center worked tirelessly on all aspects of the program. We are especially grateful to the work of Elizabeth Boylan, Shiwani Neupane, and Lauren Mack. The support of staff at the Columbia Journalism School enabled this work, and we would like to thank Elizabeth Fishman, Lauren Schaefer, Brittany Toscano Gore, and Janine Jaquet.

In putting the book together, we are especially grateful to Philip Leventhal at Columbia University Press, our fact-checkers Julie Tate and Andy Young, our manuscript editor Irene Pavitt, and our copy editor Mary Sutherland. In particular, we want to thank Jenn Henrichsen for her work in helping conceive and project manage the many fruitful events that so many people attended as part of the program. Finally, we would like to acknowledge and thank the work of Smitha Khorana, who shepherded the book through every stage of commissioning, editing, and revision. Without Smitha, this book would certainly not exist.

We want to thank Columbia University president Lee Bollinger and his staff—in particular, David Stone—and Columbia Journalism dean Steve Coll, who supported this work from the outset. Columbia's institutional commitment to freedom of the press and issues of expression have underpinned and enabled all our work.

And last, we would like to thank Edward Snowden, whose actions in 2013 shone a light on a covert world of surveillance, which has grown, without scrutiny, beyond the legitimate reach of government and outside the comprehension of most citizens.

JOURNALISM AFTER SNOWDEN

INTRODUCTION

EMILY BELL, TAYLOR OWEN,
AND SMITHA KHORANA

*It's not really about surveillance, it's about what the public understands—
how much control the public has over the programs and policies of its
governments. If we don't know what our government really does, if we
don't know the powers that authorities are claiming for themselves, or
arrogating to themselves, in secret, we can't really be said to be holding the
leash of government at all.*

EDWARD SNOWDEN, DECEMBER 2015

On May 20, 2013, the former National Security Agency analyst
and private contractor Edward Snowden flew to Hong Kong
from Hawaii, armed with a cache of documents taken from the
National Security Agency. He had been in touch with the journalist Glenn
Greenwald and the filmmaker Laura Poitras using encrypted communication, and had arranged to meet them in person. For the next eight days,
Greenwald, Poitras, and Ewen MacAskill, the investigative journalist
from the *Guardian*, reviewed the documents that Snowden had passed on
to them and became acquainted with his life story.

On June 5, 2013, the first stories reporting mass surveillance by the U.S.
government were published from the New York offices of the *Guardian*.
The *Washington Post* soon followed suit, led by the efforts of the journalist Barton Gellman, who Poitras had approached as a collaborator.

The documents revealed secret court orders requiring Verizon to pass on phone records for all its users to the government. The NSA had been making records of nearly every phone call in the United States.[1] The disclosures exposed structural details of two key NSA programs, PRISM and XKeyscore, and of Tempora, which was based in the United Kingdom under the auspices of Government Communications Headquarters (GCHQ). The surveillance program PRISM had allowed the NSA to gain backdoor entry into the data of nine giant Internet companies, including Google and Facebook.

Four days after the first stories were published, Glenn Greenwald revealed the identity of Edward Snowden to the world in an article in the *Guardian*.[2] The whistleblower who had shaken the foundations of the American surveillance system was not a lifelong government employee, as many had speculated, but a relatively junior analyst and private security contractor working with the NSA. It was surprising that a twenty-nine-year-old had managed to collect the breadth of information about the surveillance activities of the world's superpowers—the United States and its Five Eyes partner countries (the United Kingdom, Australia, Canada, and New Zealand)—without being detected.

Stand-alone stories and revelations about surveillance soon gave way to a global conversation about state power, oversight, and accountability. The NSA had surveilled citizens around the world and thirty-five world leaders, including German chancellor Angela Merkel and Brazilian president Dilma Roussef, and had accessed internal communications of international organizations like Human Rights Watch and Amnesty International.

Snowden had sought out journalists, as he reasoned that he alone could not properly evaluate the importance of or the threat attached to the documents he had obtained. His faith in the filter of journalism seemed oddly anachronistic in the context of a world that has moved progressively toward unfiltered disclosures and complete transparency. Organizations such as WikiLeaks and Anonymous started alternative news structures predicated on the idea that traditional news publishers would be neither technically competent nor sufficiently bold in their publishing strategies.

Snowden entrusted Greenwald and Poitras to evaluate the news value of the information he leaked. Selected documents were then shared with, reported on, and published by a network of traditional media institutions around the world. The collaborative nature of publishing that emerged at the time of the Snowden leaks was, in many ways, a precursor to the Panama Papers leak in 2016, when over a hundred journalists around the world worked together in secret for over a year on a massive cache of documents taken from the law firm Mossack Fonseca.[3]

The Snowden leaks took place at a time of increasing challenges for traditional news publishers. In the early 2000s, journalism had been transformed by seismic changes. Traditional advertising-revenue streams were decimated by the Internet; resources had been drained from teams doing investigative and national security reporting. The decline of print, the slimming of legacy newsrooms, and the erosion of local journalism marked a new era of post-industrial journalism.[4]

There was also the issue of trust. After September 11, legacy media organizations had consistently been criticized for being soft on national security reporting. The work of independent journalists like Glenn Greenwald and Marcy Wheeler, the blogger behind the national security blog Empty Wheel, and organizations like WikiLeaks were a reaction to this media climate. In the run-up to the Iraq War in 2003, articles by Judith Miller in the *New York Times* falsely reporting the existence of weapons of mass destruction had helped bolster the Bush administration's case for war. In the years after September 11, 2001, mainstream American news organizations had been slow to report on CIA black sites, torture, illegal detentions at Guantanamo Bay, extraordinary renditions, and the curtailing of civil liberties in the name of national security. In 2005, the *New York Times* published a warrantless wiretap story by James Risen and Eric Lichtblau after sitting on it for almost an entire year at the behest of White House officials who warned that publishing the story would have dire consequences on the country's security.[5] Snowden himself cited this as a reason that he did not take his cache of documents directly to the *Times*.

The NSA leaks marked a point where the role of publishing institutions became one of critical importance both in defending the regional governmental challenges to possession of the information and in sorting and filtering the appropriate stories. Years after Snowden's leaks, stories based on Snowden's documents have continued to be reported on and published in a variety of outlets, including the *New York Times* and the *Intercept*, the online publication started by Glenn Greenwald, Laura Poitras, and Jeremy Scahill after the Snowden leaks. These documents provided evidence and formed the foundation of subsequent reporting. In 2008, the American Civil Liberties Union filed a lawsuit, *Amnesty v. Clapper*, challenging government surveillance. It specifically addressed the constitutionality of the Foreign Intelligence Surveillance Act (FISA) Amendments Act of 2008, which had significantly expanded the NSA's mandate, allowing the agency to target any foreign citizen for surveillance.[6] Previously, only agents of foreign powers could be surveilled. Not only were all citizens anywhere in the world now possible targets of American surveillance, but the amendments allowed for the communications of Americans to be intercepted without warrants.

In February 2013, just months before the Snowden leaks, the Supreme Court, dividing 5 to 4, dismissed the case, deciding that the claims were based too much on speculation and on a "chain of contingencies." The plaintiffs could not satisfy the constitutional requirement for being allowed to sue—they lacked the evidence. Jameel Jaffer, former deputy legal director of the ACLU and founding director of the Knight First Amendment Institute at Columbia University, who argued the case, said that "the government is sort of creating this hurdle that is insuperable, this barrier to judicial review, which will ensure that nobody can ever challenge this kind of statute in court."[7]

The most striking element of NSA surveillance remains that government programs were not reviewed by the American judicial system, but instead were overseen by a separate court, the Foreign Intelligence Surveillance Court, formed only to evaluate classified programs.

Immediately after Snowden's leaks, the Obama administration insisted that the NSA had surveilled only foreigners. President Obama said, "If you are a U.S. person, the NSA cannot listen to your telephone calls." Yet the leaked documents revealed that American citizens residing within the United States were consistently caught in the surveillance dragnet. This sort of confusion and intentional obfuscation of the facts of government surveillance highlights *why* the evidence Snowden provided was so crucial. The leaks provided the evidence that had been missing in the 2008 lawsuit—and allowed the ACLU to file another lawsuit, *ACLU v. Clapper*, this time successfully.[8] On May 7, 2015, the appeals court ruled that Section 215 of the Patriot Act did not authorize the bulk collection of metadata.

Government reactions to the leaks have been strikingly different in the United States and the United Kingdom. The Snowden cache was initially housed at multiple institutions, including the *Guardian* offices in London, and with reporters from the *Washington Post*. In Great Britain, GCHQ—the British intelligence and security organization—pressured the *Guardian* to turn over the documents and threatened editors with an injunction and prosecution under the Official Secrets Act. In response to this intimidation, *Guardian* editors destroyed the MacBooks containing the Snowden documents in the presence of technicians from GCHQ.

At this point, the *Guardian* had already transferred some of the Snowden documents to the *New York Times*. The U.S. government did not formally exercise prior restraint in any of the newsrooms that were reporting on the documents. It was constrained in part by the Pentagon Papers decision of the Supreme Court, which in 1971 had "held that any attempt by the Government to block news articles prior to publication bears a heavy burden of presumption against its constitutionality." The Pentagon Papers—a body of documents leaked by military analyst Daniel Ellsberg to the *New York Times* in 1971—had offered proof that the American public had been misled about the Vietnam War. This had been the first effort by the U.S. government to enjoin publication on the ground of national security. The landmark decision in support of the *New York Times*, declaring that "the government had not met that burden," had set an important precedent.

Yet, at the time of the Snowden leaks, some questioned the sturdiness of that decision. Jill Abramson, editor in chief of the *New York Times*, consulted an external lawyer who determined that while legal action after publication couldn't be ruled out, it was unlikely that the government would take journalists or editors to court. Many were unsure to what lengths the U.S. government might go to obstruct the publication of stories about NSA surveillance. The Obama administration had already prosecuted more journalists than had any other administration in history and had gone after whistleblowers aggressively.[9] In May 2013, the Department of Justice secretly seized the phone records of journalists at the Associated Press.[10] After the Snowden leaks, the Obama administration ostensibly upheld the First Amendment in its lack of interference in publication.[11] Yet, Snowden revealed in the film *Citizenfour* that the FBI had obtained authorization to work with the CIA and a number of unnamed foreign partners, and had been tasked to use "all appropriate means"—including government pressure—"where appropriate" to persuade media to refuse publication. This uncertainty about what legal protections exist for journalists, whistleblowers, and publishers is characteristic of the so-called After Snowden period.

Ultimately, the U.S. government's reaction to the Snowden leaks focused on the source,[12] not on the publication outlets or the journalists involved. On June 21, 2013, Snowden was charged with three felonies under the Espionage Act, and the U.S. government requested his extradition. Two days later, WikiLeaks organized his departure from Hong Kong. Snowden's passport was confiscated en route to Cuba at Sheremetyevo International Airport in Moscow, where he was relegated to spend forty days in the transit zone before he was granted asylum by Russia.

The Espionage Act, which dates to World War I and which was also used to charge Daniel Ellsberg and the whistleblower Thomas Drake, prohibits a public-interest defense. "The Espionage Act does not distinguish between leaks to the press in the public interest and selling secrets to foreign enemies for personal profit," said Ben Wizner, Snowden's lawyer at the American Civil Liberties Union.[13]

Both Poitras and Greenwald had been living abroad in the months after meeting Snowden in Hong Kong, and they expressed concern that they would be served with subpoenas when they entered the United States for the first time after the leaks to accept the George Polk Award. Instead, nothing happened, and the team of journalists from the *Washington Post* and the *Guardian* who had reported on the Snowden documents went on to win the Pulitzer Prize in Public Service. The two awards—the Polk and the Pulitzer—marked a turning point in the general acceptance of the importance of the leaks and subsequent reporting.

Public support for Snowden has been bolstered over time. Through his engagement on Twitter and frequent speaking engagements, conducted remotely, Snowden has remained present in public life despite his exile. In June 2015, two years after the leaks, Congress passed the first congressional action to curtail mass surveillance. The USA Freedom Act had bipartisan support, and despite criticism of the limitations of the bill, it was an important milestone.

A survey conducted by the Pew Research Center in June 2013, just weeks after the leaks, found that while 49 percent said that the Snowden leaks served the public interest, 44 percent claimed that the public interest was harmed. Three years after the leaks, former attorney general Eric Holder publicly declared that Edward Snowden had performed a public service. In a series of articles in the spring of 2016, the *Guardian* also revealed that the Office of the Inspector General at the Pentagon and the NSA had illegally given the names of previous whistleblowers to the FBI and had destroyed evidence in these cases.[14] These whistleblowers had tried to alert their superiors to NSA surveillance years before Snowden, and these stories rendered moot the argument that Snowden should have expressed his concerns within the organization before contacting journalists outside.

In September 2016, the ACLU, Human Rights Watch, and Amnesty International organized a global campaign asking the Obama administration to pardon Edward Snowden.[15]

———— ∞ ————

Snowden's leak of classified documents and reporting from partner institutions around the world sparked an unprecedented public debate on digital privacy, the pursuit of national security, and the power of the state. It also fostered discussion about the role of journalism in democratic societies, the constitutional rights of the press, and the guarantee of free expression.

Our new and more complete knowledge of what the NSA is capable of now informs how we report and discuss a large number of the stories that dominate the news agenda—whether it is Apple contesting its right to preserve encryption technology against requests from the FBI, the burgeoning wealth and close ties to governmental power of technology companies, or the real and imagined threat of terrorism. Some scholars believe that the Snowden leaks enabled Apple to make its case public by setting the stage and educating citizens about the close collaboration between the NSA and telecommunications companies.

The Snowden disclosures provided a lens through which to view a new, converged world, one where technology companies are simultaneously becoming platforms for journalism and potential sources of government intelligence. While citizens have long known that governments spy on one another, and activists and communities of color in the United States have been surveilled by the FBI since the civil rights movement,[16] scholars of technology and security knew only limited details about how governments have sought to leverage the Internet. Until Snowden's leak, most citizens around the world were largely unaware that their electronic communications were being monitored, collected, stored, shared, and analyzed by their governments.

Since the development of modern telephony, the surveillance capability of states has been enabled by access to the personal communications of their citizens provided to them by telecoms. Wiretapping was implemented by police and intelligence officers, but authority was granted on a case-by-case basis by the judicial system and regulated by national law. The Internet changed the scale and pace of this give-and-take in two major respects.

First, the Internet allows for transmission of data covering a far wider range of interpersonal communication and personal activity than discreet telephone calls. Increasingly, our daily lives are being transmitted in a form of data that can be collected and stored. Second, the dominant business model that emerged in Silicon Valley has incentivized users to share their data in exchange for free services. The terms of service of Google, Facebook, and countless other Internet services forces users to provide their data for use by these corporations, inadvertently enabling the modern surveillance capability of governments. This culture of information sharing and very limited personal privacy in online activity has proved beneficial to both Silicon Valley companies and the NSA.

In a leaked document, the NSA describes its vast ambition to "sniff it all, collect it all, know it all, process it all, and exploit it all." This startling disclosure represents a desire to control the Internet and, with it, the majority of global information flow. As the former *Guardian* editor Alan Rusbridger states in a chapter in this anthology, "The Internet is the thing they [governments] fear. The thing they want to master. The space in which we may all find darkness as well as light. But the very reasons the state wants to tame, penetrate, and control the digital universe are the same reasons that make it an instrument of liberty."

This ongoing debate about the future of the Internet forms the backdrop of the Snowden leaks and this book. Today, the open web is increasingly challenged by both corporate control and social-media companies. Recent debates on net neutrality, online piracy, and Facebook's Free Basics highlight this uncertainty about who can access the Internet—the digital divide—and who should control it.

It is in the context of these questions that the Tow Center for Digital Journalism at the Columbia Graduate School of Journalism created the Journalism After Snowden research project to understand the mechanics of the Snowden story, and to study the legal and technical implications for journalism in the wake of these disclosures.[17] Through research, events, and writing, we embarked on a wide conversation on journalism in the age of the surveillance state.

This book is the culmination of our research program. It includes reflections on the implications of state surveillance on the practices and societal roles of journalism from some of the world's leading editors, journalists, and scholars of media, technology, journalism, and law. These authors provide a detailed look at the impact of Edward Snowden's leak: editors discuss how they dealt with the data, the reporting, and the fallout; digital-security experts speak to the technical challenges of doing journalism in a world of state surveillance; legal and governance scholars explore the constitutional implications of curtailing the rights of a free press; media scholars reflect on how this leak shifts the balance between sources and reporters; and some of the world's most prominent editors and reporters explore what all of this means for the practice of journalism.

Our one caveat is that the anthology lacks a certain diversity of perspective. We approached former members of the intelligence community and ex-civil servants to contribute. Most of these individuals declined. We are grateful that Steven Bradbury, formerly of the Department of Justice, agreed to lend his voice to this anthology, and we wish that others had chosen to participate. Academic institutions have a unique capacity in these sorts of debates to mediate conflicting claims, set the facts straight, and create a common space for discourse.

We organized the book into four sections. In part I, "The Story and the Source," we hear from individuals who were directly involved in the process of leaking and publishing the initial stories, including Edward Snowden himself. We begin with Alan Rusbridger, the former editor in chief of the *Guardian*, who argues that the Snowden leaks force us to question who is a journalist and what journalists can do in the public interest. Jill

Abramson, the former editor in chief of the *New York Times*, recounts the difficulty of making publishing decisions around national security stories at the *Times* after September 11, 2001. She explains how and why the *Guardian* transferred a copy of the Snowden documents to the *Times*.

Glenn Greenwald, a former columnist with the *Guardian* and cofounding editor at the *Intercept*, reflects on the human need for privacy. He challenges the frequent argument that government surveillance is a concern only if you are guilty—everyone needs some level of privacy. Surveillance has a chilling effect precisely because it alters daily routines and everyday behavior. Over time, ubiquitous surveillance can dampen all forms of civil disobedience, fostering a meek public and leaving people less willing to engage with radical politics and activist movements.

An edited transcript of a conversation between Tow Center director Emily Bell and Edward Snowden, conducted remotely in December 2015, carries reflections on Snowden's interactions with journalists and media organizations. "Working more closely with the journalists has radically reshaped my understanding of journalism, and that continues through to today," says Snowden. Snowden revisits his choices at the time of the leaks but also casts a unique perspective on the cascade of events that his calculated risk-taking triggered. Although we always wanted to focus the efforts of this book on the policy and practice of "what's next?" for journalism, without Snowden's voice we felt strongly that this book would be incomplete.

In this section, both Rusbridger and Abramson address the decision-making process around publishing state secrets. Despite security concerns, Abramson contends that no harm has been done by reporting on and publishing these documents, and Rusbridger leaves open the possibility that there have been repercussions, but he also urges us to place them in the context of the wider democratic conversation that emerged from this reporting. In this respect, both compel us to think carefully about who we as a society want to make the decision about what is and what is not in the public interest. Is it solely the job of the government to make these decisions? Traditionally, we have allowed other professions to engage with this process, including police, judges, and journalists. Since September 11, 2001, that responsibility has been posited primarily with governments, and the decisions underlying these processes have often been shrouded in secrecy. At the same time, citizens have tried to contest these boundaries through independent reporting, citizen journalism collectives, crowdsourcing, and small and large acts of whistleblowing. A central historical role of journalism has been to make the ultimate decision about what people should know. Journalists have the capacity to report, reveal, and contextualize information that is being withheld from citizens, and as a result they have the tools to stand up to power—be it state power, corporate power, or other forms of institutional power.

In part II, "Journalists and Sources," five leading academics, journalists, and digital-security practitioners detail the communities of action and development that have emerged to help journalists work in a post-Snowden information environment.

On the very practical end, the revelation of government surveillance capabilities, combined with the rise in U.S. prosecutions of whistleblowers, has led journalists, particularly national security and investigative reporters, to question whether they can legitimately claim to protect their sources. Source protection is central to the constitutionally protected rights of a free press. The tools needed to ensure a greater degree of security over interpersonal communications—that is, encryption—remain difficult to use and, due to human fallibility in their implementation, unreliable. But more importantly, journalists are not confident that these tools will protect their digital communications from the technical sophistication of government surveillance.

These concerns were corroborated in a survey of U.S. investigative reporters that was conducted as a partnership between the Pew Research Center and the Tow Center for Digital Journalism. The survey "Investigative Journalists and Digital Security: Perceptions of Vulnerability and Changes in Behavior" found that while two-thirds of investigative reporters surveyed believed that the U.S. government had probably collected data about their communications, fewer than half of those reporters have received digital-security training, and more than half fail to employ even the most basic security tools.[18]

One of the aims of this project was to be able to use insight for teaching, and the research allowed us to develop methods to help journalists better understand how to protect their sources, information, and interactions. The Tow Center initiatives included workshops in New York and San Francisco, extensive training sessions at the Columbia Journalism School, and published reports by Susan McGregor and by our research fellows, Christopher Walker and Carol Waters.[19]

These practical considerations have broader implications for the role of a free press in a democratic society. If a journalist can't claim to protect a source, then the escape valve that we have built into our democratic institutions and governance model—the very ability for a free press to challenge and reveal—is at risk. How do the surveillance capabilities of governments change how journalists do their jobs? Will citizens learn less about the malfeasance of government and private-sector institutions in this climate? If so, what are the implications for the societies that have placed authority, power, and responsibility in the hands of a free press?

In these chapters, our contributors provide a hard look at the vulnerabilities that journalists face, how surveillance has changed journalism practice, and the new tools available to help protect them. Even when journalists are literate in digital security, the technology and tools are constantly changing. This section is meant to broadly educate journalists about threat-modeling and the basics of source protection when using digital communications.

Steve Coll, dean of the Columbia Journalism School and staff writer at the *New Yorker*, explores the unique challenges that journalists now face when protecting their sources in the context of investigative reporting. The James Risen case shows how the government can easily determine the identity of a source without calling a journalist to testify in court. By leaving digital traces of the times when digital communication took place and the parties involved, metadata can and has been used to convict leakers and identify sources. In this climate, Coll says, it is essential that journalism schools integrate digital security and source protection into their curriculum. He pays particular attention to the concerns of international journalists who face complex challenges when reporting in authoritative states with surveillance capabilities.

David Schulz, senior research scholar in law and the Floyd Abrams Clinical Lecturer in Law at Yale Law School, and Valerie Belair-Gagnon, executive director of the Information Society Project at Yale, explore the legal concept of reporter's privilege and the wider ramifications of *United States v. Sterling* on the practice of journalism. Schulz and Belair-Gagnon examine the erosion of the reporter's privilege in the digital age. How much privilege should a journalist have to protect sources? Who qualifies for this privilege? Does he or she have a right to anonymous sources? Legally, the answer at this time is no. As they explain, "The Court of Appeals' ruling in *Sterling* is an unflinching rejection of a reporter's right to make a binding promise of confidentiality in exchange for information," and therefore, "if we take seriously the idea of the press as an agent for public accountability, we need to continue to rethink the legal privilege, the possibility for a federal shield law, and who gets to claim that privilege." Julia Angwin, a digital-security expert and senior reporter at ProPublica and the author of *Dragnet Nation: A Quest for Privacy, Security and Freedom in a World of Relentless Surveillance*, uses five case studies that were developed as part of our Tow Center digital-security workshop held in San Francisco in June 2014 to examine threat-modeling approaches and security strategies.

Trevor Timm, cofounder and the executive director of the Freedom of the Press Foundation, speaks to the need for institutional change in news organizations. Newsrooms must prioritize digital security, integrating digital hygiene into the workflows of their journalists. Even though substantial changes have been made since the Snowden leaks, including the adoption of HTTPS by the *Washington Post* and the creation of the post of director of information security by the *New York Times*, more must be done.

Nabiha Syed, assistant general counsel at BuzzFeed, argues that two groups—national security journalists and independent journalists—have been particularly disadvantaged by government secrecy. While processes like the Freedom of Information Act (FOIA) exist to allow transparency at the local and federal level, the methods to contest these processes when they fail are resource-heavy and may require institutional backing. Independent journalists rarely have access to these resources. Meanwhile, opaque national security exemptions hinder the free flow of information and complicate the reporting process even further.

Angwin, Timm, and Syed make clear just how vulnerable and targeted whistleblowers have become. When under a microscope of federal investigation, it is unlikely that any degree of digital security will be sufficient to remain anonymous. This means that at the core of this debate lies not just a technical challenge but a policy question. As noted throughout this volume by senior editors, scholars, and journalists, there is a strong case that journalists should be actively engaging in the debate over federal whistleblower legislation and aggressive prosecutions. If sources for accountability reporting disappear, then the role that journalism is constitutionally protected to serve in our society is significantly diminished.

In part III, "Governing Surveillance," six renowned scholars, journalists, and lawyers debate the political, public policy, institutional, and physical infrastructure of surveillance. They collectively ask: What are the building blocks that enable the surveillance state, and how do these elements engage with the practice and constitutional role of journalism?

Clay Shirky, journalism professor at New York University, places the relationship between press leaks and state pushback in a historical context. Transnational media networks have changed the way national press and governments have traditionally negotiated the process of publishing sensitive stories. As journalists continue to report outside of national boundaries and journalism becomes increasingly decentralized and untethered to the nation-state, leakers with vast troves of data will in turn become more common, and incentives to consult with governments will only diminish.

Steven Bradbury, who served as the head of the Office of Legal Counsel (OLC) of the Department of Justice from 2005 to 2009, offers insight into the decision-making processes that have dictated national security secrets since September 11. Although he was not working at the Department of Justice at the time of the Snowden leaks, his office oversaw the initial expansion of NSA surveillance during the George W. Bush administration, and he offers an incisive view of the perspective from the inside. Bradbury claims that the press has sensationalized its coverage of NSA programs, in particular the PRISM program. He also argues that the Pentagon Papers decision has been widely misunderstood. While most people take the Supreme Court decision to mean that newspapers are effectively protected from prior restraint and can therefore publish what they want without risk of legal ramifications, Bradbury reminds us that there *is* content that is illegal to publish, and publishing classified national security secrets can still result in an after-the-fact criminal prosecution.

The *New York Times* national security reporter David Sanger explains that the strained relationship between Silicon Valley and the U.S. government goes beyond surveillance to encompass a new complex world of cyberwarfare. Snowden "opened the world's eyes to a new world of surveillance and cyberwarfare," writes Sanger. "There, what he revealed cannot be stuffed back into a black box—and will change the way we view American power over the next decade."

Reflecting on how the practice of journalism has shifted on a particularly sensitive beat, the *Wall Street Journal* reporter Siobhan Gorman details how the Snowden leaks changed the NSA's relationship to the press. The NSA has always had an unusually insular culture, notes Gorman, and has kept the press at arm's length. After the Snowden leaks, the agency has worked to create a cohesive public-relations and branding strategy. Whether this will result in a more open culture in the future is yet to be seen.

Patrick Weil, visiting professor at Yale Law School, challenges the way the Espionage Act was used to revoke Snowden's passport while he was in transit. The right to a passport is constitutionally protected, Weil writes, as he asks how Snowden's citizenship status may be affected in the future.

The Harvard Law School professor Cass Sunstein, who was a member of President Obama's surveillance review panel, challenges the way the precautionary principle has been applied to surveillance. Typically, any effort necessary has been taken in order to prevent a terrorist attack, despite the low probability that such an event may occur. "When emotions are running high, people are prone to neglect the probability that a bad outcome will occur; they focus instead on the outcome itself. As it operates in the real world, the precautionary principle often embodies a form of probability neglect," writes Sunstein. Instead of the precautionary principle, Sunstein recommends using a risk-management principle, which would allow different risks to be weighted against one another when making public-policy decisions on everything from terrorism to environmental protection. In the case of deciding an appropriate level of surveillance, the risks presented by a potential terrorist attack would be measured against possible risks to free speech, risks to relationships with other nations, and risks of harmful effects on commerce.

Despite having different areas of focus and expertise, many of these scholars point to the clear need for greater government reform and transparency in the oversight of U.S. surveillance programs.

In part IV, "Communications Networks and New Media," five of the most thoughtful voices working at the intersection of technology and the media address how the free press has been challenged by our new information ecosystem.

Emily Bell, director of the Tow Center for Digital Journalism and coeditor of this volume, speaks to the confluence of the social-media tools that are increasingly central to the practice of journalism and the very business models and cultural practices that have enabled governments to access more of our data. Journalists, she argues, are in a bind. They must embrace the tools and platforms that are now required to reach their audiences, but at the same time must hold the companies that manage and profit of these platforms to account. These two aims may not be compatible.

Journalists, she insists, need to engage far more actively in the tools they use. Whereas media companies once owned and controlled the dissemination platforms for their content (printing presses, delivery trucks, airwaves, etc.), they have now lost control of this process. Bell states that "the fourth estate, which liked to think that it operated in splendid isolation from other systems of money and power, has slipped suddenly and conclusively into a world where it no longer owns the means of production or controls the routes to distribution." The challenge, of course, is that these corporations may be driven more by conflicting incentives than those of content producers. Within these companies, all our online movements are tracked, and the best minds of today are focusing on how to use that information to generate corporate revenue, not how to reach a broader audience or better inform a citizenry.

Ron Deibert, professor of political science and director of the Citizen Lab at the University of Toronto, used research on two surveillance tools, Finfisher and Blue Coat, to demonstrate the surveillance capabilities held by government and private corporations. Advanced surveillance systems have been used in both democratic and autocratic states, often characterized by fine-grained targeted surveillance, enabled by off-the-shelf lawful interception tools sold to regimes as spyware. Deibert reviews these risks around the world—including cyber espionage by China and targeted surveillance by the Syrian regime.

Susan Crawford, the John A. Reilly Visiting Professor in Intellectual Property at Harvard Law School, writes about a possible future of high-speed connectivity for all citizens. There is an opportunity, argues Crawford, to rethink the independence of our communications infrastructure when building new fiber-optic networks.

Eben Moglen, professor of law and legal history at Columbia University and director of the Software Freedom Law Center, makes a sweeping case that we lose our freedom to think freely when our press is not free. "Free thought requires free media. Free media requires free technology," he writes. He asks us to imagine a world where every global citizen has open access to knowledge, enabled by open source initiatives and the creative commons movement.

Ethan Zuckerman, director of the MIT Center for Civic Media, explores the concept of ubiquitous surveillance on the Internet. One is tracked not only by states but in almost all online interactions, include reading media sites. Surveillance, Zuckerman says, is the default setting of the Internet. We haven't as a society or as a media industry thought through the implications of this, and the tools available to avoid this tracking are nascent. Journalism organizations, Zuckerman argues, should think carefully about participating in and profiting from this surveillance infrastructure. His essay seems especially prescient as social-media companies increasingly track reading habits and personalize news with user data.[20]

Our goal with this project and resulting book was to illuminate a debate about the implications of the Snowden revelations on the practice and societal role of journalism. These implications include how the data were released, who they were released to, how they were reported on, how governments responded, the details of the programs and their ambitions that were revealed, and how citizens engaged with this knowledge. We hope this book adds to these conversations.

NOTES

1. Edward J. Snowden, "Edward Snowden: The World Says No to Surveillance," *New York Times*, June 4, 2015, http://www.nytimes.com/2015/06/05/opinion/edward-snowden-the -world-says-no-to-surveillance.html.

2. Glenn Greenwald, "Edward Snowden: The Whistleblower Behind the NSA Surveillance Revelations," *Guardian*, June 11, 2013, https://www.theguardian.com/world/2013/jun/09 /edward-snowden-nsa-whistleblower-surveillance.

3. International Consortium of Investigative Journalists, "The Panama Papers: Politicians, Criminals and the Rogue Industry That Hides Their Cash," https://panamapapers.icij.org/.

4. Chris Anderson, Emily Bell, and Clay Shirky, "Post Industrial Journalism: Adapting to the Present," Tow Center for Digital Journalism, http://towcenter.org/research/post -industrial-journalism-adapting-to-the-present-2/.

5. James Risen and Eric Lichtblau, "Bush Lets U.S. Spy on Callers Without Courts," *New York Times*, December 16, 2005, http://www.nytimes.com/2005/12/16/politics/bush-lets -us-spy-on-callers-without-courts.html.

6. Constitution Project, *Report on the FISA Amendments Act of 2008*, September 6, 2012, http://www.constitutionproject.org/wp-content/uploads/2012/10/fisaamendmentsactreport _9612.pdf.

7. "ACLU Blasts Supreme Court Rejection of Challenge to Warrantless Spying Without Proof of Surveillance," February 27, 2013, Democracy Now!, http://www.democracynow .org/2013/2/27/aclu_blasts_supreme_court_rejection_of.

8. Charlie Savage, "A.C.L.U. Files Lawsuit Seeking to Stop the Collection of Domestic Phone Logs," *New York Times*, June 11, 2013, http://www.nytimes.com/2013/06/12/us/aclu-files -suit-over-phone-surveillance-program.html.

9. Cora Currier, "Charting Obama's Crackdown on National Security Leaks," July 30, 2013, ProPublica, https://www.propublica.org/special/sealing-loose-lips-charting-obamas -crackdown-on-national-security-leaks.

10. Charlie Savage and Leslie Kaufman, "Phone Records of Journalists Seized by U.S.," *New York Times*, May 13, 2013, http://www.nytimes.com/2013/05/14/us/phone-records-of -journalists-of-the-associated-press-seized-by-us.html.

11. Jameel Jaffer, "A First Amendment in the Digital Age" (Peter Zenger Lecture), October 11, 2016, Just Security, https://www.justsecurity.org/33479/a-amendment-digital -age-peter-zenger-lecture/.

12. Sheila Fitzsimons, Ken MacFarlane, and Mustafa Khalili, "Revealed: The Day Guardian Destroyed Snowden Hard Drives Under Watchful Eye of GCHQ–Video," *Guardian*, January 31, 2014, https://www.theguardian.com/world/video/2014/jan/31/snowden-files -computer-destroyed-guardian-gchq-basement-video.

13. *Citizenfour*, directed by Laura Poitras (Praxis Films, 2014).

14. Spencer Ackerman and Ewen MacAskill, "Snowden Calls for Whistleblower Shield After Claims by New Pentagon Source," *Guardian*, May 22, 2016, https://www.theguardian .com/us-news/2016/may/22/snowden-whistleblower-protections-john-crane.

15. Kenneth Roth and Salil Shetty, "Pardon Edward Snowden" (op-ed), *New York Times*, September 15, 2016, http://www.nytimes.com/2016/09/15/opinion/pardon-edward-snowden.html?_r=0.

16. Dia Kayyali, "The History of Surveillance and the Black Community," February 13, 2014, Electronic Frontier Foundation, https://www.eff.org/deeplinks/2014/02/history-surveillance -and-black-community.

17. The Journalism After Snowden research project was funded by the Tow Foundation and the Knight Foundation. The Tow Center had complete editorial independence over every element of the project.

18. Jesse Holcomb, Amy Mitchell, and Kristen Purcell, "Investigative Journalists and Digital Security: Perceptions of Vulnerability and Changes in Behavior," February 5, 2015, Pew Research Center/Journalism & Media, http://www.journalism.org/2015/02/05 /investigative-journalists-and-digital-security/.

19. Susan E. McGregor, "Digital Security for Journalists," June 2014, GitBook, https://www .gitbook.com/book/susanemcg/digital-security-for-journalists/details; Christopher Walker and Carol Waters, "Learning Security: Information Security Education for Journalists," Tow Center for Digital Journalism, towcenter.org/research/learning-security-information -security-education-for-journalists/.

20. Trevor Timm, "What Media Companies Don't Want You to Know About Ad Blockers," *Columbia Journalism Review*, June 29, 2016, http://www.cjr.org/opinion/ad_blockers _malware_new_york_times.php.

I

THE STORY AND THE SOURCE

1

JOURNALISM AFTER SNOWDEN

ALAN RUSBRIDGER

ournalism after Snowden? Two big questions linger on—one about whether the very technologies that Edward Snowden revealed are compatible with independent, inquiring reporting; and one crucial question about journalism itself, which could be boiled down to: What is it supposed to be, or do?

The technologies first. Any journalist with even a cursory understanding of the Snowden stories published in 2013/2014 by the *Guardian* and the *Washington Post* would have come to an understanding that states— even liberal democracies—have the ability to intercept, store, and analyze virtually all forms of electronic communication. Faceless people in shadowy agencies (not to mention the police) can, if they wish, read your text messages and e-mails. They can see who or what you've been searching for. They can divine what you're thinking. They can access all your contacts. And they can follow you.

James Graham's play *Privacy*, at London's Donmar Warehouse in 2014, dramatized some of these capabilities by exploiting some of the information the theatergoing audience had volunteered in the act of applying for tickets online, or by having their phones and Wi-Fi connections switched on during the performance.

At one point in the first act, members of the audience with iPhones were asked to go through a number of steps—flipping through Settings → Privacy → Location Services → System Services → Frequent Locations.

Within a few seconds, there was a collective gasp as half the stalls and circle occupants discovered the extent to which their phones had been tracking and storing their every moment. There was the evidence in front of their eyes: the maps showing the addresses they had visited over previous weeks or months, together with precise timings. The log of their lives.

These were audiences of reasonably sophisticated theatergoers with a self-declared interest in the subject of the play—that of privacy. Most, I guess, vaguely suspected that mobile phones were capable of betraying information about their calls and even movements. But there was something stark and shocking about being confronted—in public—with the incontrovertible and precise evidence of their movements.

Over the seven-week run, many journalists went to see the play. How many, I wonder, altered their behavior as a result? The theater critic may have felt that she had nothing to hide and so changed nothing about her life. But what of reporters whose job involved speaking to, or meeting, sources? Did the penny drop that no source can truly be regarded as confidential if its identity can be quickly obtained by searching through the electronic trail we all leave behind us?

"If you are a law-abiding citizen of this country going about your business and your personal life you have nothing to fear," said the British foreign secretary, William Hague, in June 2013 after the early *Guardian* revelations about the extent of the mass collection and monitoring of information by state agencies. He added that these innocent people had "nothing to fear about the British state or intelligence agencies listening to the contents of your phone calls or anything like that."

Of course, most journalists and most sources are precisely that—perfectly law-abiding citizens doing nothing wrong. Equally, much of the most worthwhile work they do relies on people being prepared to talk confidentially about things of which they have direct knowledge.

Confidentiality means nothing if a third party can reasonably easily work out to whom a journalist has been talking—through their phone logs, contacts lists, e-mails, texts, or by working out who else was in a certain location at a certain time.

Nor can journalists take much comfort in Hague's assurance that the British state is not listening to the "contents" of your phone calls. A police officer or spook doesn't need to access the "content" of any communication to work out the identity of a whistleblower or source. Welcome to the world of metadata—the accompanying information, not content—often accessible with no form of warrant or judicial oversight, and which tells so much about us.

Pre-Snowden, a knowledgeable minority would certainly have known about metadata; post-Snowden, there's no excuse for anyone in journalism (or the law, or medicine, or any profession involving confidentiality). The agencies themselves have been quite open about the value of knowing the who-whom-where-when questions. Stewart Baker, the former general counsel of the NSA, said in a 2013 discussion hosted by the *Guardian* in New York: "Metadata absolutely tells you everything about somebody's life. If you have enough metadata you don't really need content. . . . [It's] sort of embarrassing how predictable we are as human beings."

Evidence that law enforcement and security agencies do, indeed, help themselves to such data on journalists' sources is all around—just as we also learned that British spooks don't have much time for lawyer–client privilege. The Obama administration's war on leaks has led to an aggressive crackdown on whistleblowers—notoriously including the Department of Justice secretly obtaining two months' worth of phone records from more than twenty separate phone lines of AP reporters and editors. In the United Kingdom, two cases came to light in 2014 in which the police had quietly (and without judicial warrant) used antiterrorism laws to find out to whom journalists on the *Mail on Sunday* and the *Sun* had been talking to. Neither case involved terrorism, or anything like it. The papers—neither of which had been notably sympathetic about Edward Snowden and his revelations—were, of course, outraged.

The agencies are unlikely to change their habits, and as we've seen over the past year or so, it is formidably difficult for congresses or parliaments to scale back laws permitting intrusive behavior by the state once they've been passed. So, lesson one of the post-Snowden era is that reporters and editors are going to have to change their behaviors.

Betraying a source anywhere is a most unforgivable crime.

In comfortable democracies, it may lead to sources losing their jobs and their careers being wrecked, or even going to prison. In less comfortable parts of the world, it can lead to far worse outcomes—including torture or death.

So journalists have a moral responsibility to absorb what Edward Snowden has been telling us. But how many have? My guess is that a tiny minority of news reporters have taken the time and effort to read up on what forms of communication are (relatively) safe and how to send and receive encrypted e-mails. How many news organizations have secure drop boxes for sources wanting safely to submit documents? How many foreign correspondents have changed their habits in terms of the phones or computer equipment they travel with? Some have. My suspicion is that most haven't.

Which leads to the second, even more profound, question raised by the Edward Snowden coverage—the essence, independence, and purpose of journalism itself.

I felt this question quite acutely in Britain, if only because quite a few of my fellow editors either did not think that the Snowden revelations were much of a story or, worse, were positively hostile to the *Guardian* and its behavior.

The security services discreetly briefed journalists about the harm done by Snowden and can hardly have believed their luck at how enthusiastically and unquestioningly so many took the bait. The *Guardian* was aggressively accused by fellow journalists of endangering British lives and of something like treason or sedition. No fewer than three papers said that journalists could be not trusted to make judgments about the public interest where national security was concerned.

To judge by the outpourings of some colleagues in the press, Snowden made a wise choice in going to the *Guardian*. Other journalists would have, at best, ignored the story or had him arrested. A former editor of the *Independent*, Chris Blackhurst, wrote at the height of the row: "If the security services insist something is contrary to the public interest, and might harm their operations, who am I despite my groundings from Watergate onward to disbelieve them?" Edward Lucas, a senior editor for the *Economist*, said that had Snowden brought the documents to him, he would have marched him straight down to a police station.

It seems to me there is an easy answer to the "who am I?" question posed by Blackhurst: you are a journalist. You are not part of the state or the government. Your job is disclosure, not secrecy. You stand aside from power in order to scrutinize it. Your job is to be fully sensitive to all the public interests raised by the story—and to publish what you judge to be significant as responsibly as you know how. Only then is informed debate possible. As a journalist, you have as much right to balance those public interests as a politician or a policeman or a judge.

These were strange times to live through, particularly as three papers arguing that the state, not newspapers, were the only possible judges of the public interest where national security is concerned and were among the most trenchant critics of any attempt at regulation of the press in the wake of the Leveson Inquiry,[1] a two-part public inquiry by the British government investigating the role of the press and police in the 2011 *News International* phone-hacking scandal.

On one hand, they demanded self regulation—because the press was a proud and independent estate. On the other hand, they effectively argued that the state must have supremacy over the press in determining what could, and could not, be published about modern-day surveillance.

This was a confusing argument for editors, of all people, to be making, but fortunately, editors in most of the rest of the world saw things very differently.

We are used to the state claiming that our journalism has caused harm. That's what the U.S. government claimed with Daniel Ellsberg over the Pentagon Papers. (Nixon's deputy assistant for national security affairs, Alexander Haig, described the leak as "a devastating . . . security breach of the greatest magnitude of anything I've ever seen.") They made similar noises over WikiLeaks. In both cases, in time, the claims of harm melted away.

This is not to claim that the Snowden revelations did no harm to the intelligence capabilities of one or two Western powers. We cannot meaningfully test those claims. I have been told on good authority that some of the Snowden revelations did impair some intelligence gathering. I have equally been told—by a number of people on what I would consider equally good authority—that the *Guardian*'s journalism caused no harm.

Whenever I hear members of the security services claiming the bad guys are "going dark" on them, I think of an essay with that very title by Peter Swire, an Internet, privacy, and encryption expert who worked at the White House and was part of President Obama's review panel into the issues raised by Snowden.

"Due to changing technology, there are indeed specific ways that law enforcement and national security agencies lose specific previous capabilities," Swire wrote in his November 2011 essay. "These specific losses, however, are more than offset by massive gains. Public debates should recognize that we are truly in a golden age of surveillance. By understanding that, we can reject calls for bad encryption policy. More generally, we should critically assess a wide range of proposals, and build a more secure computing and communications infrastructure."

In the Pentagon Papers case, the U.S. Supreme Court displayed a clearer grasp of the duties and freedoms of the press than did some British editors during this strange period in 2013. Back in 1971, the Court supported a standard that would make it virtually impossible for the state to censor the press by claiming harm.

The judgment protected the press unless a proposed story threatened "direct, immediate, and irreparable damage to our nation or its people." Two of the Supreme Court judges went further, believing the First Amendment to be absolute. Justice Black wrote: "[I]n revealing the workings of government that led to the Vietnam War, the newspapers nobly did precisely that which the Founders hoped and trusted they would do."

The majority 6 to 3 decision by the Supreme Court echoed some of the language of a judge in an earlier hearing: "The security of the Nation is not at the ramparts alone. Security also lies in the value of our free institutions. A cantankerous press, an obstinate press, a ubiquitous press must be suffered by those in authority in order to preserve the even greater values of freedom of expression and the right of the people to know."

The Pentagon Papers judgment was hugely significant because it removed the threat of prior restraint, or censorship, over such stories. In other words, the judges absolutely believed that it was appropriate for responsible journalists to make careful decisions about the public interest in publication—and not defer to the state to decide on their behalf.

That, surely, is a proper statement of the role of a truly independent press. But removing the threat of prior intervention is also enormously helpful in allowing journalists and editors to get a sense of any possible harm that might be caused by publication of stories about national security. Take away the possibility that the state will march into newspaper offices and seize material, arrest people, or injunct publication, and it's immediately possible to have a calmer conversation.

The reverse was true in Britain, where the state (after an initial lull) did the opposite: making explicit threats to prevent publication and/or seize the source material (which it did, anyway, using terror laws against Glenn Greenwald's partner, David Miranda, at Heathrow Airport).

That attitude on behalf of the British state—which, of course, can only have been bolstered by the sight of other editors and journalists deciding that the state must, indeed, have the final say—made mature conversations considerably easier in New York and Washington than in London. That's surely something to ponder in the aftermath of Snowden, and on the assumption that Chelsea Manning and Snowden are unlikely to be the last of the whistleblowers.

The spooks and officials and civil servants will surely also be pondering the question—much discussed during the story itself—of who gets to call him- or herself a journalist.

At the *Guardian*, we didn't spend very much time wondering whether Glenn Greenwald was a proper "journalist" or not. He is someone of strong passions and some rigor. He campaigns, but he also reports. He has strong views and wants to influence the debate but is also deeply knowledgeable about the things that concern, or even obsess, him. He worked very well in conjunction with our (more traditional in every sense) correspondent, Ewen MacAskill.

Other journalists, commentators, and legislators were not sure that Greenwald should be regarded as a "proper" journalist. Too passionate, too keen to sway the argument, too argumentative, and so on.

It's a pretty big issue and not only for journalists. Parts of the British state and government might have been fed up with the *Guardian*. But by insisting that the London-based source material must be destroyed, British officials showed no evidence of thinking through how, or whether, they would deal with Greenwald instead. Or even how they would deal with the fact that the *Guardian* had backup copies of documents in the offices of ProPublica and the *New York Times*.

They made us smash our hard discs. But we didn't stop publishing. To some, the image of a gouged-out *Guardian* computer circuit board was a sinister one. The mayor of Leipzig, when he visited my office, found it a chilling one, for reasons that are still within living memory of millions of Germans.

But just as there is no single public interest, there can be no single view of what happened during the Snowden affair. Over time, I began to find the image of destroyed computers both chilling and an icon of optimism—precisely because we went on publishing.

The Internet is the thing they fear. The thing they want to master. The space in which we may all find darkness as well as light. But the very reasons the state wants to tame, penetrate, and control the digital universe are the same reasons that make it an instrument of liberty. What was unpublishable in Britain was publishable elsewhere. Infuriating to the British state, no doubt. But, we would all agree, wonderful if the information in question was trying to escape the control of China or Turkey or Russia or Syria.

So Snowden opened our eyes to multiple, sometimes competing and clashing public interests—including those represented by corporations, civil libertarians, intelligence agencies, lawyers, journalists, and politicians.

It feels to me that we still have to do full credit to the full array of things to which Snowden was trying to draw our attention—the full picture of jostling public interests to do with journalism, law, intelligence, terrorism, international relations, commerce, privacy, politics, oversight, civil liberties, technology, encryption, security, confidentiality, and freedom.

Western politicians—by cleverly reducing the arguments to privacy versus security or free speech versus terror—managed to distract attention away from the substantive issues at the heart of Edward Snowden. But they remain there, and they're important—and I suspect we will still be discussing them twenty years from now.

NOTE

1. Leveson Inquiry: Culture, Practice and Ethics of the Press, The Leveson Inquiry, http://webarchive.nationalarchives.gov.uk/20140122145147/http:/www.levesoninquiry.org.uk.

2

IN DEFENSE OF LEAKS

JILL ABRAMSON

One of the most memorable conversations I had at the *New York Times* was with Punch Sulzberger. I came to his chairman emeritus office to interview him about the Pentagon Papers for a speech I was giving. Punch recalled that right before the *Times* published the first stories based on Daniel Ellsberg's leak of the classified Vietnam study, he was gardening at his weekend estate. He saw a helicopter approaching and thought, "They are coming to take me away." Although Punch was being lighthearted, his fear that the *Times* would be prosecuted for publishing the Pentagon Papers was very real. The U.S. Supreme Court had not yet issued its landmark decision *effectively* barring prior restraint of the press.

In the summer of 2013, I worried about how ironclad that decision still was. Alan Rusbridger, then the editor in chief of the *Guardian*, with whom I had worked on the WikiLeaks material, had decided to entrust me and the *Times* with a massive trove of Snowden documents involving the British intelligence service, Government Communications Headquarters (GCHQ). The *Guardian* and the *Washington Post* had already, much to my chagrin, published huge exclusives from the Snowden materials, beginning with the explosive details about PRISM, a secret, mass-surveillance, data-mining program that the NSA had begun in 2007. I was sick at heart that the *Times* had been scooped and told Alan so. Now he was approaching me because he needed the GCHQ materials safeguarded because he feared, rightfully, that the British authorities would seize them. Soon, via a trusted courier, a package arrived in my office. Immediately I placed the package in a safe in the *Times*'s legal department.

Given the massive intrusion of the government's snooping, I viewed the Snowden materials as even more consequential than the Pentagon Papers, which had revealed significant government deception. In this case, too, the government had lied about the scope of its eavesdropping programs.

No helicopters were circling above my office, but I was worried, despite reassurances from the *Times*'s in-house counsel, that the U.S. government might try to prevent us from publishing stories based on the Snowden package. I wanted independent advice. Privately, I retained a lawyer, a friend from college days, to review the case law. Bruce Birenboim, a litigation partner at Paul, Weiss, Rifkind, Wharton & Garrison LLP, was also savvy about the Obama administration and how inhospitable to press freedom it had become, as evidenced by the James Risen case, among others. His brief concluded that prior restraint was difficult to get, but he also said, ominously, "to the extent the publication of the material can be argued to violate the Espionage Act (or some other comparable statute) the government's case is improved," and noted that the Obama administration "has been more aggressive in this area than might have been expected" in moving against national security leaks.

It made me uneasy when the British ambassador to the United States asked me to go to Washington, D.C., for a meeting at his embassy. Ever so politely, as I expected, I was being asked to return the GCHQ documents. I was careful not to confirm that we had the Snowden documents. Two days after the visit, I called to say that if we had such documents, we would not relinquish them. In the meantime, the British authorities had supervised the destruction of the materials held at the *Guardian*. When I had dinner with Alan a week or so later, he showed me a souvenir. Out of his pocket came a shard of computer file that had been hacked to pieces during the document purge.

Could such a thing ever happen at the *Times*? On the same afternoon that I visited the British embassy, I went to see James Clapper, the Director of National Intelligence (DNI), to protest the way the Obama administration was dealing with the *Times*, with its criminal-leak investigations and frequent requests that we withhold stories about national security from publication. Clapper's back was troubling him, but he had come to the office in order to meet with me. Surprisingly, he did not ask whether the *Times* was working on stories based on the Snowden trove. I told him that from now on, any requests to hold stories had to come from President Obama or his national security adviser. At least they had a constitutional duty to uphold the First Amendment. "It's first for a reason," I told Clapper, who barely restrained himself from eye-rolling as I invoked the Founders and their fervent belief that the press was a bulwark protecting the people from overly centralized government authority. I was pleased with my little constitutional lesson.[1]

In the Age of Snowden, any editor with a robust national security team has to have the stomach to fight the White House. Bill Keller, my predecessor as executive editor, had gone to the White House to hear President Bush warn that the *Times* would have blood on its hands if it published the original story about the NSA's warrantless and then-illegal eavesdropping. Democrats, too, had called me, the managing editor, to implore that the *Times* not publish. "This is the crown jewel in our national security arsenal," Senator Jay Rockefeller argued in a phone call. "If you publish, you will be helping Al Qaeda," said former congresswoman Jane Harman.

The *Times* had decided to hold the story for more than a year, in part because of such national security concerns. But our reporting had sharpened over time, as had the urgency of the story. I was relieved when the story went up on the web. But Snowden, still angry over the *Times*'s delay, decided to punish the *Times* by giving his documents to the *Guardian* and the *Washington Post* instead. I was sick over being scooped and frequently reminded Rusbridger about our mutually beneficial collaboration on the WikiLeaks stories. And finally, he had come calling.

Soon we were publishing consequential stories based on the Snowden material, including a front-page story on how encryption had been rendered useless by NSA snooping. Reporters dealing with the material became conversant with how to use encryption to protect their communications. The *Times* had learned valuable lessons about publishing stories based on vast national security leaks. During WikiLeaks, we had formed a secret working group away from the main newsroom and learned how to keep classified documents in a very secure manner. We were extremely careful not to publish details that could, even inadvertently, endanger lives.

With the Snowden material, we were even more careful. A tiny group worked in a windowless storage room that was kept under security surveillance. Cell phones, which can be used as eavesdropping devices by the NSA, were not allowed in the room. Because the group was basically confined to a cramped, airless room, I made sure to take care of frequent deliveries of food and treats. I noticed that the team was gaining weight.

During the Bush and Obama administrations, I dealt on more than a dozen occasions with requests from the White House that we not publish stories based on classified national security leaks. When the *Times* was asked to withhold information from readers because of national security concerns, such requests almost always involved difficult editorial decisions. Usually the government's concerns about the sensitivity of the material were valid and worthy of careful consideration. There are circumstances where information, when published, could endanger lives or compromise ongoing military or diplomatic operations. The *Guardian*, rightfully, had redacted pages from an NSA training manual turned over by Snowden because they revealed too much about certain ongoing operations. Snowden himself has said that he was careful in what documents he chose for disclosure so as to ensure that each was legitimately in the public interest.

There was always a difficult balancing test on what and whether to publish, in which reporters and editors weigh the concerns of the government against the press's duty to inform the public. Is the public better off knowing about the government's secret massive eavesdropping programs? The answer is an unqualified yes. Has publication of these stories harmed national security? So far, the government has offered scant evidence that it has.

In the Pentagon Papers case, which covered the *Times* and Punch Sulzberger in their greatest glory, Solicitor General Erwin Griswold argued that the publication of the Ellsberg materials could do grave harm to national security. Years later, in a memoir, Griswold admitted that he knew of no actual instance of harm to the country from the publication of the Pentagon Papers.

NOTE

1. At the time the Bill of Rights was drafted, the First Amendment was intended to be the Third. It became the First by default after the first two amendments were not ratified by the states. The original First Amendment was not about freedom of the press but addressed adequate representation in Congress.

3

THE SURVEILLANCE STATE

GLENN GREENWALD

This text has been adapted from a lecture that Glenn Greenwald delivered at the Nourse Theatre in San Francisco in June 2014. The lecture was part of a book tour for *No Place to Hide: Edward Snowden, the NSA, and the U.S. Surveillance State*, which recounts Greenwald's experiences with Edward Snowden, and the reporting that came out of the Snowden documents.

It's been years since I went to Hong Kong back in June 2013 in order to meet the person whom I think is clearly one of the most important, if not the single most important, sources in the history of American journalism, Edward Snowden.

The year that followed, at least for me, was a bit intense. But it wasn't only intense for me personally; it was really intense for a lot of other people as well. It was very intense for the fine men and women at the National Security Agency, and it was also very intense for the senior national security official in the Obama administration, James Clapper, who was caught red-handedly lying to the American people through the U.S. Senate about what the NSA was and is doing. This lying is every bit as much of a felony as anything that Edward Snowden is accused of doing. Unlike Edward Snowden, who is facing many decades in prison, multiple felony charges, and has been forced to live in Moscow in order to avoid living the rest of his life in a cage, James Clapper, like every single other national security and corporate elite of the last decade who has committed egregious crimes, has faced no legal accountability of any kind. But at least it has been intense for him as well, so we can console ourselves with that. It was definitely intense for President Obama, who had to navigate the fallout of having been exposed for presiding over an extremely aggressive expansion of the very surveillance system that he vowed repeatedly in 2007 and 2008 that he would reign in.

It was a pretty intense time for lots of media outlets that had to account for their behavior over the last decade or so. It was, first and foremost, very intense for the numerous populations around the world in multiple countries and on multiple continents who learned for the first time that contrary to what they had been led to believe for many years by the U. S. government, this sprawling, limitless system of surveillance is directed not at terrorists or other national security threats but is instead directed indiscriminately at them.

The reason that I think the intensity has been so sustained for so long is because the debate that was triggered by these revelations actually ended up being about a lot more than just surveillance. In fact, the debates have been about a wide array of other issues, at least as significant as the question of surveillance. There has been for the first time globally a profound examination of what individual privacy means in the digital age and why it matters. There has been a serious debate about the dangers of vesting large governments with immense power, which they can exercise in the dark with no transparency or real accountability. There has been a serious debate about the role that the United States plays in the world generally and the enormous gap between the marketing and branding image sold to the world about Barack Obama and the reality of who he really is and what he does. There has been a really important and long-lasting debate about the proper role of journalism, and especially the proper role of a journalist, vis-à-vis those who wield the greatest power.

Over the first year after the Snowden leaks as I was doing this reporting, I was focused on specific revelations: What is this specific surveillance program, and what is it that this capability actually enables? What is the technology that has been developed that allows the NSA to invade our communications in the ways that they're invading it? A lot of that, not just from me working on the story but for those people who have been following it around the world, has somewhat obscured the broader implications of the story and the revelations in the aggregate.

So much has been said in establishment American media circles about what Edward Snowden did, about the reporting, and about what these documents show, the vast majority of which is factually false.

When you are at the center of a story that the American media is paying an enormous amount of attention to, your appreciation for just how willing and eager they are to disseminate falsehoods escalates substantially. I want to talk about a few of the principle falsehoods that they have disseminated, and about some of the things that I think the falsehoods reveal about our broader political discourse.

The first myth, the first falsehood, is the notion that Edward Snowden is a Russian spy. When I wrote my book—I went back and looked at what the discourse was in the United States in the immediate aftermath of our writing of our first story. In June 2013 when the whole story exploded, I was in Hong Kong focused on the documents and working with my source, and was mercifully ignorant of the things that American pundits were saying. When I looked back at what was being said about Edward Snowden in that story, what was so amazing to me was that what was being said then—this was a time when he was in Hong Kong and before he ended up getting trapped in Moscow—was, in the same authoritative tone: *Edward Snowden is a Chinese spy. This is an operation being run out of Beijing.*

When Snowden ended up trapped in Moscow, some of these very same accusations instantly morphed into, *oh, of course he's a Russian spy*—without any acknowledgment that they were saying something profoundly different just two weeks earlier. I am positive that if Edward Snowden were somehow been able to escape Moscow tomorrow and make his way to Lima, the very same people would say, *oh, I mean it was so obvious all along, he was a Peruvian spy.*

There is an op-ed from May 9, 2014, in the *Wall Street Journal* by Edward Jay Epstein; what he says is that he spoke to a senior Obama cabinet member who told him off the record: "[T]here are only three possible explanations for the Snowden heist: (1) It was a Russian espionage operation; (2) It was a Chinese espionage operation, or (3) It was a joint Sino-Russian operation."[1] What that translates to is: *we have absolutely no idea what happened here, but we are willing to say anything at all, no matter how evidence free it is, if it's sufficient to demean him and malign his reputation.*

The thing that I find really fascinating about this is not just that there's so much evidence that instantly negates the accusation and renders it factually untrue, it's that Snowden was in Hong Kong and was forced to leave by the Chinese government. He was told that if he didn't leave, they would turn him over to the U.S. government—which is not exactly the kind of treatment typically extended by the Chinese government to Chinese spies. When he landed in Moscow, he was forced to stay for five weeks in the transit zone in the international airport while the Putin government negotiated with the U.S. government over things the Russians could get in exchange for handing him over. This is not really the typical treatment extended by Vladimir Putin to Russian spies. But the most compelling evidence for why it's so ridiculous is that he never chose to be in Moscow in the first place. He was trapped there, forced to be there by the United States. Snowden was on his way, attempting to transit through Russia on his way to Havana and then make his way to Ecuador, where he intended to seek asylum. While he was on the plane from Hong Kong, the U.S. government unilaterally revoked his passport. Many of us did not even know the U.S. government had that power—they can just wake up one day and say, no hearing, no charges, no due process, we hereby decree that your passport is, from this point forward, invalid. You are then prevented, even if you're outside your country, from traveling over international borders. When he landed in Moscow, he was told that he was not able to leave to another country. The Russians then bullied the Cubans into rescinding the offer of safe passage so that he could no longer go through Havana.

So the U.S. government first forced him to stay in a place that he never wanted to be, Russia, then had its loyalists and apologists in the media use the fact that he was in Russia as evidence that he was a Russian spy. Had Edward Snowden wanted to engage in any kind of malicious or self-aggrandizing acts, given the archive that he had, he had a variety of options. He could have sold this material for tens of millions of dollars to multiple intelligence agencies around the world and been rich for the rest of his life. Or he could have covertly passed it to American adversaries—none of which he did. He instead did exactly what you want a whistleblower to do, which is to come to journalists at well-regarded media institutions and ask them to go through the material very carefully and vet it and publish that which is necessary to enable his fellow citizens, which he considers to be not just Americans but all human beings on the planet, to learn about what is being done to their privacy. This is so plainly a pure act of conscience—somebody who decided that his political principles were serious enough to him that he was willing to sacrifice his own interests and unravel his life in defense and in pursuit of those principles.

Ultimately what I really came to understand about what Edward Snowden did is that he was willing to engage in this act of conscience because he did not want to live for the rest of his life knowing that he had confronted this extraordinary injustice and simply acquiesced to it and done nothing. He had witnessed this mass suspicionless system of surveillance that had been constructed entirely in the dark. He told me that the pain of knowing that, of having that sit on his conscience for the rest of his life, was so great that there was nothing the United States could do to him, including putting him into prison for the rest of his life, that would be worse than that.

Because this effort on the part of media and political elites to insist that there must be some nefarious, hidden motive that drove Edward Snowden to do what he did says a great deal about the people who make the accusations, but it says almost nothing about Snowden himself. America's political and media elite don't believe he could acted out of real political conviction because they themselves have no political convictions, and they would never sacrifice for anybody else.

There's another myth worth exploring in terms of what it reveals about our political culture: that Edward Snowden did what he did because he is a "fame-seeking narcissist." The thing that amazed me about going back and looking at how this accusation emerged was when I looked at the columns that were being written and the claims that were being made on television in 2013—it was amazing how quickly this script emerged and how coordinated it was. You can find dozens of these pundits who are saying exactly the same thing, using that exact phrase over and over and over again. Many people believe that media outlets and the people who work in them get coordinated messaging, that they're all sort of told what to say, or that they coordinate what it is that they're going to say. I was quite skeptical of that claim. I never thought there was overt or active coordination. Rather, I thought they were really just like herd animals; they repeated what others were saying. But the extent to which this very specific, idiosyncratic phrase—fame-seeking narcissist—came through all their moves in such an immediate, quick period of time, almost led *me* to start entertaining that theory.

What was so striking about it was that literally within forty-eight hours after we unveiled him on June 9 as the source for these materials, a wide array of people—like David Brooks in the *New York Times* and Bob Schieffer, the host of *Face the Nation*, and Richard Cohen, the columnist at the *Washington Post*, and Jeffrey Toobin, the CNN analyst—all attached themselves to this phrase, and all apparently decided that they were capable of diagnosing him—clinically, psychologically diagnosing this person whom they had never heard of before, never met, and knew nothing about—as suffering from narcissism.

There is so much evidence that makes this accusation entirely, self-evidently absurd. The very first conversation I ever had with Edward Snowden was over the Internet in encrypted channels before I knew anything about him. He said to me, "I am absolutely determined, to the point where I don't even want to debate it or talk about it with you that I am going to come forward and publicly identify myself as the source for these disclosures. I'm going to do that very early on in the story."

The reason Snowden was so intent on doing that was twofold. One was, he said, *I believe that I have an obligation if I'm going to do something that has this much of an effect on the world, to come forward and account for why it is that I did what I did.* Secondly, he said, *I'm intent on doing it because I don't believe I'm doing anything wrong; quite the contrary, I believe that what I'm doing is the right thing to do, that it's morally compelled of me, so I'm not going to lurk in the shadows and hide as though I've done something shameful. I'm going to step forward and say, "Yes I did it, here's who I am, here's where I am and here's why I did it."* But he told me, *The minute that I do come forward and make my public accounting about who I am and why I did what I did, I'm going to disappear completely from the media spotlight. I'm not going to give interviews, I'm not going to talk to media people, I'm not going to be in public at all.* He knew that the media was going to try and personalize the story about him, which would distract attention away from where he wanted the attention to be, which was not on him but on the substance of what the NSA was doing, on the substance of the revelations.

So, after we revealed him on June 9, for the next four or five months the biggest TV stars in the United States—all those actors who play roles of journalists on TV—were calling me almost on a daily basis, pleading with me to arrange for a prime-time television interview with Edward Snowden. He could have been on prime-time television every single night for months; he could have easily been the most famous person in the world. Yet, not only didn't he want any of that but he stayed completely away from television and all other journalists for a year until he finally did an interview on NBC while still in Moscow.

There's something much more significant about the accusation, besides the fact that it's just plainly false, which is that it's indicative of how whistleblowers and people who meaningfully dissent in any way are treated. I'm talking about people who decide that the prevailing order is fundamentally so unjust that they're willing to go so far as to break the law in order to resist and confront it. These people are always subjected to the same treatment: they get depicted as suffering from some kind of psychological disorder. We were always taught when we were in elementary school and growing up in the United States that people who were dissidents in Russia were sent to mental institutions in Siberia. To this day, China takes its dissidents and puts them in mental institutions as well because it equates dissidents with mental illness. If you go back and look at how whistleblowers and dissidents in the United States are treated, it really isn't all that dissimilar to the way that Edward Snowden was maligned as suffering from a psychological affliction.

When I was growing up, my primary childhood hero was Daniel Ellsberg. I admired him for all of the obvious reasons that most people today admire him, although in 1971 when he did what he did, very few people actually looked up to him. Although I always respected Daniel Ellsberg, I found the response by the Nixon administration to learning that Daniel Ellsberg was leaking the Pentagon Papers really confounding. The Nixon administration broke into the office of Ellsberg's psychoanalyst to try and learn about his psychosexual secrets. This always mystified me because it seemed like the ultimate non sequitur. The headlines were PENTAGON PAPERS, MAJOR LEAK REVEALS THAT THE U.S. GOVERNMENT HAS BEEN SYSTEMATICALLY LYING TO THE AMERICAN PEOPLE FOR A DECADE ABOUT THE VIETNAM WAR. Then the response of the Nixon administration was going to be that Daniel Ellsberg is a swinger and has this unnatural attachment to his sister from the age of seven and that he's working it out in therapy. Why would they possibly think that would be effective?

I had the honor of becoming friends with Dan Ellsberg and serving with him on the board of the Freedom of the Press Foundation, which we cofounded with several other people. The first time I ever met him, I asked him, "Why did they think that that would be an effective strategy; it seems like an absurd non sequitur?" What he said to me was, "You are thinking about this way too rationally." He said, "This is not how human beings think." The reason that tactic is actually extremely effective is because if you can depict somebody as engaging in personally shameful behavior, or if you can make other people perceive him as psychologically unstable or even sick, you make him so radioactive that you not only distract attention away from his revelations (the old classic case of kill the messenger in order to suffocate the message) but you actually make people want nothing to do with him. Not only him personally but also the fruits of what he has decided to do. So if you're thinking about Dan Ellsberg's psychosexual secrets, you're going to not want to think about the Pentagon Papers or talk about it because the whole thing makes you uncomfortable; it makes it seem like it's a realm of psychological disturbance.

If you look at how people who have been whistleblowers or dissenters have been treated, you will find that tactic used over and over again. One of the most compelling examples that I can remember was in 2010 when WikiLeaks released the Iraq War Logs. They were unbelievably profound; they unveiled extremely vivid details of American atrocities and war crimes in Iraq, beyond what anyone had previously known. It was one of the most significant leaks in all of American history. On the day that those leaks were reported by the *New York Times*, which was partnering with WikiLeaks, an article on the front page stated that WikiLeaks documents revealed American atrocities or civilian deaths in Iraq. Right next to that article, getting at least equal play, was one by the *New York Times* pro-war reporter John Burns (this story was co-bylined with Ravi Somaiya), which was all about the odd personality quirks of Julian Assange.

The article seemed devoted to depicting Julian Assange as a bizarre paranoid freak. But the *New York Times* was so intent on depicting him as a freakish, paranoid, mentally unstable person that it even talked about his personal sanitary habits: his clothes were rumpled; he slept on sofas; his hair was unkempt. Two months later, the longtime executive editor of the *New York Times*, Bill Keller, broke the story that Julian Assange's socks are so dirty that they actually crumple up around his ankles. This was the way the *New York Times* treated this extraordinary disclosure because Assange had stepped out so far from what is considered permissible, had become this symbol of dissent, that he had to be maligned as being psychologically ill.

Then the same thing was done to Assange's heroic source, Chelsea Manning. The *New York Times* and many other media outlets worked very hard to convince us all to believe that she had done what she did, not out of any act of conscience but because she was struggling with what they were calling her "gender disorders." (Or because she had tension with her father, or because she was gay in the middle of a war zone and that led to all kinds of psychological burdens.) If you read the chats that she actually engaged in with the person who ultimately turned her in, what you find is a model of rational, stable thought. Whatever else you think of her, she had an extremely cogent idea of why she was doing what she did: she had joined the military thinking that her government was acting patriotically both in general and in the war, and instead had discovered a whole range of abuses of which she was previously unaware and did not want on her conscience. She decided that she was going to leak this information in order, in her words, to trigger reform and debate democratically about what should be done about this. She is a model of rational and conscience-driven choice.

Yet, you see again and again the very same kinds of rational, conscience-driven choices being depicted as mentally unstable or the by-product of mental disturbances. The premise that gets reinforced is that the prevailing order, the status quo, is so fundamentally good that nobody would ever possibly dissent meaningfully from it, unless she were mentally ill. The converse of that is equally reinforced, which is that if you want to be considered to be healthy and sane and mentally stable, you will acquiesce to, rather than dissent from, the prevailing order. That is a very powerful message to continually reinforce.

There's a second and probably subtler, though more insidious, premise being reinforced whenever this dynamic gets bolstered: that dissidence is synonymous with mental illness. Here, the idea is that the only people who have psychological motives at play driving what they're doing are the people who object to and confront and resist fundamental injustice. Only when somebody does something and steps out like that do we start asking what it is about him psychologically that has driven him to do what he has done. The underlying premise is that there is no psycholog- ical motive to compliance and to conformity and to acquiescence that is simply the normal, natural state of psychological being. The only time that psychological motives come into play is when somebody dissents.

What that premise is designed to do is to completely obfuscate a crucial debate. It's designed to resolve a crucial debate without even acknowledg- ing that that debate even exists. And that debate is this: What is truly the psychologically disturbed or unstable thing to do? Is it to work within a military system that is engaging in systematic war crimes in secret and to help conceal that and acquiesce to it and help perpetrate it? Or is it to object to it and disclose it and uncover it so that people around the world actually know that it's happening? Or what is the psychologically healthy choice? Is it to work within the system of secret, indiscriminate mass sur- veillance and tell nobody that it's going on so they have no idea what's happening to their privacy and can't democratically debate whether they want to live in a world where that happens? Or is it to blow the whistle and tell the world what's taking place? What is the psychologically healthy thing to do in the face of a government lying to its own citizens for ten years about the winability of a brutal, savage war? Is it to stay within the military system and adhere to what you're told are your oaths to keep it all secret? Or is it to take volumes of government documents that prove these lies and give those documents to the *New York Times*? This is really the fundamental question that we ought to be asking—that this instant, reflexive equation of dissent and whistle-blowing with mental illness con- tinuously prevents us from asking.

I want to talk briefly about one more myth that has been at the center of the Snowden discussion. This concerns what the NSA and the U.S. government defenders and loyalists of the Obama administration have been saying is the reason they have assembled and expanded this system of mass surveillance. They tell us that they have expanded the system of mass surveillance and implemented it so aggressively because the people who are running it have a deep, internal, almost uncontrollable desire to protect all of us from really dangerous things, especially from the terror- ists. That's the claim that gets made over and over.

The idea of constantly invoking the word "terrorism" as a fear-mongering tactic has been what has justified almost everything the U.S. government has done over the past twelve years, from invading and destroying a country of 26 million people in an aggressive invasion to erecting a worldwide system of torture. They have kidnapped people off the streets with no due process and sent them to the worst human-rights abusers on the planet; put them in cages on an island in the middle of the sea, thousands of miles from their home, for more than a decade without so much as bothering to charge them with any crime; ended the lives of many women and children and innocent men in predominantly Muslim countries again and again and again through the use of drones. The word "terrorism," which gets invoked in every single instance as a debate-ending mechanism. It really is a word that almost has no meaning, and yet it's used to justify essentially everything.

There are so many reasons why we shouldn't take these tactics seriously—beginning with the fact that almost every story that we've been able to report on about what the NSA is actually doing has nothing to do with "terrorism." Whether it's spying on democratically elected allies like the Brazilian president Dilma Rousseff or the German chancellor Angela Merkel, or spying on economic conferences arranged regionally with our allies, or spying on oil companies like the Brazilian oil giant, Petrobras, or subjecting entire populations to indiscriminate surveillance on the grounds of absolutely no suspicion, we've learned of all kinds of actual espionage activities that plainly have nothing to do with the ostensible objective that they claim.

But there's a better and easier reason to know that that claim—"we're just doing this to protect you from the terrorists"—is deceitful and that it's a lie. And that reason is, through a great stroke of luck, we just so happen to have tens of thousands of NSA documents where, when they thought nobody was listening, they describe what their mission actually is: indiscriminate surveillance on the grounds of absolutely no suspicion.

The phrase, the motto of the CIA is "Collect It All." That is its motto. Not collect the terrorist communications or collect some or collect a lot, it's "Collect It All." The NSA is criticized by a lot of people, including me, and it gets bashed all the time in many different ways. I think a lot of that is deserved, but it sometimes does deserve credit and gratitude. In this instance, I have to say it does deserve credit and definitely has my gratitude for creating documents that are unbelievably clear about what its real mission is. These documents, many of which I've published in *No Place to Hide* and then put online simultaneously with the book's publication, repeat "Collect It All" over and over again. There is one document, however, that is my favorite NSA document because of its clarity in terms of just how comprehensive it is. At the top of the document, it says "new collection posture." This is the NSA describing its new collection position, and right underneath is a really ugly, though helpful, circle with six points on it. Each of the six points has a different phrase that elaborates on the "Collect It All" mandate. So you go clockwise around the circle, and at the top it says "Sniff It All" and then it says "Know It All," "Collect It All," "Process It All," "Exploit It All," and then the last one is "Partner It All."

This, then, is the institutional mandate of the NSA—it is collecting billions and billions of telephone calls and e-mails every single day from populations and nations all over the world, including our own. It is a system of ubiquitous spying. And it is the largest and most invasive systems of suspicionless surveillance ever created. The goal of the NSA, its true goal, is the complete elimination of privacy in the digital age. Its mission is to collect and store and, when it wants, monitor and analyze every single communication event by and between human beings that takes place electronically, meaning by telephone or over the Internet. That is its real goal. When you confront it with that evidence, though, it is no longer able to sustain these myths.

I did a debate with General Michael Hayden, the former NSA and CIA director under George W. Bush, who actually implemented and then oversaw the expansion of many of these surveillance programs.[2] Hayden stood up before I was able to speak and put on a very kind of grandfatherly, friendly face, and he said, "You know we're just struggling like all of you to keep our children safe. We live in this really dangerous world and I know there's a lot of claims about how we want everything, but I promise you we don't, we're only interested in knowing what terrorists who want to blow up this auditorium are actually saying." So when I was able to stand up and talk about and describe the document that said "Sniff It All, Know It All, Collect It All, Process It All, Exploit It All, Partner It All," Hayden again stood up and said, "Well I think what I really need to get you to understand is that when we say collect it all, we don't mean collect it all."

One of the reasons why the debate around surveillance and privacy has resonated to the extent that it has is that there's such little faith in most public institutions for good reasons, including journalistic ones.

If I were to report just that the NSA was engaged in these activities but didn't have the documents, it would not have resonated to the extent that it did. The reason for that is because citizens can go and look at the documents themselves, and that in itself does indeed end the debate about what the NSA is really about.

Privacy matters so fundamentally to who we are as human beings and to what it means when we talk about individual freedom, but in fact it's actually a difficult argument to make. People have a very easy time on a visceral level understanding why other values are immediately compelling to them, like the ability to feed their children or to have health care or a job. Privacy tends to be more remote and more ethereal.

The typical claim that gets made to dismiss the value of privacy and to say the reasons why we need not value it or care when it's violated is that there are really bad people on the planet doing really bad things, and those people want to hide what they're doing. Anyone who is not one of those bad people does not have anything to hide and shouldn't care if people know what he or she is doing. This mind-set was expressed in its most repugnant form by Eric Schmidt, the longtime CEO of Google. When asked in an interview about all the different ways that his company is profoundly invading people's privacy by making all sorts of personal information and information about their activities available publicly, he said in an aggressive and snide way, "If you have something that you don't want anyone to know, maybe you shouldn't be doing it in the first place."

Less than a year after that, Eric Schmidt demanded that every employee at Google cease talking to the online digital magazine *CNET* because it had published an exposé about Schmidt himself using information available from Google. That underscores a crucial point that the people who say that they don't care about their own privacy because they're not doing anything wrong, often do not actually believe it. Those are the very same people who put passwords on their e-mails and social-media accounts, and who put locks on their bedroom and bathroom doors. We all instinctively know that all of us need places where we can go and think and choose and be and explore without the judgmental eyes of other people being cast upon us.

There is a mountain of social-science evidence demonstrating that when we think we are being watched, our behavior changes substantially.

The range of options that we entertain dramatically shrinks. When we think we're being watched, we tend to make behavioral choices that we believe other people want us to make. It is a natural human desire to avoid the sense of shame or societal condemnation. We all want to avoid those kinds of judgments. A person who believes she's being watched is a person who'll make behavioral choices that are much more compliant and much more conformist and much more submissive.

And that is why every state loves surveillance because it breeds an easy-to-control and conformist population. There are all kinds of things that we want to hide from other people, things that we would tell our psychiatrist or lawyer or doctor or best friend or spouse or some stranger on the Internet, things that we wouldn't want anybody else to know. Things that have nothing to do with wrongdoing or criminality but have to do with who we are as people. It's only in a realm where we know that we can make choices and where we're not being judged and not being watched that we can really test the limits of who we want to be. It's in the private realm where dissent and creativity and personal exploration exclusively reside.

So a world in which privacy is being eliminated in the digital age, a world in which you are going to know that everything you're doing is susceptible to being monitored by authorities is a world in which human freedom has been dramatically diminished in a very individual and fundamental way.

This idea that if I'm not doing anything wrong, I have nothing to hide is actually a truly pernicious idea. It translates to the idea that the only people who want privacy, the only people who think privacy is important, are those who should be regarded as suspicious because they are the ones who are doing wrong and bad things.

That's actually the way the NSA thinks. In its warped mind, it looks for people on the Internet who use encryption to protect their e-mails because it thinks that if people are trying to prevent us from knowing what it is that they're doing, that's probably fairly good evidence that they are indeed doing bad things, and we therefore ought to consider them to be targets. It really turns privacy into evidence that you're a bad person.

There's one other implication to this debate—the idea that if you're not doing anything wrong, you don't have to worry about surveillance. After the first week of the reporting that I did in Hong Kong, I wrote five different articles, I'd unveiled Snowden, and I went on MSNBC and was interviewed by the prime-time host, Lawrence O'Donnell. He asked me a bunch of questions, and at the end of the interview he issued his pronouncement about the NSA surveillance stories. He decreed the following—he said, "[Y]ou know, Glenn, I have listened to your reporting; I've listened to what you've said with an open mind, and what I have concluded is that I'm actually not worried. This does not bother me at all. I do not feel threatened in any way by what you've told me the government is doing." I remember reacting with an extreme amount of irritation when he said that. I couldn't really quite figure out why that bothered me so much. It sat with me for a little while, and some time later I read a column by Ruth Marcus, the longtime columnist of the *Washington Post*, who is a big supporter of President Obama and whose husband served in a senior position in the Obama administration as chairman of the Federal Trade Commission. She had a similar attitude, and she wrote, "The government is probably collecting everybody's metadata, but you know what, I seriously doubt they're looking at mine." A long-established columnist for the *New Yorker*, Hendrik Hertzberg, who's also a very good Democrat, wrote something quite similar. He said, but in a *New Yorker* kind of way, "The threat of these privacy invasions are conjectural and abstract and therefore I don't really feel immediately threatened by them."

If you look at the people who say those things, in this instance, they all have something in common: they wake up every single day and more or less defend those who wield the greatest amount of political power. Of course, they're not people who are threatened by a surveillance system—they're probably right, they probably don't have anything to worry about. Or there are people who say, *You know what, I have made myself so unthreatening, I am such an impotent, politically passive person, that I seriously doubt the government is interested in the recipes that I'm exchanging with my aunt.* I hear that all the time.

There's an implicit bargain that they have accepted when they say something like *I know that if I'm willing to make myself so unthreatening to people who wield power that in exchange, I won't have to worry about what they might do to me. Therefore, since I am a person who is completely unthreatening to those who wield political power,* or in the case of people like Lawrence O'Donnell and Ruth Marcus and Hendrik Herzberg, *if I am somebody who is a devoted servant to those who are in political power,*

I feel like I don't have anything to worry about. It is indeed critical to recognize that even in the most oppressive tyrannies, the people who accept
that bargain are never the people who are targeted with government
oppression. If you look at Mubarak's Egypt, the people who just stayed in
their houses and said they didn't really care if we have democracy and if
Mubarak continues—those who were government supporters weren't the
people who were gunned down in the street or put in prison and tortured.
The people who *were* subjected to those abuses were the ones who made
themselves threatening to those in power, who went into the squares of
Cairo and demanded Mubarak's release. The measure of how free a society is not how the good, subservient citizens are treated; it's how its dissidents are treated.

What I ultimately realized about what bothered me so much about what
Lawrence O'Donnell and others said was that if you go into an American
Muslim community, or if you go and speak with African Americans who
have a long history of surveillance abuses, or if you go and speak to activists within Occupy, WikiLeaks, Anonymous, all online activists fighting
on behalf of Palestinian rights—you will never hear any of those people
say, "Oh, I'm not worried about the system of surveillance that has been
constructed." This is something that you can say only if you've accepted
that really corrupt bargain.

Many people ask about the Snowden leaks: What has really changed?
What in reality has been altered as a result of these revelations? The premise embedded in those questions in a lot of ways misapprehends how
political change typically takes place. It's important to recognize that
the U.S. government is the most powerful government on the earth. The
national security state is the most powerful faction of that most powerful
government. The walls of the National Security Agency are not going to
collapse in on themselves because we publish some of their documents
and because there is some public anger in the world: this is not how
change happens. But there is a lot of reason to believe that truly meaningful change will take place.

One place that one should not look for that meaningful change to
take place is the U.S. Congress or the U.S. government itself. The U.S.
government is not walking around thinking about how best to limit its
own power: that is not the way power is exercised. The tactic of the U.S.
government will probably be to pass some kind of legislation that likely

has the word "reform" in the title, and that particular legislation it can then call "reform," which will let the president go before the world and give a patented, pretty speech that says that he and we have heard your anger and we have recalibrated, in response, the balance between security and privacy. Which, in reality, will simply be the illusion of reform that is designed to do nothing other than protect and strengthen the system and let it continue more or less impeded. And that is the tactic of the United States when faced with some sort of public standoff.

But there are lots of other ways that there is serious pressure being put on the U.S. government. One is through the coalition of other countries around the world that are genuinely indignant about these kinds of revelations and are working together to undermine U.S. hegemony over the Internet. Another is through the tech companies, the tech giants in Silicon Valley like Facebook and Google and Yahoo and Microsoft. They do not care in the slightest about your privacy or the privacy of any of their users, which they demonstrated conclusively by eagerly cooperating with the NSA beyond what the law requires, when they thought there was no cost to doing so because they were doing it in secret. Now they can't do it in secret anymore, and now there is a cost to that cooperation so those tech companies are in full-blown panic about the impact of this system of surveillance on their future business prospects. They are petrified that the world's fourteen- and twelve- and ten- and eight-year-old kids—their future users—are going to be very vulnerable to the appeal by Brazilian and Korean and German competitors that you should not use Facebook and Yahoo and Google because they'll turn your private data over to the NSA and we won't. So they are really applying serious pressure on the U.S. government to reign in this surveillance.

The U.S. government doesn't care at all about public anger or public-opinion polls that show widespread concern about the NSA, but it does listen to the panic of Silicon Valley billionaires. This is a really important pressure point that can result in some serious reform, even though it's motivated by pure self-aggrandizement. The much better and more significant prospect for change is through individual action. Usually when there's a political injustice that gets revealed, it's very hard for individuals to find what they can do about it. This, however, is an exception. There are all sorts of things that individuals can do that are not just symbolic but that can actually meaningfully rein in the surveillance system.

One is to refuse to use the services of companies that are collaborators of the NSA. There are all kinds of companies in the world that have genuine commitments to protecting your privacy, even more so now than a year ago. There are individuals all over the world who now realize the extent to which their privacy is being compromised who are now using things like encryption and other technologies to try to build a brick wall around their communications, one that the NSA truly can't invade. If enough individuals do that, it will be a meaningful step in preventing what was supposed to be, and still could be, the greatest invention of human democratization and liberalization—the Internet—and thus prevent it from being turned into the greatest and most potent means of social coercion and social control.

The lesson that I personally learned from having worked with Edward Snowden is one that will profoundly shape the way I view the world and my life and my own acts as an individual for the rest of my life. The lesson is this: I've been writing about politics for nine years now, and I have mostly focused on the large injustices that have taken place in the wake of the War on Terror. These injustices have been perpetrated by the democratically unaccountable American national security state and the massive corporations that are its partners. Early on, I realized that if you go around and just talk about those injustices and dissect and analyze and document them, there's a serious danger that you can spread some gloomy defeatism. Many people feel that these powers are too entrenched, that these injustices are too enormous for any individual ever to do anything about them.

This is a temptation to which we all have the danger of succumbing. It's a temptation that many people who wield power deliberately cultivate. They want you to believe that you're too weak and powerless to ever meaningfully challenge them. It's a form of learned helplessness, an extremely potent human temptation in some ways because it relieves us of the obligation as individuals to do anything. We tell ourselves it's too big and there's nothing we can do, but it also plays on our fears.

Edward Snowden was a twenty-nine-year-old kid who grew up poor, lower-middle class, didn't finish high school, had no family connections, no power, no position, no prestige, was a completely ordinary, fairly low-level employee of this massive, global corporation. Yet, through nothing more than an act of consciousness, through an act of fearless commitment to his own values, he literally changed the world.

There are all kinds of examples of completely obscure and powerless people who through acts of conscience change the world. Whether it's Rosa Parks for refusing to sit at the back of a bus or a Tunisian street vendor setting himself on fire and sparking a regional conflagration and revolution against some of the world's most brutal and entrenched dictators—there are historical examples, distant and recent, that ought to teach us the lesson that any structure built by human beings, no matter how formidable or entrenched or powerful that structure might seem, can always be torn down and replaced by other human beings. I think the real lesson of Edward Snowden is that we should forever have the antidote to giving in to this kind of defeatism. No matter who you are as an individual, you really do have within yourself the ability to change the world, whatever that might mean.

NOTES

1. Edward Jay Epstein, "Was Snowden's Heist a Foreign Espionage Operation?" *Wall Street Journal*, May 9, 2014, http://www.wsj.com/articles/SB10001424052702304831304579542402390653932.

2. "State Surveillance: Be It Resolved State Surveillance Is a Legitimate Defence of Our Freedoms . . . ," May 2, 2014, Munk Debates, http://www.munkdebates.com/debates/state-surveillance.

4

A CONVERSATION WITH
EDWARD SNOWDEN

Emily Bell spoke to Edward Snowden over a secure channel about his experiences working with journalists and his perspective on the shifting media world. This is an excerpt of that conversation, conducted in December 2015.

EMILY BELL: Can you tell us about your interactions with journalists and the press?

EDWARD SNOWDEN: One of the most challenging things about the changing nature of the public's relationship to media and the government's relationship to media is that media has never been stronger than it is now. At the same time, the press is less willing to use that sort of power and influence because of its increasing commercialization. There was this tradition that the media culture we had inherited from early broadcasts was intended to be a public service. Increasingly we've lost that, not simply in fact, but in ideal, particularly due to the twenty-four-hour news cycle.

We see this routinely even at organizations like the *New York Times*. The *Intercept* recently published The Drone Papers, which was an extraordinary act of public service on the part of a whistleblower within the government to get the public information that's absolutely vital about things that we should have known more than a decade ago. These are things that we really need to know to be able to analyze and assess policies. But this was denied to us, so we get one journalistic institution that breaks the story; they manage to get the information out there. But the majors—specifically the *New York Times*—don't actually run the story; they ignore it completely. This was so extraordinary that the public editor, Margaret Sullivan, had to get involved to investigate why they suppressed such a newsworthy story. It's a credit to the *Times* that they have a public editor, but it's frightening that there's such a clear need for one.

In the U.K., when the *Guardian* was breaking the NSA story, we saw that if there is a competitive role in the media environment, if there's money on the line, reputation, potential awards, anything that has material value that would benefit the competition, even if it would simultaneously benefit the public, the institutions are becoming less willing to serve the public to the detriment of themselves. This is typically exercised through the editors. This is something that maybe always existed, but we don't remember it as always existing. Culturally, we don't like to think of it as having always existed. There are things that we need to know, things that are valuable for us, but we are not allowed to know, because the *Telegraph* or the *Times* or any other paper in London decides that because this is somebody else's exclusive, we're not going to report it. Instead, we'll try to "counter-narrative" it. We'll simply go to the government and ask them to make any statement at all, and we will unquestioningly write it down and publish it, because that's content that's exclusive to us. Regardless of the fact that it's much less valuable, much less substantial than actual documented facts that we can base policy discussions on. We've seemingly entered a world where editors are making decisions about what stories to run based on if it'll give oxygen to a competitor, rather than if it's news.

I would love to hear your thoughts on this, because while I do interact with media, I'm an outsider. You know media. As somebody who has worked in these cultures, do you see the same thing? Sort of the Fox News effect, where facts matter less?

BELL: It's a fascinating question. When you look at Donald Trump, there's a problem when you have a press which finds it important to report what has happened, without a prism of some sort of evaluation on it. That's the Trump problem, right? He says thousands of Muslims were celebrating in the streets of New Jersey after 9/11, and it's demonstrably not true. It's not even a quantification issue, it's just not true.

Yet, it dominates the news cycle, and he dominates the TV, and you see nothing changing in the polls—or, rather, him becoming more popular.

There are two things I think here, one of which is not new. I completely agree with you about how the economic dynamics have actually produced, bad journalism. One of the interesting things which I think is hopeful about American journalism is that within the last ten years there's been a break between this relationship, which is the free market, which says you can't do good journalism unless you make a profit, into intellectually understanding that really good journalism not only sometimes won't make a profit, but is almost never going to be anything other than unprofitable.

I think your acts and disclosures are really interesting in that it's a really expensive story to do, and it is not the kind of story that advertisers want to stand next to. Actually people didn't want to pay to read them. Post hoc they'll say, we like the *Guardian*; we're going to support their work. So I agree with you that there's been a disjuncture between facts and how they are projected. I would like to think it's going to get better.

You're on Twitter now. You're becoming a much more rounded-out public persona, and lots of people have seen *Citizenfour*. You've gone from being this source persona, to being more actively engaged with Freedom of the Press Foundation, and also having your own publishing stream through a social-media company. The press no longer has to be the aperture for you. How do you see that?

SNOWDEN: Today, you have people directly reaching an audience through tools like Twitter, and I have about 1.7 million followers right now [this number reflects the number of Twitter followers Snowden had in December 2015]. These are people, theoretically, that you can reach, that you can send a message to. Whether it's a hundred people or a million people, individuals can build audiences to speak with directly. This is actually one of the ways that you've seen new media actors, and actually malicious actors, exploit what are perceived as new vulnerabilities in media control of the narrative, for example Donald Trump.

At the same time, these strategies still don't work . . . for changing views and persuading people on a larger scope. Now this same thing applies to me. The director of the FBI can make a false statement or some kind of misleading claim in congressional testimony. I can fact-check, and I can say this is inaccurate. Unless some entity with a larger audience—for example, an established institution of journalism—sees that themselves, the value of these sorts of statements is still fairly minimal. They are following these new streams of information, then reporting out on those streams. This is why I think we see such a large interplay and valuable interactions that are emerging from these new media self-publication Twitter-type services and the generation of stories and the journalist user base of Twitter.

If you look at the membership of Twitter in terms of the influence and impact that people have, there are a lot of celebrities out there on Twitter, but really they're just trying to maintain an image, promote a band, be topical, remind people that they exist. They're not typically effecting any change, or having any kind of influence, other than the directly commercial one.

BELL: Let's think about it in terms of your role in changing the world, which is presenting these new facts. There was a section of the technology press and the intelligence press who, at the time of the leaks, said we already know this, except it's hidden in plain sight. Yet, a year after you made the disclosures, there was a broad shift of public perception about surveillance technologies. That may recede, and probably post-Paris, it is receding a little bit. Are you frustrated that there isn't more long-term impact? Do you feel the world has not changed quickly enough?

SNOWDEN: I actually don't feel that. I'm really optimistic about how things have gone, and I'm staggered by how much more impact there's been as a result of these revelations than I initially presumed. I'm famous for telling Alan Rusbridger that it would be a three-day story. You're sort of alluding to this idea that people don't really care or that nothing has really changed. We've heard this in a number of different ways, but I think it actually has changed in a substantial way.

Now when we talk about the technical press, or the national security press, and you say, this is nothing new, we knew about this, a lot of this comes down to prestige, to the same kind of signaling where they have to indicate we have expertise, we knew this was going on. In many cases, they actually did not. The difference is, they knew the capabilities existed.

This is, I think, what underlies why the leaks had such an impact. Some people say stories about the mass collection of Internet records and metadata were published in 2006. There was a warrantless wiretapping story in the *New York Times* as well. Why didn't they have the same sort of transformative impact? This is because there's a fundamental difference when it comes down to the actionability of information between knowledge of capability, the allegation that the capability *could* be used, and the fact that it *is* being used. Now what happened in 2013 is we transformed the public debate from allegation to fact. The distance between allegation and fact, at times, makes all the difference in the world.

That, for me, is what defines the best kind of journalism. This is one of the things that is really underappreciated about what happened in 2013. A lot of people laud me as the sole actor, like I'm this amazing figure who did this. I personally see myself as having a quite minor role. I was the mechanism of revelation for a very narrow topic of governments. It's not really about surveillance; it's about what the public understands—how much control the public has over the programs and policies of its governments. If we don't know what our government really does, if we don't know the powers that authorities are claiming for themselves, or arrogating to themselves, in secret, we can't really be said to be holding the leash of government at all.

One of the things that's really missed is the fact that as valuable and important as the reporting that came out of the primary archive of material has been, there's an extraordinarily large and also very valuable amount of disclosure that was actually forced from the government, because they were so back-footed by the aggressive nature of the reporting. There were stories being reported that showed how they had abused these capabilities, how intrusive they were, the fact that they had broken the law in many cases, or had violated the Constitution.

One of the biggest issues is that we have many more publishers competing for a finite, shrinking amount of attention span that's available.

When the government is shown in a most public way, particularly for a president who campaigned on the idea of curtailing this sort of activity, to have continued those policies, in many cases expanded them in ways contrary to what the public would expect, they have to come up with some defense. So in the first weeks, we got rhetorical defenses where they went, nobody's listening to your phone calls. That wasn't really compelling. Then they went, "It's just metadata." Actually that worked for quite some time, even though it's not true. By adding complexity, they reduced participation. It is still difficult for the average person in the street to understand that metadata, in many cases, is actually more revealing and more dangerous than the content of your phone calls. But stories kept coming. Then they went, well alright, even if it is "just metadata," it's still unconstitutional activity, so how do we justify it? Then they go—"well, they are lawful in this context, or that context."

They suddenly needed to make a case for lawfulness, and that meant the government had to disclose court orders that the journalists themselves did not have access to, that I did not have access to, that no one in the NSA at all had access to, because they were bounded in a completely different agency, in the Department of Justice.

This, again, is where you're moving from suspicion, from allegation, to factualizing things. Now of course, because these are political responses, each of them was intentionally misleading. The government wants to show itself in the best possible light. But even self-interested disclosures can still be valuable, so long as they're based on facts. They're filling in a piece of the puzzle, which may provide the final string that another journalist, working independently somewhere else, may need. It unlocks that page of the book, fills in the page they didn't have, and that completes the story. I think that is something that has not been appreciated, and it was driven entirely by journalists doing follow-up.

There's another idea that you mentioned: that I'm more engaged with the press than I was previously. This is very true. I quite openly in 2013 took the position that this is not about me, I don't want to be the face of the argument. I said that I don't want to correct the record of government officials, even though I could, even though I knew they were making misleading statements. We're seeing in the current electoral circus that whatever someone says becomes the story, becomes the claim, becomes the allegation. It gets into credibility politics where they're going, "Oh, you know, well, Donald Trump said it, it can't be true." All of the terrible things he says put aside, there's always the possibility that he does say something that is true. But because it's coming from him, it will be analyzed and assessed in a different light. Now that's not to say that it shouldn't be, but it was my opinion that there was no question that I was going to be subject to a demonization campaign. They actually recorded me on camera saying this before I revealed my identity. I predicted they were going to charge me under the Espionage Act; I predicted they were going to say I helped terrorists, blood on my hands, all of that stuff. It did come to pass. This was not a staggering work of genius on my part; it's just common sense; this is how it always works in the case of prominent whistleblowers. It was because of this that we needed other voices, we needed the media to make the argument.

Because of the nature of the abuse of classification authorities in the United States, there is no one that's ever held a security clearance who's actually able to make these arguments. Modern media institutions prefer never to use their institutional voice to factualize a claim in a reported story; they want to point to somebody else. They want to say this expert said, or this official said, and keep themselves out of it. But in my mind, journalism must recognize that sometimes it takes the institutional weight to assess the claims that are publicly available, and to make a determination on that basis, then put the argument forth to whoever the person under suspicion is at the time, for example, the government in this case, and go—"look, all of the evidence says you were doing this. You say that's not the case, but why should we believe you? Is there any reason that we should not say this?"

This is something that institutions today are loath to do because it's regarded as advocacy. They don't want to be in the position of having to referee what is and is not fact. Instead, they want to play these both-sides games where they say, "Instead we'll just print allegations, we'll print claims from both sides, we'll print their demonstrations of evidence, but we won't actually involve ourselves in it."

Because of this, I went the first six months without giving an interview. It wasn't until December 2013 that I gave my first interview to Barton Gellman of the *Washington Post*. In this intervening period, my hope was that some other individual would come forth on the political side, and would become the face of this movement. But more directly, I thought it would inspire some reflection in the media institutions to think about what their role was. I think they did a fairly good job, particularly for it being unprecedented, particularly for it being a segment in which the press has been, at least in the last fifteen years, extremely reluctant to express any kind of skepticism regarding government claims at all. If it involved the word "terrorism," these were facts that wouldn't be challenged. If the government said, "Look, this is secret for a reason, this is classified for a reason," journalists would leave it at that. Again, this isn't to beat up on the *New York Times*, but when we look at the warrantless wiretapping story that was ready to be published in October of an election year [2012], that [election] was decided by the smallest margin in a presidential election, at least in modern history. It's hard to believe that had that story been published, it would not have changed the course of that election.

BELL: Former *Times* executive editor Jill Abramson has said her paper definitely made mistakes, saying that she wishes she had not withheld stories. [Abramson said, in a Tow Center lecture, "I've come to believe that unless lives are explicitly in danger such as during wartime, when you might be disclosing things that could endanger troops, or involving putting people who are under cover in danger, almost all of these stories should be brought out in public, except in certain circumstances."][1] What you're saying certainly resonates with what I know and understand of the recent history of the U.S. press, which is that national security concerns post-9/11 really did alter the relationship of reporting, particularly with administration and authority in this country. What we know about drone programs comes from reporting; some of it comes from the story which the *Intercept* got hold of, and Jeremy Scahill's reporting on it, which has been incredibly important. But a great deal of it has also come from the ground level. The fact that we were aware at all that drones were blowing up villages, killing civilians, crossing borders where they were not supposed to be really comes from people who would report from the ground.

Something interesting has definitely happened in the last three years, which makes me think about what you are telling us about how the NSA operates. We're seeing a much closer relationship now between journalism and technology and mass-communication technology than we've ever seen before. People are now completely reliant on Facebook. Some of that is a commercial movement in the U.S., but you also have activists and journalists being regularly tortured or killed in, say, Bangladesh, where it's really impossible to operate a free press, but they are using these tools. It is almost like the American public media now *is* Facebook. I wonder how you think about this. It's such a recent development.

SNOWDEN: One of the biggest issues is that we have many more publishers competing for a finite, shrinking amount of attention span that's available. This is why we have the rise of these sorts of hybrid publications, like a BuzzFeed, that create just an enormous amount of trash and cruft. They're doing A/B testing and using scientific principles. Their content is specifically engineered to be more attention getting, even though they have no public value at all. They have no news value at all. Like here's ten pictures of kittens that are so adorable. But then they develop a news line within the institution, and the idea is that they can drive traffic with this one line of stories, theoretically, and then get people to go over onto the other side.

Someone's going to exploit this; if it's not going to be BuzzFeed, it's going to be somebody else. This isn't a criticism of any particular model, but the idea here is that the first click, that first link is actually consuming attention. The more we read about a certain thing, that's actually reshaping our brains. Everything that we interact with, it has an impact on us, it has an influence, it leaves memories, ideas, sort of mimetic expressions that we then carry around with us that shape what we look for in the future, and that are directing our development.

BELL: Yes, well, that's the coming singularity between the creation of journalism and large-scale technology platforms, which are not intrinsically journalistic. In other words, they don't have a primary purpose.

SNOWDEN: They don't have a journalistic role, it's a reportorial role.

BELL: Well, it's a commercial role, right? So when you came to Glenn [Greenwald] and the *Guardian*, there wasn't a hesitation in knowing the primary role of the organization is to get that story to the outside world as securely and quickly as possible, avoiding prior restraint, protecting a source.

Is source protection even possible now? You were extremely prescient in thinking there's no point in protecting yourself.

SNOWDEN: I have an unfair advantage.

BELL: You do, but still, that's a big change from twenty years ago.

SNOWDEN: This is something that we saw contemporary examples of in the public record in 2013. It was the James Risen case where we saw the Department of Justice, and government more broadly, was abusing its powers to demand blanket records of e-mail and call data, and the AP case where phone records for calls that were made from the bureaus of journalism were seized.

That by itself is suddenly chilling, because the traditional work of journalism, the traditional culture, where the journalist would just call their contact and say, "Hey, let's talk," suddenly becomes incriminating. But more seriously, if the individual in question, the government employee who is working with a journalist to report some issue of public interest, if this individual has gone so far to commit an act of journalism, suddenly they can be discovered trivially if they're not aware of this.

I didn't have that insight at the time I was trying to come forward because I had no relationship with journalists. I had never talked to a journalist in any substantive capacity. So, instead, I simply thought about the adversarial relationship that I had inherited from my work as an intelligence officer, working for the CIA and the NSA. Everything is a secret, and you've got two different kinds of cover. You've got cover for status, which is: You're overseas, you're living as a diplomat because you have to explain why you're there. You can't just say, "Oh, yeah, I work for the CIA." But you also have a different kind of cover, which is what's called cover for action. Where you're not going to live in the region for a long time; you may just be in a building, and you have to explain why you're walking through there; you need some kind of pretext. This kind of trade-craft unfortunately is becoming more necessary in the reportorial process. Journalists need to know this; sources need to know this. At any given time, if you were pulled over by a police officer and they want to search your phone or something like that, you might need to explain the presence of an application. This is particularly true if you're in a country like Bangladesh. I have heard that they're now looking for the presence of VPN [virtual private network software] for avoiding censorship locks and being able to access uncontrolled news networks as evidence of opposition, allegiance, that could get you in real trouble in these areas of the world.

At the time of the leaks, I was simply thinking, alright the government—and this isn't a single government now—we're actually talking about the Five Eyes intelligence alliance [the United States, the United Kingdom, New Zealand, Australia, and Canada] forming a pancontinental superstate in this context of sharing—they're going to lose their minds over this. Some institutions in, for example, the U.K., can levy D notices [official British news-censoring system]; they can say, "Look, you can't publish that, or you should not publish that." In the United States, it's not actually certain that the government would not try to exercise prior restraint in slightly different ways, or that they wouldn't charge journalists as accomplices in some kind of criminality to interfere with the reporting without actually going after the institutions themselves, single out individuals. We have seen this in court documents before. This was the James Risen case, where the DOJ had named him as sort of an accessory—they said he was a co-conspirator. So the idea I thought about here was that we need institutions working beyond borders in multiple jurisdictions simply to complicate it legally to the point that the journalists could play games, legally and journalistically more effectively and more quickly than the government could play legalistic games to interfere with them.

BELL: Right, but that's kind of what happened with the reporting of the story.

SNOWDEN: And in ways that I didn't even predict, because who could imagine the way a story like that would actually get out of hand and go even further: Glenn Greenwald living in Brazil, writing for a U.S. institution for that branch, but headquartered in the U.K., the *Washington Post* providing the institutional clout and saying, "Look, this is a real story, these aren't just crazy leftists arguing about this," and *Der Spiegel* in Germany with Laura [Poitras]. It simply represented a system that I did not believe could be overcome before the story could be put out. By the time the government could get their ducks in a row and try to interfere with it, that would itself become the story.

BELL: You're actually giving a sophisticated analysis of much of what's happened to both reporting practice and media structures. As you say, you had no prior interactions with journalists. I think one of the reasons the press warmed to you was because you put faith in journalists, weirdly. You went in thinking I think I can trust these people, not just with your life, but with a huge responsibility. Then you spent an enormous amount of time, particularly with Glenn, Laura, and Ewen [MacAskill] in those hotel rooms. What was that reverse frisking process like as you were getting to know them? My experience is as people get closer to the press, they often like it less. Why would you trust journalists?

SNOWDEN: This gets into the larger question: How did you feel about journalists, what was the process of becoming acquainted with them? There's both a political response and a practical response. Specifically about Glenn, I believe very strongly that there's no more important quality for a journalist than independence. That's independence of perspective, and particularly skepticism of claims. The more powerful the institution, the more skeptical one should be. There's an argument that was put forth by an earlier journalist, I. F. Stone: "All governments are run by liars and nothing they say should be believed." In my experience, this is absolutely a fact. I've met with Daniel Ellsberg and spoken about this, and it comports with his experience as well. He would be briefing the Secretary of Defense on the airplane, and then when the Secretary of Defense would disembark right down the eight steps of the plane and shake hands with the press, he would say something that he knew was absolutely false and was completely contrary to what they had just said in the meeting [inside the plane] because that was his role. That was his job, his duty, his responsibility as a member of that institution.

Now Glenn Greenwald, if we think about him as an archetype, really represents the purest form of that. I would argue that despite the failings of any journalist in one way or another, if they have that independence of perspective, they have the greatest capacity for reporting that a journalist can attain. Ultimately, no matter how brilliant you are, no matter how charismatic you are, no matter how perfect or absolute your sourcing is, or your access, if you simply take the claims of institutions that have the most privilege that they must protect, at face value, and you're willing to sort of repeat them, all of those other things that are working in your favor in the final calculus amount to nothing because you're missing the fundamentals. There was the broader question of what it's like working with these journalists and going through that process. There is the argument that I was naïve. In fact, that's one of the most common criticisms about me today—that I am too naïve, that I have too much faith in the government, that I have too much faith in the press. I don't see that as a weakness. I am naïve, but I think that idealism is critical to achieving change, ultimately not of policy but of culture, right? Because we can change this or that law, we can change this or that policy or program, but at the end of the day, it's the values of the people in these institutions that are producing these policies or programs. It's the values of the people who are sitting at the desk with the blank page in Microsoft Office, or whatever journalists are using now.

BELL: I hope they're not using Microsoft Office, but you never know.

SNOWDEN: They have the blank page . . .

BELL: They have the blank page, exactly.

SNOWDEN: In their content-management system, or whatever. How is that individual going to approach this collection of facts in the next week, in the next month, in the next year, in the next decade? What will the professor in the journalism school say in their lecture that will impart these values, again, sort of mimetically into the next cohort of reporters? If we do not win on that, we have lost comprehensively. More fundamentally, people say, "Why did you trust the press, given their failures?" Given the fact that I was, in fact, quite famous for criticizing the press.

BELL: If they had done their job, you would be at home now.

SNOWDEN: Yeah, I would still be living quite comfortably in Hawaii.

BELL: Which is not so bad, when you put it that way.

SNOWDEN: People ask how could you do this, why would you do this? How could you trust a journalist that you knew had no training at all in operational security to keep your identity safe because if they screw up, you're going to jail. The answer was that that was actually what I was expecting. I never expected to make it out of Hawaii. I was going to try my best, but my ultimate goal was simply to get this information back in the hands of the public. I felt that the only way that could be done meaningfully was through the press. If we can't have faith in the press, if we can't sort of take that leap of faith and either be served well by them, or underserved and have the press fail, we've already lost. You cannot have an open society without open communication.

Ultimately, the test of open communication is a free press. If they can't look for information, if they can't contest the government's control of information, and ultimately print information—not just about government but also about corporate interests—that has a deleterious impact on the preferences of power, on the prerogatives of power. You may have something, but I would argue it's not the traditional American democracy that I believed in.

So the idea here was that I could take these risks because I already expected to bear the costs. I expected the end of the road was a cliff. This is actually illustrated quite well in *Citizenfour* because it shows that there was absolutely no plan at all for the day after.

The planning to get to the point of working with the journalists, of transmitting this information, of explaining, contextualizing—it was obsessively detailed, because it had to be. Beyond that, the risks were my own. They weren't for the journalists. They could do everything else. That was by design as well, because if the journalists had done anything shady—for example, if I had stayed in place at the NSA as a source and they had asked me for this document, and that document, it could have undermined the independence, the credibility of the process, and actually brought risks upon them that could have led to new constraints upon journalism.

BELL: So nothing you experienced in the room with the team, or what happened after, made you question or reevaluate journalism?

SNOWDEN: I didn't say that. Actually working more closely with the journalists has radically reshaped my understanding of journalism, and that continues through to today. I think you would agree that anybody who's worked in the news industry, either directly or even peripherally, has seen journalists—or, more directly, editors—who are terrified, who hold back a story, who don't want to publish a detail, who want to wait for the lawyers, who are concerned with liability.

You also have journalists who go out on their own and they publish details which actually are damaging, directly to personal safety. There were details published by at least one of the journalists that were discussing communication methods that I was still actively using, that previously had been secret. But the journalists didn't even forewarn me, so suddenly I had to change all of my methods on the fly.

Which worked out OK because I had the capabilities to do that, but dangerous.

BELL: When did that happen?

SNOWDEN: This was at the height of public interest, basically. The idea here is that a journalist ultimately, and particularly a certain class of journalist, they don't owe any allegiance to their source, right? They don't write the story in line with what the sources desires; they don't go about their publication schedule to benefit, or to detriment, in theory, the source at all. There are strong arguments that that's the way it should be: public knowledge of the truth is more important than the risks that knowledge creates for a few. But at the same time, when a journalist is reporting on something like a classified program implicating one of the government's sources, you see an incredibly high standard of care applied to make sure they can't be blamed if something goes wrong down the road after publication. The journalists will go, "Well, we'll hold back this detail from that story reporting on classified documents, because if we name this government official it might expose them to some harm, or it might get this program shut down, or even if it might cause them to have to rearrange the deck chairs in the operations in some far away country."

That's just being careful, right? But ask yourself: Should journalists be just as careful when the one facing the blowback of a particular detail is their own source? In my experience, the answer does not seem to be as obvious as you might expect.

When you think about what an intelligence agency is, all they are is the government's secret journalists. The idea of a case officer, for example, in the Central Intelligence Agency, this is what we would imagine in Hollywood. They call it a CIA agent; in reality, it's a case officer. A case officer is simply someone who runs a number of sources. Now these are clandestine sources that have actually been developed, these aren't people who came to journalists. But this is actually someone whose full-time job is to meet a bunch of individuals, assess their access, assess their vulnerability to manipulation, to coercion, and eventually over time, develop them to the point where they can be recruited.

They'll sign a piece of paper that completely implicates them, because then you know they're psychologically bought into it. They've signed their name, they know what they're doing, and they'll be the most committed source that a journalist could ever hope for, because of course, a spy agency can promise more than a journalist.

BELL: Right, and there are, as you say, really strong contingencies. From my own experience, journalists and police are very similar. There's an information exchange.

One of the interesting things that challenges us here at Columbia when we're looking at the future, is that we are entering an era of surveillance technology being universally available.

Journalists are now being challenged, ethically, to think about all of the technologies and methods that they can apply to surveying and inferring. Intelligence agencies would have been using these technologies fifteen, twenty years ago. Journalists are now going to be able to use those facilities themselves, and they are now cost-effective methods. When you can survey the whole world, if you can obtain information in ways that you never could, should you?

SNOWDEN: There was an idea you touched on there, which was the difference in capabilities—but commonality of intentions—of journalists, spies, and police. It's interesting to me, because you can actually depoliticize the conversation. Instead of talking about police or spies, or journalists and their sources, simply refer to them as "informants." That's really what they are, even for journalists, the source is an informant. They're providing some sort of information that was not previously public, not previously accessible. Then the journalists actually serve as the *public's* informant.

This was how I described myself. The pivot was that I used to work for the government; now I work for the public. They are not quite the same thing anymore. There is a growing distinction between the state and the public, in terms of their interests. We see in many cases that the desires of the state or the government are actually contrary in intention to the desires of the public.

Today, we've fundamentally rejected the policies of total war; we specifically try to minimize civilian casualties. But we maintain the same intelligence policies that were born out of total war policies. Are they the same, are they appropriate?

What was a spy agency supposed to do traditionally? Post-9/11, and actually since the beginning of the Cold War—if you go back far enough—you can say it's a by-product of the policies of total war that were born after World War II. If you're willing to incinerate an entire city with atomic fire, the idea of having agents of government engaged in sabotage or arson or assassination is really not so controversial.

What does an intelligence community actually do? When you strip out those military powers, which are actually separate from and contrary to the traditional work of an intelligence agency, what are you left with? What you're left with is an intelligence agency that's literally tasked to produce information and reports to inform policy makers with the highest quality information that's secretly gathered—whether it's through diplomatic discussions, whether it's through electronic intercepts, whether it's through human sources and penetrations—so that they can inform their policy decisions. That's all an intelligence agency is supposed to do.

They're not supposed to be involved in drone strikes; they're not supposed to be involved in assassinations; they're not supposed to be involved in sabotage, or regime change, or anything like that. Those operational acts are not a part of the traditional intelligence-gathering process. This is one of the most controversial and least discussed things to come out of the evolution of the Central Intelligence Agency and the National Security Agency. Particularly in the Bush administration in the wake of 9/11, they increasingly became militarized, or identifying as paramilitary organizations.

The National Security Agency—they're technically subordinate to the Department of Defense. The Central Intelligence Agency is a purely civilian agency. During the time that I worked there, they used military language for everything they did. The motto is "Mission First." They would self-nominate to be what was described as a paramilitary organization. This is a radical change here, but when we think about it in the context of journalism, if the state increasingly embraces what could be described as direct-action capabilities, they move beyond the intelligence-gathering perspective and they start going, "How can we use this information in the most effective manner. We're actually achieving our policy goals directly, not just informing decisions, but actually taking action. We're going to pull this guy off the street; we're going to render him from one country to another country; we're going to torture him for further information; we're going to use that information to enable raids; we're going to drop missiles on the bases of the people that he named; we're going to subvert technologies and critical infrastructure of entire countries on the basis that the people that we were investigating said they used it for certain purposes."

What happens when you're creating incentives within society where increasingly private and secretive organs of the state have more capacity than the public has to contest or direct through journalism? What happens when journalists feel that they can't get the information they need to educate the public, even about the most basic facts, through things like the FOIA [Freedom of Information Act] process, because they are being rejected? We have officials, the most powerful officials, for example Hillary Clinton, who are trying to exempt themselves from these processes of governments, because they go, "Look, I really don't want my e-mails being FOIA'd, so I'll create my own separate system for that."

Will journalists feel pressure to embrace direct-action methods with people who feel themselves as aligned with the ideological effort of journalism—which is not simply documenting the claims that are made at a given time, but discovering the facts of the reality of the modern world at any given point? This would be, for example, hacktivists, who are probably the purest avatar of this thinking. But whistleblowers increasingly are becoming the same thing. Whistleblowers are becoming the mechanism that journalists are forced to rely upon because of weaknesses in access to information. At the same time, the power or the policies, the structures of gating off domains of knowledge are becoming increasingly common.

SMITHA KHORANA: Do you foresee a world where someone won't have to be a whistleblower in order to reveal the kinds of documents that you revealed? What kinds of internal mechanisms would that require on behalf of the government? What would that look like in the future?

SNOWDEN: That's a really interesting philosophical question. It doesn't come down to technical mechanisms, that comes down to culture. We've seen in the EU a number of reports from parliamentary bodies, from the Council of Europe, that said we need to protect whistleblowers, in particular national security whistleblowers. In the national context, no country really wants to pass a law that allows individuals rightly, or wrongly, to embarrass the government. But can we provide an international framework for this? One would argue, particularly when espionage laws are being used to prosecute people, they already exist. That's why espionage, for example, is considered a political offense, because it's just a political crime, as they say. That's a fairly weak defense, or fairly weak justification, for not reforming whistle-blower laws. Particularly when, throughout western Europe they're going, "Yeah, we like this guy, he did a good thing. But if he shows up on the doorstep we're going to ship him back immediately, regardless of whether it's unlawful, just because the U.S. is going to retaliate against us." It's extraordinary that the top members of German government have said this on the record—that it's realpolitik; it's about power, rather than principle.

Now how we can fix this? I think a lot of it comes down to culture, and we need a press that's more willing and actually eager to criticize government than they are today. Even though we've got a number of good institutions that do that, or that want to do that, it needs a uniform culture. The only counterargument the government has made against national security whistleblowing, and many other things that embarrassed them in the past, is that, well, it could cause some risk, we could go dark, they could have blood on their hands.

Why do they have different ground rules in the context of national security journalism?

We see that not just in the United States but in France, Germany, the U.K., in every Western country, and of course, in every more authoritarian country by comparison they are embracing the idea of state secrets, of classifications, or saying, "You can't know this, you can't know that."

We call ourselves private citizens, and we refer to elected representatives as public officials, because we're supposed to know everything about them and their activities. At the same time, they're supposed to know nothing about us, because they wield all the power, and we hold all of the vulnerability. Yet increasingly, that's becoming inverted, where they are the private officials, and we are the public citizens. We're increasingly monitored and tracked and reported, quantified and known and influenced, at the same time that they're getting themselves off and becoming less reachable and also less accountable.

BELL: But Ed, when you talk about this in those terms, you make it sound as though you see this as a progression. Certainly there was a sharp increase, as you demonstrated, in overreach of oversight post-9/11. Is it a continuum?

It felt from the outside as though America, post-9/11, for understandable reasons, it was almost like a sort of national psychosis. If you grew up in Europe, there were regular terrorist acts in almost every country after the Second World War, though not on the same scale, until there was a brief, five-year period of respite, weirdly running up to about 2001. Then the nature of the terrorism changed. To some extent, that narrative is predictable. You talk about it as an ever-increasing problem. With the [USA] Freedom Act in 2015, the press identified this as a significant moment where the temperature had changed. You don't sound like you really think that. You sound as though you think that this public/private secrecy, spying, is an increasing continuum. So how does that change? Particularly in the current political climate where post-Paris and other terrorist attacks we've already seen arguments for breaking encryption.

SNOWDEN: I don't think they are actually contradictory views to hold. I think what we're talking about are the natural inclinations of power and vice, what we can do to restrain it, to maintain a free society. So when we think about where things have gone in the USA Freedom Act, and when we look back at the 1970s, it was even worse in terms of the level of comfort that the government had that it could engage in abuses and get away with them. One of the most important legacies of 2013 is not anything that was necessarily published, but it was the impact of the publication on the culture of government. It was a confirmation coming quite quickly in the wake of the WikiLeaks stories, which were equally important in this regard. That said, secrecy will not hold forever. If you authorize a policy that is clearly contrary to law, you will eventually have to explain that.

The question is, can you keep it under wraps long enough to get out of the administration, and hopefully for it to be out of the egregious sort of thing where you'll lose an election as a result. We see the delta between the periods of time that successive administrations can keep a secret is actually diminishing—the secrets are becoming public at an accelerated pace. This is a beneficial thing. This is the same in the context of terrorism.

There is an interesting idea—when you were saying it's sort of weird that the U.S. has what you described as a collective psychosis in the wake of 9/11 given that European countries have been facing terrorist attacks routinely. The U.S. had actually been facing the same thing, and actually one would argue, experienced similarly high-impact attacks, for example, the Oklahoma City bombing, where a federal building was destroyed by a single individual or one actor.

BELL: But it's kind of interesting, because in the op-ed you wrote for the *New York Times* in June 2015 when you were talking about a change in global awareness, you described a post-terror generation and wrote, "One that rejects a worldview defined by a singular tragedy." You said, "For the first time since the attacks of September 11, 2001, we see the outline of a politics that turns away from reaction and fear, in favor of resilience and reason."

The idea that we're not going to have a generation that will be defined by a singular tragedy—there is something very interesting and differ-ent going on, and it's your generation, right? In terms of ISIS or similar movements, there is a kind of war which has a shape that we don't fully understand, because it is post-national, it's post-geographic, it's post–nation-state. This is where everything that you think about, and you have just extraordinary prior knowledge on all of these matters, is really beginning to crystallize.

SNOWDEN: The idea of the post-terror generation is already sinking in, and not just in the youth cohort, who have grown up where this has always been the way it is: there are always terrorist attacks, but life goes on. It's very similar to how the IRA eventually experienced a diminishing effect in response to their attacks. Even when the U.K. and London started to put up the iron ring, they were still detonat-ing bombs and breaking windows on shopping streets, but within a few hours people would be on the same street, shopping again, hav-ing swept up the glass. It's not just the fact that life must continue, because there is no alternative. It's that policy makers are begin-ning to understand this. They won't champion it publicly, because they're afraid of being attacked by their opponents and media for being soft on terrorism. Politicians still feel a necessity to inoculate themselves against the emotional resonance of vulnerability of the public. Nobody wants to feel unsafe. So they feel they must do something, make a statement, change some policy, even if they've already assessed these policies, even if they know they're not helpful. For example, the Obama White House in 2015 said we're not going to ban encryption, we're not going to ask for backdoors, we're not going to do anything like that, because we already looked at this stuff and we found it's not very effective.

Now there's a policy debate that has been started on the back of Paris to exploit the tragedy, to create more expansive powers for the surveillance agencies, but the White House has actually, actively resisted this. They've done it in a very careful way where they've tried not to take a position on it, and they made a speech where they peripherally referenced it. . . . We also see many more opinion pieces written by prominent authors. . . . Although it's still limited to people who . . . have tenure, people who don't have a lot to risk politically, they're recognizing that if we look at the calculus of threat, the common statistic, bathroom falls and police officers kill more Americans than terrorists do. If we were really serious about addressing safety, about addressing vulnerability, about saving lives, we would be declaring a war on heart disease, on automobile accidents, on cancer, rather than on terrorism, which is an emotionally high resonance at scale event, because it is amplified in the media. It is not an exaggeration to say far more people, not just in America, but in every country, in every city all over the world, have lost more family members to cancer or heart disease, than they have to terrorist attacks.

Yet, we are not only allocating finite monetary resources to combat what is ultimately a limited impact threat. In a coldly practical, pragmatic sense, we're paying with something far more costly, which are the tremendously rare enumerated rights that exist in a free society. When we lose these things on a conditional basis, on an exceptional basis, at an edge case, we have in the sweep of history seen that all too often that means we have lost them in a total and final sense. The prerogatives of power are such that when they pass an emergency provision, when they entitle themselves to a new power for the sake of a state of emergency, all too often those powers are not given up, that state of emergency does not end. Instead, it becomes legitimated through a new function of policy or law or regulation, through some way or another.

This is where it's necessary that not just political figures but media figures realize that the post-terror generation ultimately begins and ends with them. We get the cohort who has internalized these things, who intuits the relationship between the presentation of the threat and the reality of the threat. There is a far larger body of population which, in democratic societies, is critically important. They can only be reached when the writing class, when the communicative class, is willing to take that same stand and say, this is not political. This is not "alleged to be," these are the *facts*; we face greater threats than terrorism. That's not to say that terrorism is not a threat, but it is to say that through any calculus that you might present, it is not the sole one.

BELL: So what is the right level of surveillance?

SNOWDEN: So where should surveillance be? The easiest way to answer this is to understand that what's changed in recent history is that we've moved from targeted investigation, the way that law enforcement and intelligence services always functioned in the past, because it was all that was technically available to them, to indiscriminate surveillance. This is what the government calls bulk collection and what the public refers to as mass surveillance.

What's interesting is we're finally getting public evidence, and unfortunately events like the San Bernardino attacks and Paris attacks are the strongest evidence we've had, that mass surveillance simply does not work.

Now we know this from even the White House's own public reviews of classified programs, where they looked at all the classified information available. The Privacy and Civil Liberties Oversight Board and President's Review Group on Intelligence and Communications Technologies both found that the mass-surveillance programs exemplified, for example, by telephonic metadata collection, had never stopped a single terrorist attack in the United States. Moreover, they went further, and said, and these are their words, "They had never made a concrete difference in a single terrorism investigation in the United States."[1]

It's the same thing in Paris, when you look at their actual electronic communications that did occur that are on public record now. They used an unencrypted cell phone, some unencrypted text messages.

They'd carried that cell phone to their safe house, which is terrible operational security. The problem is that when you collect everything, you understand nothing. When you cast your net so wide that you're watching everybody, you're scrutinizing every communication for some context of threat, you miss the actual targeted, rigorous scrutiny of an enumerated list of direct criminal suspects.

Beyond that, there's actually a question of, and this is far less discussed, whether this is something intelligence agencies should be involved in at all. Is terrorism really a national security threat, or is it a law-enforcement problem? There's an argument to be made that when you militarize the threat, when you put it under the national security shield, you make the sharing of information much more difficult. You make the powers much less accountable; you cripple the oversight of these authorities. You limit the amount of people involved in the pursuit of them, which necessarily actually hamstrings it. It's not a strength to have a secret program of a small group of people trying to fight terrorism, because you're limiting the brain-share that's involved in them.

Quickly you go from having the world's population and everybody who could be involved in encountering these threats, to only people who can pass a top-secret security clearance—not only can pass it, but have passed it.

BELL: What do you think about the relationship between governments asking Facebook and other communications platforms to help fight ISIS?

SNOWDEN: Should we basically deputize companies to become the policy enforcers of the world? When you put it in that context, suddenly it becomes clear that this is not really a good idea, particularly because terrorism does not have a strong definition that's internationally recognized. If Facebook says, we will take down any post from anybody who the government says is a terrorist, as long as it comes from this government, suddenly they have to do that for the other government. The Chinese allegations of who is and who is not a terrorist are going to look radically different than what the FBI's are going to be. But if the companies try to be selective about them, say, "Well, we're only going to do this for one government," they immediately lose access to the markets of the other ones. So that doesn't work, and that's not a position companies want to be in.

However, even if they *could* do this, there are already policies in place for them to do that. If Facebook gets a notification that says this is a terrorist thing, they take it down. It's not like this is a particularly difficult or burdensome review when it comes to violence.

The distinction is the government is trying to say, "Now we want them to start cracking down on radical speech." Should private companies be who we as society are reliant upon to bound the limits of public conversations? And this goes beyond borders now. I think that's an extraordinarily dangerous precedent to be embracing and, in turn, irresponsible for American leaders to be championing.

The real solutions here are much more likely to be in terms of entirely new institutions that bound the way law enforcement works, moving us away from the point of military conflict, secret conflict, and into simply public policing.

There's no reason why we could not have an international counter-terrorism force that actually has universal jurisdiction. I mean universal in terms of fact, as opposed to actual law.

In places like Afghanistan and Yemen, the reason that terrorism is a problem is because there is a vacuum there—a vacuum which the international community can occupy immediately and directly. There's an argument to be made that journalists actually have an ethical responsibility not to exploit tragedy, and in fact to downplay terrorism and mass shootings, because we have documented cases, we've got timelines, we've got a huge amount of academic evidence that shows media coverage of mass killings inspires copycats. This is not to say the media should ignore a terrorist incident, but that how they cover it, how they shape their coverage, the language they use, is important. During the Bush administration, they were afraid to use the word "torture." They should get rid of language like "masterminds" of terrorist attacks, and things like that. Anything that glorifies or increases the level of sophistication, particularly when there's no evidence to say that these individuals were particularly sophisticated. In the wake of the Paris attacks, where they said we're doing this manhunt to try and find this individual, all of the press, the U.K. is particularly bad, I apologize.

BELL: No, don't—I should be apologizing to you.

SNOWDEN: Just the abuse of rhetoric in headlines and things like that.

BELL: Yes.

SNOWDEN: They really go for it in headlines. Saying these individuals are masterminds, when they're using unencrypted cell phones, despite the fact that in the last two years journalists aren't even using unencrypted cell phones anymore.

BELL: Right, though interestingly, that sort of information, kind of the inflation of drama, and as you say, the U.K. press—part of it comes from that actual tradition of editorializing. So there is a kind of a paradox and a tension in what you were saying earlier about how we should use language which is much more aligned, in a way, with advocacy. Ironically, the way that that can go badly wrong is if you look at some aspects of the U.K. press, which are actually nothing but advocacy outlets.

SNOWDEN: The question here is: Is it advocacy when what you're actually talking about is the restraint of language for which there's no evidence? Particularly in this case we're talking about the word "mastermind," where there are a ton of other words you could use like "ringleader," or a completely value-neutral words like "organizer."

BELL: Well, you know, having been through this, the BBC produce[s] a guideline handbook, picks which words should be used when, and how, and when that shifts—or at the *Guardian*, our use of language disadvantaged us in search engines (so there's a technology problem as well). People would look for the word "terrorist" or "guerrilla" in the political sense. And we would be calling them freedom fighters, or activists, so nobody would read our stuff, because we weren't using the mass terminology.

SNOWDEN: That's interesting. The counterargument would be that there is some audience out there who's actually searching for the contrary. There's another way that you could argue, and this is just SEO [search-engine optimization]—I mean we're talking in-the-weeds technical stuff here—where you could actually create alt text.

BELL: Yeah, alt text—that's what we used to do.

SNOWDEN: It's not presented in the article.

BELL: Yeah, no, we did that—we had alt text of really terrible terms that we put against our journalism, just because nobody could see it. But it would be found by the search engine.

You're now a director at the Freedom of the Press Foundation; what's the nature of your work there? Are you actively doing stuff on a daily basis?

SNOWDEN: I work with some journalists, a number of technologists, and academics about what these problems are and how they can be fixed. One of the ideas that's really fascinating to me now is can we enforce human rights through new means, when we encounter the limitations of the law? Because human rights are things which are not granted by governments, they're inherent to our nature. . . . When we see that governments beyond this border or that border don't respect those rights, can we use the technology that they are dependent on, as with every other state, to actually enshrine and guarantee the rights to their citizens, to which they would not otherwise be entitled?

This seems like a really radical idea, and it's clearly bothering a lot of governments. It's actually not so radical, I think. This is what the universal declaration of human rights was about. This is really what international law has always been about. The problem with international law is that it has no force, it has no teeth.

Can our increasing mastery of science provide a way, at least in most basic ways, to guarantee some fragmentary rights? If we can do it in one case, a single case, even an edge case, we can radically redefine what human rights actually mean for the civilian.

What I would like to do, and this is another Freedom of the Press thing, but it's further down because the technology is so primitive, is re-create that sort of Deep Throat parking garage, but it's in your home, the whistleblower's home, a café, or whatever, you can have private spaces, private conversations, regardless of distance, and they're protected spaces, they're safe spaces.

Moreover, the fundamental problem with this now is it's being developed by companies like Facebook. They're going to want you to login, to use your e-mail, use your credit card, use some strong selectors. I believe very strongly that what we have to do to is fix this—and governments are really, really not happy about this.

BELL: You don't say.

SNOWDEN: The challenge here is that journalism is a niche market, and it has very little money in it. The *Washington Post* doesn't want to give money for security and things like that. They do, but it's painful for them; it's a tiny amount. How do we expand that space? I think the only way of doing this is to find universal uses for this and, for example, I think this use case we were talking about earlier could apply in other contexts.

But I'm proud of how the newspapers that were involved in reporting the disclosures handled this, because everybody makes mistakes, right? There are things that could have been done better. For example, the *Guardian*, I think their largest failing wasn't an editorial decision; it was the fact that they kept the story exclusive to themselves. I think more than anything, what dampened the U.K. response was it wasn't like the U.S., where there were a bunch of newspapers covering it who wanted in, and had sources. Nobody in the U.K. had national security sources, because they've got a history of saying, "Well, we don't comment, we never comment, we don't do anything like that." So there's nowhere to go to, there's no way they could have expanded the story on that.

KHORANA: As you are talking about international human rights law and technology, there's a question about your own asylum status. In *Citizenfour*, you spoke about predicting that the Espionage Act would be used against you. Did you also expect that your passport would be revoked, or was that a surprise? Are you concerned about the politicization that goes on in dealing with these issues in international law? You've seen that in your own situation, in your own difficulty in getting political asylum anywhere. Are you worried about living, potentially, as a stateless person for the rest of your life?

SNOWDEN: For me, the answer about my passport is easy: I wasn't really thinking about it. The endgame was not my primary focus, because obviously—if you put yourself in my position, right, I had a lot of advantages that most people didn't. I had worked in both human intelligence and signals intelligence. So I had seen both sides, and that's extraordinary and rare; normally, you'd be in one agency or the other. They don't normally work both sides. They would in a management capacity, but not in an operational capacity. I knew what these programs were capable of; I knew what was going on; I knew what was being watched. I didn't really imagine that one person would be able to pull this off. So I was focused on maximizing the chances that I could. I didn't really have time to consider the consequences, particularly once the ball was rolling, and the journalists were in motion.

In the context of international human rights law and being a state-less person, it's becoming less material in a really unusual way.

BELL: From a really personal point of view, you're in Russia, do you worry about becoming a tradable asset in what's now a rapidly shifting diplomatic situation?

SNOWDEN: No, because that's always been the case. The fact that I was trapped in Russia by the State Department, frozen in place, certainly didn't disappoint Russia, because they knew that I didn't have anything, I couldn't do anything. That's a bargaining chip; it's something they could always flip over at some point. Honestly, I don't even think about this stuff, because I have no control over it. I have no way to influence it whatsoever, and it's always been the case. At the same time, I don't care, because I accepted these risks a very long time ago before I left Hawaii. The fact that I've been able to accomplish as much as I have, to contribute in a much more substantial way than I could have conceived, means that no matter what happens tomorrow, I can live with that.

NOTES

1. Jill Abramson, "In Defense of Leaks," December 3, 2014, YouTube, https://www.youtube.com/watch?v=ueDd-Vkvkzg; Smitha Khorana, "Journalism After Snowden: Jill Abramson," December 11, 2014, Tow Center for Digital Journalism, http://towcenter.org/jill-abramson-speaks-at-tow-center/.

2. Quoted in Michael Isikoff, "NSA Program Stopped No Terror Attacks, Says White House Panel Member," December 20, 2013, NBC News, http://www.nbcnews.com/news/other/nsa-program-stopped-no-terror-attacks-says-white-house-panel-f2D11783588.

II

JOURNALISTS AND SOURCES

5

SOURCE PROTECTION IN THE
AGE OF SURVEILLANCE

STEVE COLL

C riminal hacking and state surveillance challenge journalists to better protect the identities of confidential sources in an age of ubiquitous digital records. The threats to reporters and sources require a new conversation about best journalistic practices, one that will produce updated norms of professional conduct designed to strengthen First Amendment protections. Yet the challenge to source protection is intensifying at a time when legacy publishers and broadcasters have lost economic stability and professional confidence. The new structure of professional journalism is one of mind-boggling diversity. The question of who is a journalist and, therefore, who has the right to seek protection before the courts under First Amendment privileges is unsettled. Diverse criminals and intelligence services increasingly exploit Internet communication for their own ends, without sentimentality about journalism or its ideals. For reporters who seek to inform the public with help from sources whose names are not ripe for publicity, these are risky times.

One set of reasons that source protection is under threat arises from the general inadequacy of defenses against hacking by criminals and states. The theft and public revelation of Sony Corporation's e-mail is a warning to newsrooms and reporters. Imagine a similar public dumping of all the e-mail coming and going from a news organization involved in sensitive source protection. In her book *Dragnet Nation*, Julia Angwin documented related threats to journalistic source protection, involving the vulnerability of open-archived data sets to exploitation by a party wishing to identify a particular journalist's contacts.[1]

A second distinct universe of threats arises from public policy. Across Democratic and Republican presidencies since Watergate, until the Obama administration, the struggle between reporters and federal prosecutors was in a state of fairly stable equilibrium. During the Bush administration, the enactment of secret, warrantless mass surveillance to thwart terrorism created the conditions for more extensive, automated monitoring of journalists' sources in national security cases. During the Obama administration, through resort to the Patriot Act and other authorities, including the antiquated Espionage Act, the Justice Department has prosecuted more journalistic sources for leaking classified information than had all previous administrations combined.

Why? A particular president's frustration about leaks to journalists may have been a factor, but Obama's pique has been shared by virtually all his recent predecessors. It seems more likely that Obama-era prosecutors benefited from two advantages their predecessors did not enjoy. One was the proclivity of reporters and sources to communicate about sensitive matters over unencrypted e-mail, which has proven easier for intelligence services to capture, search, and sort than was the content of voice telephonic conversation in the analog era. Another advantage for prosecutors has been the Patriot Act and its more recent amendments, which have empowered the FBI to collect e-mail and other electronic communications at a lower threshold of suspicion than would be required under Fourth Amendment jurisprudence. Prosecutors have been able under these new laws to convert intelligence information into criminal evidence by using internal procedures that are opaque and ripe for abuse.

For journalists, all this should be understood as an upending of professional assumptions. In the years ahead, newsroom best practices of source protection must be reconsidered and rewritten. In particular, the use of unencrypted e-mail communication and social-media outreach, which has become routine in reporting, must be reexamined. In the vanishing analog era, responsible journalists kept their promises of confidentiality to sources by staying mum and by using face-to-face meetings for the most sensitive conversations. They also vowed to go to jail, if necessary, for contempt of court, should a judge demand that a reporter reveal a confidential source's identity. In the era of mass digital surveillance and the

Patriot Act, such journalistic bravado is less relevant to a sources' security. One person qualified to remark on this change is John Kiriakou, a former CIA officer and commentator for ABC News, and an admitted journalistic source for ABC and others about the subject of CIA abusive interrogations of Al Qaeda prisoners. Kiriakou was released from the Federal Correctional Institute in Loretto, Pennsylvania, in February 2015. The story of his conviction is a case study of the new perils of national security journalism.

⸎

In the spring of 2009, guards at the U.S. military prison at Guantánamo Bay found thirty-two pages of photographs in the cells of Al Qaeda prisoners. The photos depicted CIA officers, they later learned. Some of the officers had worked at the agency's Counterterrorism Center, which oversaw the brutal interrogation of Al Qaeda suspects in secret offshore prisons, mainly between 2002 and 2006. Shocked by the discovery of the photos and fearful that Al Qaeda prisoners might target CIA officers for assassination, the CIA urged the Justice Department to investigate the matter. The following year, Attorney General Eric Holder appointed U.S. Attorney Patrick Fitzgerald to take charge. Fitzgerald organized a special team of prosecutors and FBI agents.[2]

It turned out that the photographs did not reflect any Al Qaeda conspiracy to target CIA officers. The pictures had been assembled as part of an effort to provide legal counsel to Al Qaeda prisoners who might have been tortured by the CIA. The "John Adams Project" (named after the second U.S. president, who believed that even British enemies deserved proper lawyers when put on trial) recruited attorneys to voluntarily represent Guantanamo prisoners. These lawyers sought to enable their clients to introduce facts about their abuse in CIA prisons at their military trials. They hired a private investigator, John Sifton, to compile as many names as possible of CIA officials who might have been involved with the secret prisons and to obtain their pictures. Sifton downloaded most of the photos from the Internet that were later discovered in the Guantanamo cells. These were pictures of CIA officers who had retired or otherwise had made themselves known to the public. In two cases, Sifton surreptitiously photographed officers who were not under cover but were not publicly known.

In other instances, during his investigation, after consulting with John Adams Project attorneys, he refrained from photographing certain CIA officers who might still be working clandestinely. This prudence probably kept him and his colleagues out of jail.

For two years, Fitzgerald and the FBI investigated secretly whether Sifton or any of the John Adams lawyers had broken the law. Ultimately, Fitzgerald concluded that they had not. Yet along the way, apparently by sweeping up and examining e-mails written by many people connected to Sifton, including professional journalists and their sources, Fitzgerald developed another criminal case. In the end, this new matter would result in the prosecution of a journalistic source—John Kiriakou.

It is not clear what surveillance or subpoena authorities Fitzgerald and the FBI relied on during their investigation. But from court documents, it seems likely that federal investigators took advantage of the Patriot Act's loose standards for collecting e-mail in intelligence investigations. The questions that Fitzgerald was originally charged to look into, those concerning how Al Qaeda prisoners acquired photos of CIA officers, would certainly have qualified under the new laws as grounds for e-mail collection for intelligence or counterterrorism purposes. It seems likely that the FBI used intelligence warrants to follow a branching trail of e-mails until they landed upon the diverse electronic communications of Kiriakou, who, as it happened, had nothing to do with the offending photos, the John Adams Project, or its defense of Guantanamo prisoners.

Kiriakou grew up in western Pennsylvania. He attended George Washington University, studied Middle Eastern affairs, and in 1990 entered the CIA as an analyst. Later, he became an operations officer, trained to recruit sources and thwart terrorists as a member of the Counterterrorism Center. During a tour in Greece, Kiriakou clashed with his superiors. After September 11, he said, he was asked to train as an interrogator, to work in the CIA's secret prisons. He declined the offer and retired in 2004. Yet because of his work in counterterrorism, he had a glimpse of the brutal interrogation regime, then deeply secret. In retirement, Kiriakou consulted on Hollywood films and spoke about intelligence issues on television and to print reporters. As a cooperative retiree with an interesting CIA career, he moved swiftly onto the contact lists of a number of reporters who covered the CIA, including those at the *New York Times*.

According to court records, Kiriakou freely chatted with reporters over unencrypted e-mail and even used that medium to provide, confidentially, the names and backgrounds of CIA officers who might have been involved in the torture of Al Qaeda suspects.[3]

In 2012, an FBI agent phoned Kiriakou and asked for a meeting. Thinking that he was being solicited for advice, Kiriakou turned up without a lawyer at the bureau's Washington field office. The meeting was a trap. The FBI had already obtained reams of Kiriakou's e-mails with journalists, including communiqués that touched upon the identities of formerly undercover CIA officers. Prosecutors ultimately indicted Kiriakou for leaking classified information to two reporters, including one of the *Times*'s most experienced intelligence beat writers.

Notably, because they had such a full record of e-mail communications involving Kiriakou and the reporters, the Justice Department never subpoenaed journalists to participate in the prosecution. Therefore, prosecutors avoided any First Amendment conflict over the right of journalists to protect confidential sources. Thanks to the e-mail they accessed by unknown authorities, the prosecution had all the evidence it required to put the defendant under pressure. Kiriakou eventually pleaded guilty; no reporter was asked to testify.

"The extent of Patriot Act abuse is still unknown because of excessive secrecy enshrouding its use," the ACLU reported. The ACLU documented a number of worrisome cases where the zealous use of warrantless searches led to miscarriages of justice, such as the mistaken detention of Brandon Mayfield following secret searches of his home, computers, and communication. One reason that the full extent of such errors and abuses is unknowable is that the Patriot Act and its successors prohibit recipients of FBI national security requests for e-mail and other communications from telling anyone that they have been subpoenaed or why.[4]

The Patriot Act also makes no requirement that the FBI or the secret FISA (Foreign Intelligence Surveillance Act) court disclose publicly how, exactly, e-mail obtained under loose intelligence warrants is converted into criminal evidence, as may have happened in the Kiriakou case. For defendants such as Kiriakou , the new electronic-surveillance regime may appear Orwellian. For journalists working on sensitive national security subjects, there is a related conundrum: how to prevent future Kiriakous from being inadvertently exposed to prosecution by leaving a trail of indiscreet electronic communication records.

———— ∞∞ ————

Surveillance is emerging as a threat to source protection at the same time that the Justice Department has undermined the more traditional, if tentative, rights of journalists to avoid entanglement in criminal cases. The most prominent example is the case of James Risen, an investigative reporter in the Washington bureau of the *New York Times*.

In 2003, Risen prepared a story about a covert CIA effort to undermine Iran's nuclear program. Before publishing, he informed the CIA of his findings and asked for comment. On April 30, 2003, according to a subsequent Justice Department court filing, CIA Director George Tenet and National Security Adviser Condoleezza Rice met with Risen and Jill Abramson, then the *Times*'s Washington bureau chief. Tenet and Rice urged the *Times* to hold Risen's story because, they said, it would "compromise national security" and endanger the life of a particular CIA recruit. (The agent is referred to in the Justice Department's filing as "Human Asset No. 1.") Eventually, the *Times* informed the CIA that it would not publish Risen's story.[5]

The following year, Risen and a colleague, Eric Lichtblau, learned of a National Security Agency surveillance program that collected details of Americans' telephone and e-mail communications without reference to a search warrant—the beginning of the years-long expansion of surveillance that Edward Snowden would eventually expose. Some of Risen's sources inside the NSA thought that the program was unconstitutional.

In October 2004, Risen and Lichtblau drafted a story about the surveillance program. They again informed the Bush administration of what they had discovered. The White House launched "an intense lobbying campaign" to persuade senior *New York Times* editors that the story "would severely damage national security," Risen later wrote.[6] The *Times* decided not to go forward. That left Risen frustrated and concerned.

He took a leave of absence from the newspaper to write a book. In the summer of 2005, he finished his manuscript. He included his reporting about the CIA's flawed Iran operation and, with Lichtblau's consent, their discoveries about the NSA warrantless surveillance program. Risen found a willing publisher at Free Press. When he informed his editors at the *Times* about his book-publishing plans, he later wrote, "They were furious."[7]

Rather than be scooped by their reporter and Free Press, the *Times*'s brass reconsidered their decision about the NSA warrantless surveillance reporting. In December 2005, the *Times* finally printed Risen and Lichtblau's work. The coverage caused an immediate sensation and later won a Pulitzer Prize. Yet the *Times* did not reverse its decision to withhold Risen's reporting about the CIA's covert operation to undermine Iran's nuclear program.

On January, 5, 2006, Free Press brought out *State of War*, Risen's first book, which contained, in chapter 9, a critical account of "Operation Merlin." In this covert action of the Clinton administration, according to Risen, the CIA recruited a Russian scientist to provide flawed nuclear weapons designs to Iran in hopes of delaying the country's progress toward constructing a bomb. Instead, by Risen's account, the scientist pointed out the design flaws to the Iranians, which may have helped them.

After *State of War* came out, the Justice Department launched a grand jury investigation into how Risen had acquired his scoops. In 2010, a grand jury issued a ten-count indictment against Jeffrey Alexander Sterling, a former CIA operations officer who had left the agency in 2002. The indictment accused Sterling of violating the Espionage Act of 1917 by providing state secrets to Risen for his Iran chapter.

In prosecuting Sterling, the Justice Department took positions that came close to criminalizing the act of professional reporting on classified subjects. In a pretrial filing, prosecutors in the U.S. Attorney's office for the Eastern District of Virginia argued vehemently that Risen was a key eyewitness to a felony because the reporter had allegedly interviewed Sterling and obtained classified information. Although the Justice Department did not indict Risen, this theory of the case cast Risen's reporting as a form of co-conspiracy in a serious Espionage Act felony.

The Justice Department also took the position that it could not convict Sterling at trial unless Risen testified about whether Sterling had been his source. It was apparent that Risen knew Sterling; the reporter had published a profile of him in the *Times*, after Sterling left the CIA. Prosecutors also submitted metadata telephone records showing that Sterling had called Risen. Yet they insisted that only Risen's courtroom testimony could win a conviction. For his part, Risen made clear that he would not testify about his sources under any circumstances, even if it meant that he would be held in contempt of court and jailed indefinitely. Judge Leonie Brinkema found that the prosecutors had plenty of evidence to go forward without Risen's testimony, yet the Department of Justice appealed her ruling. Earlier that year, Holder backed down and decided not to force Risen to testify at trial. The prosecutors went forward against Sterling and won a swift conviction by introducing the telephone metadata and other circumstantial evidence, a demonstration that Justice could have obtained the result it sought without damaging the First Amendment further.

The question of when a reporter may avoid testifying about sources or newsgathering is complicated. Forty states and the District of Columbia have enacted "shield laws" that define how and when a reporter can avoid testimony in cases that involve state law. Generally, these shield laws ask judges to apply a balancing test to particular facts, weighing the unique value of a reporter's information to litigants against the need to protect a free press. There is no federal shield law, however, as of yet. When, in the absence of a federal statute to rely upon, reporters have attempted to assert a privilege under the First Amendment, they have struggled to succeed. The controlling Supreme Court case, *Branzburg v. Hayes*, which dates to 1972, is in some respects ambiguous, and appellate judges have interpreted its meanings variously over the years. Yet in criminal cases such as the one involving Risen and Jeffrey Sterling, *Branzburg* has never offered subpoenaed journalists reliable protection.

In some instances, judges have considered whether a reporter acted in a professional manner while maintaining source confidentiality—whether, for example, the reporter spoke indiscreetly about a source's identity to newsroom colleagues. Such cases highlight how adherence to journalistic "best practices" of source protection can affect the integrity of First Amendment claims. This is one reason why, in order to defeat surveillance and prosecutorial intrusions and to strengthen the rights of journalists before the courts, particularly in federal national security cases, it is essential that journalists update their own rules and norms for the age of surveillance.

———— ❧ ————

The use of encryption is clearly one response that journalists must consider. Yet it presents two challenges. It is difficult even for encryption specialists to keep up with the cat-and-mouse contests between individuals who encrypt and states or hackers who seek to break down their walls. If technically illiterate journalists are to continually adapt their encryption practices to reduce their and their sources' vulnerability, they will need well-resourced and systematic assistance.

A related challenge involves usability. Even where a newsroom may have the resources and leadership commitment to develop policies guided by expert advice and continually updated, IT specialists will face challenges in crafting tools and processes that journalists can adapt to the rapid-fire flow of deadline communication. In "Digital Security for Journalists: A 21st Century Imperative," a Tow Center paper, Susan McGregor spoke with a number of working reporters. She discovered, "Those who understood and applied digital security practices to their reporting, even occasionally, were either themselves covering sensitive topic areas . . . and therefore came to these understandings of professional necessity—or, like me, they had a sufficiently technical background to parse these topics for themselves."

To move from the ad hoc start McGregor describes to a more encompassing and sustainable change in journalistic practice, a place to start is journalism education. There is an opportunity to incorporate digital security into journalism curricula, as McGregor is helping to do at the Columbia Graduate School of Journalism. As with the efforts to integrate journalism instruction with computer science, the best approach may be not to teach prescriptive software or encrypted tools, which can become obsolete or counterproductive quickly. The best approach may be to orient journalism students to the underlying field of digital security, teach them how to conduct their own threat assessments, provide contextual knowledge about the Internet's vulnerabilities, introduce basic digital sanitation methods, and then prepare students to embrace source and other journalistic security as a continual endeavor. This approach to instruction would be analogous to teaching war correspondents how to manage their physical security amid continuously evolving contours of political violence.

Teaching digital security and teaching physical security to journalists are in fact related opportunities. Both require thinking internationally and assessing the changes created by the global digital age. Covering the Islamic State's violence in the era of online beheadings presents different risk-management problems to aspiring war correspondents than do wars between formal armies or a tear gas–clouded protest in Baltimore. Equally, teaching digital security effectively requires curricula grounded in global knowledge. Journalists must understand how to assess threats from diverse sources, at home and abroad, no matter where they are based. This includes study of the capabilities of authoritarian states to look into the electronic communications of national journalists or travelers using national telecommunication systems even for a short time.

The principles mentioned here also apply to strategies for professional development in American and global newsrooms. Those newsrooms also require fresh thinking about legal, ethical, and professional norms involving threat assessment, surveillance, and communication with sources. Ideally, conversation and standard setting about securing journalistic communication would be led by influential commercial newsrooms, as well as by new entrants in investigative reporting such as First Look Media and ProPublica, which have hard-won experience with these dilemmas.

The discourse across the profession should also account for the needs and relative isolation of independent, freelance journalists, who may require dedicated resources and education programs. Even routine news-gathering practices not involving confidentiality must be reviewed and protected from surveillance and other governmental intrusion, especially outside of the United States, where authoritarian crackdowns have lately pinched the press even in notionally democratic societies such as Turkey.

In the analog era, the Associated Press and other leading professional organizations published their stylebooks, codes, and ethical requirements as forms of professional service. How can a more fragmented, less confident profession rally to the cause of source protection in the age of surveillance, to define and publicize best practices, in America and globally?

There are many questions that such an undertaking might consider. They might include:

- In a large newsroom publishing breaking stories on tight deadlines, how should newsroom policymakers train and require reporters to recognize circumstances when encryption or other protections in source communication must be adopted?
- How should journalists communicate with confidential sources about these issues of vulnerability?

- For American journalists, what are the particular vulnerabilities of newsgathering and source communication to (1) criminal hacking, (2) foreign government surveillance, and (3) U.S. government surveillance? How should newsroom policies be developed and articulated around these distinct vulnerabilities?

- For international journalists, what are the risks and benefits of using encrypted tools to evade the surveillance of an authoritarian state where both journalist and source may be vulnerable to prosecution if identified? What strategies for offshore reporting may be most effective? For traveling journalists passing through authoritarian states but returning to more open societies, what are best security practices?

- If a rough consensus around best practices is developed, comparable to the consensus about ethical issues such as misrepresentation in reporting or the need to defend source confidentiality even under the threat of contempt of court, how can such new norms be articulated, distributed, and made relevant for independent journalists as well as legacy newsroom employees?

- What is the preferred role of analog reporting methods in the digital era? How can reporters trained and enabled by social media be trained most effectively to consider the risks and benefits of unencrypted electronic communication with sources?

- How can journalism resource public-interest encryption specialists—in nonprofits, academia, the open source movement, or elsewhere—to continually review, adapt, and make usable for journalists to best encryption technologies and practices?

Too often in recent journalism history, it has required a crisis—the discovery of a fabricator who has run riot in a newsroom, or the exposure of criminal phone-hacking by British tabloids—to force a reckoning within newsrooms, at journalism schools, and across the profession. Absent changes in source protection practice by journalists, it may only be a matter of time before a major news organization is embarrassed or worse by a hack of the Sony scale or by the imprisonment of a source exposed through avoidably sloppy professional practice. If journalists and their claims to First Amendment protection are to be taken seriously by courts and the public, journalism institutions must take the initiative.

NOTES

1. Julia Angwin, *Dragnet Nation: A Quest for Privacy, Security and Freedom in a World of Relentless Surveillance* (New York: Times Books, 2014).

2. This section of the chapter is adapted from Steve Coll, "The Spy Who Said Too Much," *New Yorker*, April 1, 2013.

3. See the e-mail quoted in the indictment, *U.S. v. John C. Kiriakou*, United States District Court for the Eastern District of Virginia, 2012.

4. "Myths and Realities About the Patriot Act," American Civil Liberties Union, https://www.aclu.org/myths-and-realities-about-patriot-act.

5. "COMPROMISE NATIONAL SECURITY . . . HUMAN ASSET NO. 1": Unclassified version of the Justice Department's brief to the United States Court of Appeals for the Fourth Circuit in *U.S. v. Jeffrey Alexander Sterling and James Risen*, 11–5028, January 13, 2012.

6. James Risen, *State of War: The Secret History of the CIA and the Bush Administration* (New York: Free Press, 2006), 270. This section of the chapter is adapted from Steve Coll, "The Reporter Resists His Government," *New York Review of Books*, February 19, 2015.

7. Risen, *State of War*, 272.

6

RESCUING A REPORTER'S RIGHT TO PROTECT THE CONFIDENTIALITY OF SOURCES

DAVID A. SCHULZ AND VALERIE BELAIR-GAGNON

The Snowden revelations of massive government surveillance of communications unveiled a fundamental shift in the relation between the government and the governed since September 11. It also prompted an international debate on the need to protect confidential communications, including reporter–source communications. Over the past decade, two strategies adopted by the Obama Justice Department in pursuing leak investigations have significantly undermined the legal protection afforded to reporters' communications. The first asserted that there is no "reporters' privilege" that permits reporters to avoid disclosing their confidential sources upon the request of a prosecutor. The second reinterpreted long-standing Justice Department guidelines in expansive new ways to permit prosecutors to seize reporters' phone records and e-mail communications secretly. The chilling impact of these actions has been palpable.

No matter how the broader debate over security and privacy is resolved, a way must be found to restore meaningful legal protections for the confidential communications between reporters and their sources. A foundation of trust is essential for effective investigative reporting, and a journalist must be able to make a credible promise of confidentiality that will be respected by the courts in most circumstances. Otherwise, a great deal of information needed for effective public oversight will never be disclosed.

In this chapter, we explore the importance of reporter–source confidentiality and the legal protections that came to exist in the years following Watergate. We then describe the assault on that confidentiality brought on by post–September 11 national security concerns. We finally propose a path forward to build legal principles that will preserve a meaningful zone of confidentiality around reporters' communications.

THE IMPORTANCE OF CONFIDENTIAL COMMUNICATIONS

Reporters understand that confidential sources contribute in critical ways to effective and rich investigative reporting, and have forcefully argued in many forums that their ability to pledge confidentiality is essential to their ability to uncover and report on government missteps and misconduct. In 1933, the American Newspaper Guild's Code of Ethics first emphasized the importance of reporter–source confidentiality for journalists to function as watchdogs of democracy. The guild asserted as a fundamental ethical principle that "newspapermen shall refuse to reveal confidences or disclose sources of confidential information in court or before judicial or investigative bodies."[1]

Examples of the central role played by confidential sources can readily be found. "Deep Throat" of Watergate fame became the iconic example of a confidential source in the public mind.[2] More recent examples of important stories that first came to light through confidential disclosures range from national security reporting on the operation of secret CIA prisons and massive domestic surveillance by the NSA to reports of the administrative failings of the Department of Veterans Affairs and mismanagement of Walter Reed Army Hospital. The fundamental importance of a reporter's ability to make a binding pledge of confidentiality to a source is indisputable. As editors at the *New York Times* have underscored, "American history is full of examples of whistleblowers who were able to inform the public of malfeasance only through reporters who were able to guarantee them confidentiality."[3]

In American culture, the critical role of confidential sources is a matter of logic and should require no empirical proof. In 1941, U.S. Attorney

General Robert Jackson refused to release FBI reports to Congress because some of the most valuable information obtained by the FBI "can only be obtained upon a pledge not to disclose its sources." As Jackson explained, compelled disclosure of sources "would be of serious prejudice to the future usefulness of the Federal Bureau of Investigation."[4] The same principle applies to investigative reporters.

EVOLUTION OF A REPORTERS' PRIVILEGE IN THE UNITED STATES

To ensure that citizens benefit from information reporters can gain only on a confidential basis, the law has developed a legal privilege for reporters to resist efforts to compel the disclosure of their sources through various means. Thirty-seven states and the District of Columbia have established such a privilege through legislation, known as "shield laws." Most state courts have also recognized some form of privilege through judicial decisions. These states have recognized a reporters' privilege as a common law evidentiary privilege or as a constitutional privilege implicit within the protections of free speech and a free press.

Every state except Hawaii and South Dakota currently recognizes a reporters' privilege in some form as a matter of state law. The scope of protection, however, varies from state to state. Florida, for example, extends to a professional reporter only a qualified privilege not to disclose a confidential source.[5] Such a qualified privilege can be overcome on a showing of a compelling need and the absence of alternative sources for critical evidence in the hands of a reporter. New York, on the other hand, provides an absolute privilege against disclosure of confidential sources that can never be overcome, and a qualified privilege against the compelled disclosure of any unpublished journalistic work product, confidential or not.[6]

Several federal courts have also accepted a constitutional privilege. The First, Second, Third, Fourth, Fifth, Ninth, Tenth, Eleventh, and D.C. Circuits have all recognized the existence of a qualified privilege in some circumstances, either under the First Amendment or as a matter of common law. But there is no statutory federal shield law.

Seymour Public Library
176-178 Genesee Street
Auburn, NY 13021

The development of a federal constitutional reporters' privilege can be traced back to the Vietnam era and the case of *Branzburg v. Hayes*, the only decision by the U.S. Supreme Court to date that has addressed the constitutional protection of the relationship between reporters and their sources. In the late 1960s and the 1970s, and in the wake of the Pentagon Papers disclosures, the role of investigative press and the importance of confidentiality for sources were at the forefront of public opinion.[7] Along with the professionalization of journalism, the demand for watchdog and legal protection to support the profession was heightened. A growth in successful investigative revelations and positive public opinion about those stories came with a heightened appreciation in public opinion. In response, legal scholars started proposing doctrines and statutory protections to expand this blooming investigative institution.[8]

Branzburg v. Hayes reached the Supreme Court in 1972. The case began when Paul Branzburg, a reporter for Louisville's *Courier-Journal*, published an article that exposed local illicit drug manufacturing and distribution. Branzburg had obtained the information from sources involved in the drug trade on a promise that he would not reveal their identities. Branzburg was then subpoenaed to appear in front of a local grand jury and refused to attend, claiming a right not to reveal the identity of his sources. Facing charges for contempt in Kentucky state court, Branzburg asserted both a statutory and a constitutional privilege against testifying. The Kentucky courts rejected Branzburg's claim of privilege. Several months later, following the publication of another news story about drug use in Frankfort, Kentucky, Branzburg was subpoenaed for the identities of additional sources. Again, he refused to appear before the grand jury. This time, he was unsuccessful in persuading the Kentucky courts to permit him to protect the confidentiality of his sources.

Both Branzburg's cases were accepted for review by the Supreme Court and were consolidated with another case raising the same issue of whether there is a constitutional privilege for a reporter to refuse to appear before a grand jury. Each case involved a news report that was possible only because the reporter obtained access based on an explicit promise of confidentiality. In each case, the journalist asserted the right to live up to his promise and refused to testify before a grand jury. In an enigmatic and closely divided decision, a majority of the court held that the reporters had no First Amendment right to refuse to testify when properly summoned to appear before a grand jury.

The majority opinion rejected the argument that recognition of a constitutional privilege was needed for journalists to perform effectively as government watchdogs. The opinion observed that "from the founding of our country, the press has operated without constitutional protection for press informants, and the press has flourished."[9] It then dismissed the evidence put forward by the reporters as insufficient "to demonstrate that there would be a significant constriction of the flow of news to the public" if the reporters' claims of privilege were rejected.[10] The majority found no factual basis to conclude that the public interest in law enforcement could be overcome by the uncertain burden that might possibly be imposed on the press if reporters were compelled to testify before a grand jury like any other witness.

Justice Powell provided the crucial fifth vote in the 5 to 4 majority and wrote separately. Powell agreed with the majority opinion that there was no constitutional privilege for a reporter to refuse to appear before a grand jury. He suggested that an evidentiary privilege might protect reporters from being compelled to disclose information in certain circumstances. Explaining his understanding of the court's holding, Powell wrote: "[I]f the newsman is called upon to give information bearing only a remote and tenuous relationship to the subject of the investigation, or if he has some other reason to believe that his testimony implicates [a] confidential source relationship without a legitimate need of law enforcement, he will have access to the court on a motion to quash."

Powell's handwritten conference notes make clear that he agreed with the majority that there should be no constitutional privilege, observing that it would be too hard to define who is a journalist eligible to assert the privilege. But his notes equally make clear that Powell supported a common law, evidentiary privilege "which courts should recognize and apply . . . to protect confidential information."[11]

Over the subsequent decades, lower courts widely came to agree that the Powell concurrence combined with the four votes in dissent created a majority on the court that recognized some form of privilege. A reporters' privilege won wide acceptance in the federal courts in a variety of contexts. Most federal circuit courts adopted a three-part test to determine whether the reporters' privilege could be used to protect confidential sources and information, asking:

- Is the information relevant?
- Is there a compelling need for the information?
- Is the information available elsewhere?

A broad consensus developed, and reporters came to believe that the existence of a privilege was well established in the fabric of the law.

While the *Branzburg* ruling afforded protection to reporters from subpoenas to testify in federal criminal investigations, another development occurred after disclosures of President Nixon's misuse of government investigatory powers against "enemy" reporters. The Justice Department adopted strict internal rules respecting the confidentiality of reporters' communications in federal criminal investigations. Guidelines issued by the attorney general in 1970 severely limited the occasions when federal prosecutors could subpoena reporters or secretly obtain reporters' records. Official Justice Department policy forcefully recognized that "freedom of the press can be no broader than the freedom of reporters to investigate," and committed to respect "a reporter's *responsibility*" to cover controversial public issues. The rules expressly restricted federal prosecutors from issuing any form of compulsory process that "might impair the newsgathering function." Under the guidelines, reporters could be subpoenaed only if the evidence was essential to a prosecution and was not reasonably available from any other source. The guidelines also required the personal approval of the attorney general to be obtained before any subpoena could be issued to a reporter or a news organization, and mandate that such subpoenas must be as narrowly drawn as possible. For four decades, these departmental rules provided a broad restraint that severely limited the issuance of federal subpoenas to reporters.

TERRORISM, NATIONAL SECURITY, AND THE EROSION OF THE PRIVILEGE

After September 11, the reporters' privilege came under attack on several fronts. In the courts, the Justice Department became very aggressive in seeking reporters' sources in cases involving national security leaks. In one high-profile case, immortalized in the movie *Fair Game*, starring Naomi Watts and Sean Penn, a special prosecutor sought to discover who had leaked to the press that Valerie Plame was a covert CIA agent. The leak apparently had aimed to punish Plame's husband, Ambassador Joe Wilson, for disclosing that a key memo cited by President Bush in his call for a war on Iraq was widely considered a fake, and the president's team knew it. The *New York Times*'s Judith Miller and *Time*'s Matthew Cooper were served with grand jury subpoenas but refused to disclose their sources. The federal district court rejected Miller's and Cooper's claims of privilege and held them in contempt for refusing to testify.

The U.S. Court of Appeals of the District of Columbia Circuit upheld the contempt orders. Citing *Branzburg*, the appellate court rejected a First Amendment privilege to refuse to testify before a grand jury and concluded that any common law privilege that might exist was overcome on the facts of the case. The district court judge then ordered Miller's imprisonment for her continuing contempt of its order to comply with the prosecutor's subpoena. In contrast, Cooper avoided jail time when his employer, *Time* magazine, decided it would comply with an order separately requiring it to turn over documents containing the name of Cooper's source.

On July 6, 2005, Miller began serving a term of up to eighteen months' imprisonment for her contempt. Bill Keller of the *New York Times* hailed Miller's stand as "a brave and principled choice."[12] After serving for eighty-five days in a federal detention center in Alexandria, Virginia, Miller finally named her source after the source voluntarily and personally released her from her promise of confidentiality.

The post–September 11 assault on the privilege continued through a number of other leaks investigations, and culminated in a 2013 ruling by the Fourth Circuit Court of Appeals in *United States v. Sterling*. That decision denies that any reporter's privilege exists, constitutional or evidentiary, so that a prosecutor's demand for a reporter's information cannot be reviewed or restricted by a judge absent clear prosecutorial abuse. This ruling came in the prosecution of Jeffrey Sterling, a former CIA agent who was indicted for having disclosed national defense information in violation of the 1917 U.S. Espionage Act 18 U.S.C. § 793(d) and (e). Sterling was alleged to have disclosed classified information about a covert CIA operation targeting the Iranian nuclear program to Pulitzer Prize–winning reporter James Risen, who used this information in his 2006 book *State of War: The Secret History of the CIA and the Bush Administration.*

In May 2011, Attorney General Eric Holder issued a trial subpoena asking Risen to reveal the identity of his source and to confirm that the statements in the book were in fact provided by the source. Risen asserted a reporter's privilege and moved to quash the subpoena. The district court agreed with Risen, concluding that Risen's testimony was not even needed by the prosecutors to make their case, given all the other evidence pointing to Sterling's guilt. The district court thus quashed the Risen subpoena, holding that journalists have "a qualified First Amendment reporter's privilege that may be invoked when a subpoena either seeks information about confidential sources or is issued to harass or intimidate the journalist."[13]

In July 2013, the Fourth Circuit Court of Appeals in Richmond reversed. A divided court accepted the argument of the Justice Department prosecutors that no privilege, constitutional or evidentiary, allowed Risen to refuse to identify his source in a criminal prosecution, and the Supreme Court declined to review the holding. The majority rejected the constitutional privilege, saying the issue already had been decided in *Branzburg*: "There is no First Amendment testimonial privilege, absolute or qualified, that protects a reporter from being compelled to testify by the prosecution or defense in a criminal proceeding about criminal conduct that the reporter personally witnessed or participated in, absent a showing of bad faith, harassment or other such non-legitimate motive."[14]

The majority read *Branzburg* also to have rejected the existence of any common law privilege. It concluded that only the Supreme Court has the authority to change this holding and recognize a privilege. The majority observed that it would decline to recognize a common law privilege even if they had the power to do so. It agreed with the *Branzburg* majority that there was no evidence of any significant chilling effect caused by the absence of a privilege, and that public policy did not justify preserving anonymity for " 'those confidential informants engaged in actual criminal conduct.' "[15] In 2014, the Supreme Court declined to review the Fourth Circuit holding.

The Court of Appeals' ruling in *Sterling* is an unflinching rejection of a reporter's right to make a binding promise of confidentiality in exchange for information. In its view, there is no privilege of any type. The question of whether to require a reporter to reveal a source rests solely with the prosecutor, and there is no competing interest for a court to weigh.

The protections afforded by the U.S. attorney general's guidelines limiting the use of subpoenas to reporters have also suffered since September 11. In its devotion to hunt down government whistleblowers, the Justice Department reinterpreted the rules in expansive new ways. In one leak investigation, the department secretly seized records for twenty phone lines used by dozens of Associated Press reporters in three different bureaus in a period extending over two months. The Justice Department issued this broad subpoena even though it knew the names of the two reporters involved and knew the specific days when the leak occurred. In another investigation, the department told a court that there was probable cause to believe that James Rosen, a Fox News reporter, had violated the Espionage Act by asking a government source for confidential information on newsworthy developments. The department made this unprecedented charge of criminality by a reporter to obtain a search warrant for the reporter's e-mail, even though it had no intention to prosecute Rosen for the crime he allegedly had committed. The department asserted an Espionage Act violation only so it could secretly get his e-mail.

A press uproar ensued when the department's seizures of reporters' information became public and caused President Obama to instruct Attorney General Eric Holder to review and improve the department's rules for obtaining information from reporters. When Holder released revised rules, they set off new alarms. The revisions updated the rules to cover modern forms of communication and closed the specific loopholes that permitted the secret AP and Fox seizures. They also added new discretion for prosecutors to subpoena reporters and watered down the message that subpoenas should rarely be issued to reporters. For example, Holder replaced an explicit instruction to Department of Justice prosecutors not to "impair the newsgathering function" during their criminal investigations with a vague admonition to avoid issuing subpoenas if they "might *unreasonably* impair *ordinary* newsgathering activities." The revised Holder rules provided no guidance for prosecutors about what constitutes "ordinary newsgathering," and seemed likely to invite more subpoenas directed at investigative journalists. The revised rules also contained new provisions that could be read to eliminate altogether the safeguards for reporters' communications upon request of the Director of National Intelligence (DNI).

The uproar was immediate and intense over these alterations of the guidelines, which seemed certain to result in more subpoenas being issued to reporters by federal prosecutors. After a constant drumbeat of criticism from the press, in January 2015—just weeks before stepping down from his office—Attorney General Holder rescinded the objectionable new language. The phrase "ordinary newsgathering" was removed from the guidelines, input from the DNI on any subpoena decision was clarified to be purely advisory, and new language was added to make clear that any information obtained from a reporter was to be "closely held" within the Department of Justice and used only for proper law-enforcement purposes.

RESCUING A PRIVILEGE

In light of these upheavals, if we want to rescue a meaningful federal reporters' privilege, we need a new approach. The courts must be convinced of the importance of legal protection for reporter–source communications. They must also be educated about their institutional role in ensuring the flow of valuable information to the public, a role they can perform only if some type of privilege is recognized to exist. A four-part strategy could turn the tide against the misunderstandings evident in the Fourth Circuit's holding and the Justice Department's relaxation of standards that worked well for decades.

ESTABLISHING THE NEED FOR CONFIDENTIAL COMMUNICATIONS

The first key is for journalists to establish more tangibly why the ability of sources to speak confidentially with reporters is crucial for our democracy. One would think that role of confidential sources in so many news stories, and the importance of a reporter's ability to make a promise of confidentiality would be readily understood as a simple fact of human nature.

Former Attorney General Robert H. Jackson made just this commonsense point in objecting to the congressional subpoena for FBI sources. Then, why is it so difficult to get some courts to recognize the value to society in allowing a reporter to make a binding promise of confidentiality to a source?

In arguing for a privilege in the past, reporters have pointed to seminal stories that could be obtained only from a confidential source:

- A confidential source provided the press with the Pentagon's secret history of America's involvement in Vietnam, which famously became known as the "Pentagon Papers."
- Journalist Walter Pincus relied on confidential sources in reporting that President Carter planned to move forward with development of a "neutron bomb" that could inflict massive casualties without extensive destruction of property.
- The reports by CBS News and *New Yorker* journalist Seymour Hersh on the abuse of detainees at Abu Ghraib prison in Iraq were based on a leaked report that was "not meant for public release."
- Based on confidential source reporting by James Risen, the *New York Times* informed the public long before the Snowden revelations that the National Security Agency was monitoring phone calls and e-mails into and out of the United States involving suspected Al Qaeda operatives, without seeking approval from federal courts.
- The *Washington Post* relied on confidential sources to report on the CIA's network of secret prisons—known as "black sites"—for terrorism suspects, while the *Times* and other news organizations relied on confidential sources in reporting on the use of "harsh interrogation tactics" against terrorism suspects in U.S. custody.

These examples illustrate the kinds of information about government conduct that would not be likely ever to reach the public if a journalist could not credibly make a binding promise of confidentiality to a source. As stressed by Yale professor Alexander Bickel, who represented Branzburg before the Supreme Court, "Forcing reporters to divulge . . . confidences would dam the flow to the press, and through it to the people, of the most valuable sort of information."[16]

In *Branzburg*, the Supreme Court brushed off these examples. The court concluded that "reliance by the press on confidential informants does not mean that all such sources will in fact dry up because of the later possible appearance of the newsman before a grand jury."[17] This suggests that it would be valuable to develop empirical proof to address the question posed by the *Branzburg* majority: Where is the evidence that a privilege is needed? In 1985, a study concluded that two-thirds of the stories nominated for Pulitzer Prizes relied to a significant extent on confidential sources.[18] But such analyses beg the question of whether sources would still talk in the absence of any recognized privilege. Those who have attempted to develop the proof the Supreme Court sought have bemoaned the fact that it requires "proving the negative," and have found the empirical evidence to be largely inconclusive.[19]

Reporters could help the cause to some extent by doing the reporting needed to make the case that the cloak of confidentiality has tangible societal benefits and promotes the functioning of democracy. We can document how the reporting on the neutron bomb caused such a public outcry that the United States abandoned plans for such a weapon or how the disclosure of the CIA's interrogation techniques precipitated objections from Congress and ultimately led President Obama to prohibit them. In light of these examples, we need to ask: What has been done to determine the impact of the WikiLeaks disclosures on the Arab Spring in 2011 and in the Middle East? Or what has been done to document the political response to disclosures about mismanagement at the Veterans Administration? Such follow-up impact reporting would be valuable to have when the issue of a privilege is taken up again in the courts.

CORRECTING THE MISTAKEN READING OF *BRANZBURG*

A second step is to correct the mistaken reading of *Branzburg v. Hayes* embraced by the Fourth Circuit and other courts. The recent rejection of the privilege in the courts is built on a misreading of Justice Powell's concurrence in *Branzburg*. For instance, the *Sterling* court reads *Branzburg* to hold that there is no privilege in a criminal proceeding absent "bad faith, harassment or other such non-legitimate motive." This is not a fair reading of what Justice Powell had to say about a privilege in *Branzburg*. In his critical concurrence, Justice Powell wrote:

> The Court does not hold that newsman, subpoenaed to testify before a grand jury are without constitutional rights with respect to the gathering of news or the safeguarding of sources.
>
> [I]f the newsman is called upon to give information bearing only a remote and tenuous relationship to the subject of the investigation, or if he has some other reason to believe that his testimony implicates [a] confidential source relationship without a legitimate need of law enforcement, he will have access to the court on a motion to quash.
>
> The asserted claim to privilege should be judged by the striking of a proper balance between freedom of the press and the obligation of all citizens to give relevant testimony. . . . The balance of these vital constitutional and societal interests on a case by case basis accords with the tried and traditional way of adjudicating such questions.[20]

While rejecting a constitutional privilege for a reporter to refuse even to appear before a grand jury, Justice Powell plainly voiced support for an evidentiary privilege that could be applied "on a case by case basis." A privilege that a reporter could assert in response to a specific question, which a judge would then decide whether an answer had to be given by "striking . . . a proper balance between freedom of the press and the obligation of all citizens to give relevant testimony." The Fourth Circuit has fundamentally misread the Powell concurrence and misunderstood its significance as a recognition of the need for an evidentiary privilege.

CHANGING THE VOCABULARY OF THE PRIVILEGE

Another prong of the strategy may be to reconceptualize the privilege as an "anonymous source" privilege, rather than a reporters' privilege. This would respond to criticism that "reporter's privilege places the professional needs of journalists above the community's need for law enforcement."[21]

The Supreme Court decided *Branzburg* in an era when the Court repeatedly refused to read the First Amendment as creating any "special rights" for the institutional press. A request to recognize a "reporter's privilege" thus arrived at the court with a heavy burden on the press because it smacks of special rights. But the privilege is not really about the needs of reporters; it is about the needs of citizens for information that can come only from sources willing to speak on an anonymous basis.

It is hard to reconcile the unwillingness of some courts to impose any burden at all on prosecutors to overcome some qualified protection when they want to know the identities of those who speak confidentially to reporters, with the uniform willingness of courts to impose burdens on those who seek to know the names of individuals who speak directly to the public through anonymous online posts. In case after case, courts have required an adequate justification a request to unmask an anonymous online poster. Courts regularly apply a "stringent" standard to protect an anonymous expressive speech, a standard that weighs both the value of the speech and the needs of the party seeking to identify the speaker.[22]

Courts appreciate that anonymous commentators have long advocated for political, social, cultural, and economic change. Indeed, many have noted that *The Federalist Papers* were published pseudonymously. In *McIntyre v. Ohio Elections Commission*, Justice Thomas recounted how some members of the Continental Congress in 1779 wanted to compel a newspaper publisher to identify the author of a column criticizing that body, but their efforts were defeated by arguments that "the liberty of the Press ought not to be restrained" in such a manner.[23] Such historical facts led him to conclude that the Framers "believed that the freedom of the press included the right to publish without revealing the author's name."

As observed in *McIntyre*, even though "the right to remain anonymous may be abused when it shields fraudulent conduct," it remains the case that "our society accords greater weight to the value of free speech than to the dangers of its misuse."[24] While courts fully understand the importance of protecting those who speak anonymously, many do not seem to grasp that the same concerns should warrant a level of protection to those who wish to speak anonymously through a reporter. Reframing the privilege as an anonymous-source privilege would "acknowledge the initial communicator" and thus highlight the concerns for speaker privacy and antiretaliation that are addressed by the privilege as well as the public interest in increasing the flow of information and enhancing self-governance.[25]

RECRUITING THE COURTS AS DEFENDERS
OF DEMOCRACY

The final step is to defend the privilege for anonymous sources not just as essential for the information flow but as fundamental to the way U.S. government operates. If there is no privilege, then the issue of whether and when to compel a reporter to reveal sources rests solely with a prosecutor—the judiciary has no role to play at all in weighing the competing needs of the criminal justice system against the burdens imposed on important First Amendment activity when a reporter is called to testify. Second Circuit Judge Robert Sack noted in a 2006 dissent in *New York Times v. Gonzales* that this surrender of unreviewable power to the executive branch is inconsistent with principles of the separation of powers and the role of judges in our system as the arbiters of conflicting constitutional interests.

Judge Sack made this point in a case upholding a subpoena for the telephone records of the *New York Times* reporter Judith Miller in another leak investigation. This case arose from an investigation into a leak involving an Islamic charity in Chicago. In searching for the leaker, the U.S. attorney in Chicago went to New York to issue a subpoena for Miller's phone records, and the *New York Times* went to court to assert a privilege over the disclosure of those records. While a majority concluded that any common law privilege that might exist was overcome on the facts presented, Judge Sack dissented. He urged that the decision of whether to recognize a privilege ultimately boils down to the question of whether the courts have any role to play in balancing the competing interests that are present: society's interest in maintaining a flow of important information and society's interest in criminal justice: "Without such protection, prosecutors, limited only by their own self-restraint, could obtain records that identify journalists' confidential sources . . . virtually at will."[26]

Judge David S. Tatel made much the same point in concurring in the result upholding the contempt order against Miller in the Plame leak investigation. As he observed, it is the courts that "must weigh the public interest in compelling disclosure, measured by the harm the leak caused, against the public interest in newsgathering, measured by the leaked information's value."[27] Recasting the reporters' privilege as an evidentiary privilege that must be recognized to protect anonymous sources, and that the courts—not prosecutors—are the proper arbiters of the competing constitutional concerns, may provide a theoretical base to salvage judicial recognition of a privilege.

THE FUTURE OF A PRIVILEGE

The digitization of news media has increased the diversity of online voices. While the web offers promises of democratic debate in the public sphere, it has put pressures on the definitional crisis of journalism. "Who is a journalist" poses several problems in defining a reporter's privilege. And since pressures on the privilege have increased considerably since the Snowden revelations, the ability of the press to act independently has been weakened. If we take seriously the idea of the press as an agent for public accountability, we need to continue to rethink the legal privilege, the possibility for a federal shield law, and who gets to claim that privilege.

NOTES

1. Kenneth C. Bryant, "Newsmen's Immunity Needs a Shot in the Arm," *Santa Clara Law Review* 11, no. 1 (1975): 56–71; Sanford V. Teplitzky and Kenneth Weiss, "Comment, Newsman's Privilege Two Years After *Branzburg v. Hayes*: The First Amendment in Jeopardy," *Tulsa Law Review* 49, no. 417 (1975); Paul Marcus, "The Reporter's Privilege: An Analysis of the Common Law, *Branzburg v. Hayes*, and Recent Statutory Developments," *Arizona Law Review* 5 (1983): 815–67.

2. Matt Carlson, *On the Condition of Anonymity: Unnamed Sources and the Battle for Journalism, History of Communication* (Champaign: University of Illinois Press, 2011), http://www.press.uillinois.edu/books/catalog/92gpe7fw9780252035999.html.

3. "And Strikes a Blow at a Strong Press" [editorial], *New York Times*, June 28, 2005, http://www.nytimes.com/2005/06/28/opinion/28tue3.html.

4. Quoted in Edward Levi, "Address by the Honorable Edward H. Levi Attorney General of the United States before the Association of the Bar of the City of New York," 1975, Department of Justice, https://www.justice.gov/sites/default/files/ag/legacy/2011/08/23/04-28-1975.pdf.

5. Fla. Stat. §90.5015.

6. N.Y. Civ. Rights Law § 79-h.

7. "The Newsman's Privilege After *Branzburg v. Hayes*: Whither Now?" *Journal of Criminal Law and Criminology* 64, no. 2 (1973): 218–39; Lars Willnat and D. H. Weaver, "Public Opinion on Investigative Reporting in the 1990s: Has Anything Changed Since the 1980s?" *Journal of Media and Communication Quarterly* 75, no. 3 (1982): 449–63.

8. Anthony Lewis, "Cantankerous, Obstinate, Ubiquitous: The Press," *Utah Law Review* (1975): 75, 78.

9. *Branzburg v. Hayes*, 408 U.S. 665 (1972), at 699.

10. Ibid., at 693.

11. Adam Liptak, "A Justice Scribbles on Journalists' Rights," *New York Times*, October 7, 2007, http://www.nytimes.com/2007/10/07/weekinreview/07liptak.html?_r=0

12. Adam Liptak and Maria Newman, "*New York Times* Reporter Jailed for Keeping Source Secret," *New York Times*, July 6, 2005, http://www.nytimes.com/2005/07/06/politics /06cnd-leak.html?pagewanted=all&_r=0.

13. *United States v. Sterling* 818 F. Supp.2d 945 (E.D. Va. 2011), at 951.

14. *United States v. Sterling* 724 F.3d (2013), at 492.

15. Ibid., at 504, quoting *Branzburg v. Hayes*, at 691.

16. Alexander M. Bickel, *The Morality of Consent* (New Haven, Conn.: Yale University Press, 1975), 84–85.

17. *Branzburg*, 408 U.S. at 693–94.

18. John E. Osborn, "The Reporter's Confidentiality Privilege: Updating the Empirical Evidence After a Decade of Subpoenas," *Columbia Human Rights Law Review* 17 (1985): 73–74.

19. RonNell Anderson Jones, "Rethinking the Reporter's Privilege," *Michigan Law Review* 1221 (2013): 1243–44.

20. *Branzburg v. Hayes*, 408 U.S. 665, 709–10 (1972) (Powell, J., concurring).

21. Gabriel Schoenfeld, book discussion on *Necessary Secrets: National Security, the Media, and the Rule of Law* (New York: Norton, 2010), at Hudson Institute, May 25, 2010, http://www.hudson.org/events/1097-a-book-discussion-on-necessary-secrets-national -security-the-media-and-the-rule-of-law-52010.

22. Mara J. Gassman, Matthew E. Kelley, and Ashley Kissinger, "Anonymous Online Speech," in *Communications Law in the Digital Age 2015* (New York: Practising Law Institute, 2015), 13–196, http://www.lskslaw.com/documents/Chapter11_Comm_Law_2015_Vol_02 _CC101500594030165108.pdf.

23. *McIntyre v. Ohio Elections Commission*, 514 U.S. 334 (1995), at 361–62; citation omitted.

24. Ibid., at 357.

25. Jones, "Rethinking the Reporter's Privilege."

26. *New York Times v. Gonzales*, 459 F.3d 160 2d Cir. (2006).

27. *In re Grand Jury Subpoena* (Judith Miller) (D.C. Cir. 2006).

7

DIGITAL SECURITY FOR JOURNALISTS

JULIA ANGWIN

I n 1972, a secret source known as "Deep Throat" revealed key elements of the Watergate scandal to *Washington Post* reporters Bob Woodward and Carl Bernstein. His identity remained secret until thirty-three years later, in 2005, when former FBI official Mark Felt revealed himself as Deep Throat.

On June 6, 2013, a secret source provided secret documents to the *Washington Post* and the *Guardian* about the National Security Agency's PRISM spying program. Within forty-eight hours, the NSA claimed that it had identified the leaker as Edward Snowden.

Forty-eight hours versus thirty-three years. That is the stark difference between the confidentiality that sources can expect today and what they used to be able to expect. Of course, it's always been difficult to keep secrets. Over the years, several people correctly guessed Deep Throat's identity—including Carl Bernstein's wife, Nora Ephron,[1] and the journalist Jack Limpert[2] at *Washingtonian* magazine.

But keeping a secret is arguably far more difficult in today's world, where nearly every form of communication—from e-mails, phone calls, and text messages to even face-to-face meetings—can leave a digital trace that can and likely will be analyzed for clues in a leak investigation.

Despite the challenges, journalists still must try to keep secrets. I admit that it is strange to talk about secrecy as a goal for journalists, since much of our work involves exposing secrets. But, paradoxically, journalists often need secrecy to increase transparency. In many cases, journalists cannot hold institutions accountable for their actions without relying on secret sources within those institutions who provide crucial information.

And so, the question becomes "how" can journalists keep secrets in an era of ubiquitous surveillance? There are no silver bullets, no one single technological tool that will solve all problems of keeping a source confidential. Most newsrooms are not well equipped with digital-security tools and guidance. And there are remarkably few authoritative sources that working journalists can rely on.

I was lucky that I was able to build my digital-security arsenal with the help of leading computer-security experts across the world. In 2009, I was a technology reporter at the *Wall Street Journal*. I was fascinated by the crop of new tech companies like Facebook whose business models relied on digital surveillance. To study this new phenomenon, I launched a series of articles titled "What They Know."[3]

As I reported on the rise of surveillance during the subsequent years, I met researchers around the world who had devoted their lives to building antisurveillance technologies. Many of them would communicate only through encrypted means. And so, slowly, painfully, I learned to communicate using the tools that they preferred.

It was far from easy. I still remember the two hours that one researcher spent helping me set up an encrypted instant-messaging session—and how I still managed to screw it up the next time we chatted. Or the months I spent wondering why no one was sending me encrypted mail, until I realized that I had not uploaded my public key to the directory. And the many, many times I thought I was sending encrypted messages but mistakenly had sent them unencrypted.

Despite the headaches, using the technology was rewarding. Slowly but surely, new sources starting reaching out to me through encrypted channels. I realized that I had a competitive advantage with a certain group of sources who were savvy about digital security.

But my setup was fragile, and it wasn't supported by my newsroom. I had to secretly use tools that weren't approved by the corporate technology team. Every software upgrade sent me into a panic that I might not be able to duct-tape my system back together. I often had to call the developers who made my tools for help. Eventually I moved to a newsroom, ProPublica, that supported my tools and had experts on staff to help me.

Even so, my setup isn't bulletproof. Experts disagree vehemently about almost every aspect of the security, and so every one of my chosen tools comes with its own army of vociferous critics.

Post-Snowden, there are more resources available to journalists than previously, but there is still a lot of work to be done. Many journalists are reluctant to discuss their digital-security measures—in part because they fear inadvertently revealing information that could unmask a source, but mostly because they don't take any security measures to speak of. And computer-security experts are deeply divided about the best techniques to recommend.

Another problem is that technologists often have little knowledge about journalists' workflow and the intricacies of reporting; and journalists often lack technological literacy. To bridge this gap and help develop some concrete guidance for journalists, the Columbia University Tow Center for Digital Journalism gathered about forty top technologists, lawyers, and privacy experts for a day in San Francisco in 2014 to thrash out best security practices for journalists.

We broke into small groups, and each group pondered how a journalist might approach the security and confidentiality of a specific reporting challenge. In each case, we considered what we were trying to keep secret, from whom we were trying to keep it secret, techniques for keeping those secrets, and what the consequences could be if we failed. I used the outcomes from these sessions to help shape this chapter's recommendations. I also relied on my own experience and input from my kitchen cabinet of computer security professionals.

First, some basic requirements. You can't properly protect your sources if you don't protect your own data. That means using strong passwords, keeping your computer software updated so that is less vulnerable to attacks, and not clicking on suspicious links in e-mail that might contain spyware or a computer virus.

In addition to those basic steps, I also cover all my computer cameras with stickers so that they cannot be commandeered by hackers to film me surreptitiously. I use a privacy screen on my laptop so that when I am taking notes at a conference or writing an article on the airplane, people around me cannot read what I'm writing. I am also careful where I store my drafts and notes; for some sensitive stories, I have been known to carry all my files on an encrypted USB stick that I keep with me at all times.

Second, preparation is extremely important. Just as a journalist who prepares questions for an interview is more successful, journalists who prepare strategies for secure communications before they need them are likely to be more successful at winning over nervous sources. There is no better case in point than the story of how Edward Snowden sought out the journalist Laura Poitras in large part because of her ability to use secure communication tools.

I was lucky that I built my digital-security arsenal before I had to use it for anything other than communicating with digital-security experts. By the time I started talking to sources through encrypted channels, I had worked out many of the kinks of the system. You should consider setting up these tools even if you aren't quite sure yet if and when you will use them.

Third, not every source requires the same approach. Protecting a source from the NSA, with its vast surveillance system and computational power, is far different from protecting a source from being identified by a corporate boss. Figuring out which type of surveillance you are worried about is called building your "threat model."

Generally speaking, governments—whether local or national—have greater powers of surveillance and coercion. For government-threat models, journalists may need to be careful about borders and telecom networks that might be controlled by the government, for instance.

Other institutions, such as corporations, generally have fewer resources but often have total control over their employees' digital lives—surveilling their web searches, their e-mails, their faxes, their phone calls, and even the copier machine. For corporate-threat models, journalists need to be wary of any activities that a source does within his or her workplace.

Finally, it's important to think strategically about digital security. It's easy to get excited about the latest cool tools—and thankfully in the post-Snowden era, existing tools are getting better and new tools are popping up every day. But not every tool is right for every scenario.

Strategically, I find it helpful to think of two main categories of information I'm trying to protect—content and metadata. Content includes notes, documents, photos, and other information collected in the course of reporting. Metadata is the data about reporting—the name of a source, meeting dates and times, phone call logs.

I came up with acronyms to describe the various strategic approaches for protecting each category of data.

For content, the strategies are Hide, Encrypt, and Mask—or HEM for short. Hide means hiding the existence of a piece of content by placing it in a secret compartment either physically or digitally. Encrypt means to make the content unreadable to outsiders using cryptographic techniques. Mask means disguising the reporting content as an innocuous other type of content.

For metadata, the strategies are Add Noise, Cloak, and Evade—or ACE for short. Add Noise means confusing an observer by adding false connections or false content to the communications. For example, a reporter calling a source in the mayor's office could call every person in the office so that the call logs show a blitz of calls rather than a single call to an identifiable source. Cloak means masking metadata by using alternative identities or locations. Evade means avoiding metadata collection by meeting in person and not using digital forms of communication.

The journalist scenarios outlined in the following sections are my attempt to illuminate these strategies. In your reporting, you most likely will not encounter the exact scenarios as described. But I hope that the scenarios provide a starting point for thinking through the challenges you face.

Critics will point out that there are ways to circumvent nearly every strategy we dreamed up. And the critics will be right. An attacker with an unlimited budget and legal authority can probably unravel any of our strategies. And all these strategies can be subverted by an attacker who finds a way to plant spyware on your computer or phone that hijacks your clicks and words before they can be encrypted or rerouted. Being smart about computer hygiene—using updated software and not downloading suspicious files or links that arrive in e-mail—can help fight off such attacks. As we have seen from the Snowden revelations, a well-financed spy agency can have an incredible arsenal of tools.

Luckily, not every attack on journalists' confidentiality is unbounded. Some sources just need to be shielded from their boss or a bad cop. And for their part, journalists have an obligation to make it hard for attacks on their sources to be successful.

Of course, by the time you read this, some of the tools that we suggest could be out of date and supplanted by new, better tools. But hopefully, the strategic approach we outline can inform your search for updated tools.

SCENARIO ONE

You are a business journalist who meets a potential source, Bob, who works at the local chamber of commerce, at a party. You are investigating some local business corruption and are worried that the chamber of commerce is monitoring your movements. You want to Bob's help but don't want to freak him out. What is an easy and nonthreatening way to set up a secure channel with Bob?

- *Strategic goal.* Your initial goal is to hide the fact that you are talking to Bob from his employer (i.e., avoid metadata surveillance). You will also want to hide the content of your conversation, but first you have to find a way for him to be anonymous.
- *Threat.* Bob's employer, the chamber of commerce.
- *Tactics.* This is one the hardest, unsolved problems in digital security: establishing trust with a new source without leaving a digital trail. And once you have established a digital trail, it's impossible to erase.

Still, some metadata strategies can be helpful. If you plan to exchange e-mails or calls with Bob at his workplace, you could add noise to your relationship with an agreed-upon cover story developed at the party. Something along the lines of "I know your employer might not approve of us talking about work, so let's keep our e-mails to a shared love of cooking."

You could also try to cloak your identities by using disposable e-mail addresses to communicate. But he would have to make sure not to use that e-mail address from work, where e-mails are sure to be monitored.

You could also try to cloak identities by using burner phones. (A burner phone is a prepaid cell phone bought with cash at a location far from your usual commute, so as not to be tied to your identity.) You could ask Bob if he would be willing to communicate via burner phones and then mail him a burner phone after the meeting.

You could also try to evade metadata by asking Bob for a follow-up, in-person meeting at a coffee shop or somewhere else that you think would not be monitored by his employer. You could even take a page from Deep Throat, who asked Woodward to move a flowerpot on his balcony to request a meeting, and ask Bob if you and he could establish offline signals to set up meetings.

Another way to evade metadata collection is to use postal mail. The U.S. Post Office scans the metadata on envelopes, but if you don't put a return address it's harder for the Post Office to trace the origin. Since your threat model is Bob's employer, not the government, you could send Bob a letter in the mail describing the importance of the story you are working on and asking for a future meeting.

Once you get Bob on your side, you could protect the content using encryption. You could ask Bob if he'd like to communicate with you via Signal—a free iPhone app that enables encrypted text messages and voice calls. (The Android versions are called RedPhone, for voice calls, and TextSecure, for texting.) However, if his employer has access to his phone these apps could raise red flags.

SCENARIO TWO

You are a prominent national security reporter in Washington, D.C. Rumor has it that anyone you e-mail inside the White House will be under automatic investigation for potentially leaking classified information (even if the questions you ask are innocuous). How do you talk to your sources now, even just to set up an in person meeting?

- *Strategic goal.* Protect metadata about contact with White House sources.
- *Threat.* The White House.
- *Tactics.* This is another difficult metadata challenge that calls for the use of the ACE strategies under the eyes of a watchful employer.

You could *add noise* to your reporting by calling or e-mailing everyone at the White House every day to create a metadata trail that would be difficult to analyze. Of course, this could be impractical or could backfire.

You could also cloak your identity by getting a burner phone, setting up a disposable e-mail account, or using the instant-messaging protocol Off-the-Record (OTR), which masks your identity. Off-the-Record messaging is a protocol for sending and receiving encrypted instant messages. Used in combination with Tor,[4] a web browser that provides anonymity by bouncing user's Internet traffic to various servers around the world, it can hide the identities of people talking over instant messaging.

The challenge would be to find a way to convince sources to use the same technology on their end—and to do it from home instead of the office where computers will be monitored.

Your best bet is probably to evade metadata collection by visiting sources at home or some other place where you can find them offline (make sure to turn off your phone so you don't leave a metadata trail). At that meeting, you can establish a cloaking strategy for future communications—such as exchanging burner phones, disposable e-mail addresses, or Off-the-Record usernames.

SCENARIO THREE

You are a journalist who has had a long relationship with Alicia, an insider in a political hierarchy who has provided some on-the-record and some off-the-record information in the past. Now, Alicia wants to give you some documents exposing wrongdoing by her boss. But Alicia is not very tech-savvy and doesn't have administrative rights on her work computer, so can't install encryption software—not to mention that she fears that installing encryption software would draw unwanted attention.

- *Strategic goal.* Protect Alicia from detection as she securely transfers the documents to you. You need to protect some metadata and content of the documents during the transfer.
- *Threat.* Alicia's employer.
- *Tactics.* In this scenario, you and Alicia must protect both metadata and content related to the transfer of documents. But since you have a digital trail already, you should take care to keep your observable communication consistent with previous patterns.

Now, for the document transfer. If the documents are in paper form, Alicia could hide them and transport them to a copier that is not at the office. (Most copiers have hard disks that store records of each copy made, so copying at the office could leave a metadata trail that leads back to Alicia.)

She could then evade metadata collection by bringing the documents to you in person, as long as both of you leave your phones at home. She could also potentially evade metadata collection by mailing the documents to you in an envelope without a return address.

If Alicia can securely obtain a digital copy of the files, she could also cloak the transfer of files by using OnionShare from her home computer to upload the files to a secure Internet location from which you could retrieve them.

OnionShare is software that allows people to share large files anonymously over the Internet. The sender downloads OnionShare software and uploads the file to a secret address on Tor, the anonymous web browser. However, you and Alicia would have to arrange a time in advance for the transfer, because both computers need to be online at the same time for it to work.

One cautionary note about documents: Journalists should take care to scrub the metadata from the documents before publishing them—as the metadata can perhaps reveal a source. (Converting a Word document to PDF can scrub metadata; there is also software available for scrubbing metadata from other types of files.)

SCENARIO FOUR

You are a journalist, and you are nearing the end of writing a sensitive article about local law enforcement. You are starting to worry that you are being followed and that your computer might be compromised. What can you do at this point in your reporting to minimize the risk to existing sources Jose and James?

- *Strategic goal.* Protect metadata and content collection of future communications with Jose and James, while trying to find out if previous conversations have been compromised.
- *Threat.* Local law enforcement.

- *Tactics.* Unfortunately, it's very difficult to determine if a computer or phone you are using has been compromised. All you can do is stop using the potentially compromised device.

Experts at places such as the Citizen Lab at the University of Toronto can determine if your computer has been compromised, but they don't take every case. If provable, however, the compromise of your computer could be an important part of the story.

In the meantime, you should transfer your work to a new machine. Print the documents from the original computer and refer to them that way. It's not safe to transfer the documents to the new machine because they might be infected with malware.

You should then discuss the possible compromise with your sources. You could develop a cover story so that if they are found to have been talking with you, they can offer a plausible explanation. But they may feel safer revealing their identities in the article, if they feel they can use it to seek legal protection as whistleblowers.

For future communications, you could cloak your communications with James and Jose by supplying them with burner phones bought in another city (outside the range of your local law-enforcement agency) to use to communicate with you. Establish weekly or daily times in which they are to turn on the phones to communicate with you from a location that is not their home, office, or regular haunt.

To prevent police from using a Stingray device to track their movements, Jose and James should turn off their cell phones and burner phones if they are meeting you in person. To prevent malware on the phone from secretly keeping it powered on, they could put it in a Faraday cage—a case that is lined with a thin sheet of metal that blocks all signals.

You could also cloak your communications through Off-the-Record instant messaging with Jose and James on computers they use at home. If you have the money, you could even buy them cheap Windows laptops on eBay and install Tails, a computer operating system that is set up with privacy defaults. Tails routes user Internet traffic automatically through Tor and is set up for default use of encrypted e-mail and instant messaging. The good thing about Tails is that the entire operating system is booted up from a USB drive or CD, so the computer itself doesn't contain any information if it is searched.

If you need documents from Jose and James, you could also ask them to evade metadata collection by mailing them from postal boxes outside the city.

They can also cloak their identities by sending documents using SecureDrop, an encrypted dropbox that newsrooms can install to allow sources to send documents in an encrypted and anonymous fashion. Sources must download Tor and follow a few simple instructions to send documents through SecureDrop.

SCENARIO FIVE

You are a journalist in the China bureau of a major national newspaper. You know that the Chinese government is monitoring your electronic communications. How can you discuss stories, transmit data, and talk about sources with your editors back in New York without compromising your sources?

- *Strategic goal.* Protect the identity of sources while still providing content to your editors that assures them of the credibility of your sources.
- *Threat.* The Chinese government.
- *Tactics.* With a threat as large and powerful as the Chinese government, you face long odds. But you can and should still try to obscure the content of your communications with editors in New York.

One well-known masking strategy—known as steganography—is the use of code words in plain sight. For example, when meeting with editors in New York, you could establish innocuous-sounding code words or phrases to indicate certain levels of confidence in a source, something like "the smog is getting worse" or the "smog is getting better" that you can use in communications between China to New York that you know are being monitored.

If you *must* transmit a source's real identity to your editors in New York, you should encrypt it, preferably on a Tails computer that you can be sure has not been tampered with by the government (which may not be easy to procure).

And when you transmit it, you should try to cloak your identity by using Tor, the anonymous web browser. However, because China tries to block Tor, your news organization would likely need to set up a Tor Bridge or a virtual private network to allow you access to the Tor network. A Tor Bridge is a private connection to Tor and is not listed in the public Tor directory.

SCENARIO SIX

You are a filmmaker who has snuck into Syria to film the civil war. You shoot some harrowing footage and want to get back to the United States right away to edit it. How do you get your footage safely over the Syrian border?

- *Strategic goal.* To protect the content of the film footage from Syrian border guards and Syrian electronic eavesdropping.
- *Threat.* The Syrian government.
- *Tactics.* Your first move should be to encrypt the film files. Once you have encrypted them, you may even want to delete the raw files. When she was making *Citizenfour*, the documentary filmmaker Laura Poitras encrypted all the video she took of Edward Snowden and then deleted the raw files at the end of every day so that she never had raw footage with her that could be seized.

Once the files are encrypted, you could try to hide them, either physically or digitally. You could try to hide the footage in a physical secret compartment in your luggage or a fellow traveler's belongings (but this is a highly risky strategy that relies on physical border searches being incomplete).

You could also try to hide the files digitally using a disk encryption program such as Microsoft's BitLocker, which can store encrypted files in a disguised portion of your computer that would be undetectable to all but the most tech-savvy border guards.[5]

You could even mask the footage as a music CD or some other innocuous content (but this risks it getting confiscated at the border).

But your best bet is to transfer the digitally encrypted files back to the United States before you leave the country, while cloaking your identity. You could use OnionShare to upload the video to a colleague back in the United States and then delete it from your computer once they have it. Or if your organization has SecureDrop, you could upload the files to it before you leave the country.

Of course, not all these tools are easy to use. Some tools are simple—such as Tor, just download it and away you go. But others are not at all simple, mostly because they are volunteer projects that have scarce resources for improvements. The GPG-encrypted e-mail program, for instance, is a tool that is very finicky and easy to screw up—in large part because it is maintained by one guy in Germany who until recently was running out of money. (After I wrote about his plight, he got funded.)[6]

Despite its challenges, I use GPG almost every day, and my ability to use the software has brought me many sources and connections that I could not have made any other way.

So I would advise journalists who are concerned about their tech-savviness to consider two strategies:

1. Don't be afraid to fail. I have failed many times as I have learned these tools. It's better to fail early, before you have a big story, than to try to get up to speed for a big story.
2. Reach out to the computer-security community for advice. Many of the people who build these tools are doing it because they are passionate about protecting journalists and sources, and they will be happy to answer your questions via Twitter or e-mail.

Journalists should also try to urge their newsrooms to support them in adopting better practices around secure communications. Many newsrooms view spending on computer security as an unnecessary cost, but I think it should be viewed as a competitive advantage that will quite likely result in better scoops. It makes sense for newsrooms to invest in tools such as Tor Bridges and SecureDrop (which are free but require time to install and maintain).

My newsroom, ProPublica, has invested time and energy in hosting SecureDrop and has enabled HTTPS—which allows your web pages to be delivered over an encrypted connection—across its website.

And finally, remember that there is no perfect solution to any of these questions. You can set up a secure and anonymous encrypted channel with your source, only to find that source's spouse let a crucial detail slip at the country club that unmasks all your efforts. Digital security is an arms race: as technology evolves, institutions are upgrading their surveillance capabilities, and journalists will likely be one step behind.

But the fact that the technology isn't perfect and that our adversaries are well funded is no reason to give up. Even in the face of the risks, we have a moral obligation to do as much as we can to minimize the risks for our sources and ourselves. The good news is that although the threats are great, the range of technical solutions is increasing by the day. One day, I hope we will look back at this time and see that we were at the cusp of a new, safer era of journalism.

GLOSSARY OF JOURNALIST SECURITY TOOLS

AIR-GAPPED COMPUTER   An air-gapped computer is not—and has never been—connected to an insecure network, such as the Internet. It is used for the most sensitive journalistic operations, such as storing the Snowden documents.

BURNER PHONES   Burner phones are prepaid cell phones that are bought with cash at a location far from your usual commute, so as not to be tied to your identity.

DISPOSABLE E-MAIL ADDRESS   A disposable e-mail address is an e-mail account that is not tied to your identity. Best practice is to set up the account while using Tor anonymizing software, because most e-mail providers store the location from which an account was set up. However, not all e-mail providers allow Tor users to set up an account.

FARADAY CAGE   A Faraday cage is a container that is lined with material that blocks radio signals—ensuring that your phone is not transmitting your location.

GPG   Gnu Privacy Guard[7] is free software that enables e-mail encryption. Most people access it through the Mac version, GPGTools,[8] or the Windows version, GPG4Win. Many people refer to it as PGP—or Pretty Good Privacy—which is the paid version of this software.

ONIONSHARE   OnionShare is software that allows people to share files anonymously over the Internet.[14] The sender downloads OnionShare software and receives a secret web address. The recipient must use Tor to visit the web address and download the file.

OTR   Off-the-Record messaging is a protocol for sending and receiving encrypted instant messages[15]. Most people use it through the Mac version, Adium,[16] or the Windows version, Pidgin.[17] I will use OTR to refer to all instant messaging programs that use the protocol.

OTR + TOR   Off-the-Record messaging used over the Tor system offers the best of both worlds: anonymity *and* encryption. However, it requires some tech savvy to configure OTR programs to work with Tor. (E-mail provider Riseup.net offers a decent tutorial.)

SECUREDROP—SecureDrop is an encrypted dropbox that newsrooms can install to allow sources to send documents in an encrypted and anonymous fashion. Sources must download Tor and follow a few simple instructions to send documents through SecureDrop.[9]

SIGNAL   Signal is an iPhone app that allows users to make encrypted calls and send encrypted texts to each other. For Android phones, it is called RedPhone for voice calls and TextSecure for text messaging.[10]

TAILS   Tails is a computer operating system that is set up with privacy defaults. Tails routes user Internet traffic automatically through Tor and is set up for default use of encrypted e-mail and instant messaging. Users must boot up their computer using a USB drive or CD installed with Tails. Tails is specifically designed to be secure even if the computer you are using has been compromised.[11]

TOR   Tor is an anonymity network that works by bouncing user's Internet traffic to various servers around the world so that the user appears to be in a different location.[12]

TOR BRIDGES   Tor Bridges are private connections to Tor that are not listed in the public Tor directory.[13] They are often used in places like China that attempt to block Tor traffic. For even more extreme situations, Tor offers an even more secret hookup called Tor pluggable transports. I will use Tor Bridges to refer to both categories of secret connections to Tor.

NOTES

1. Nora Ephron, "Deep Throat and Me: Now It Can Be Told, and Not for the First Time Either," *Huffington Post*, May 31, 2005, http://www.huffingtonpost.com/nora-ephron /deep-throat-and-me-now-it_b_1917.html.

2. Jack Limpert, "Deeper into Deep Throat," *Washingtonian*, July 31, 1974, http://www .washingtonian.com/1974/07/31/deeper-into-deep-throat/.

3. "What They Know," *Wall Street Journal*, http://blogs.wsj.com/wtk/.

4. Tor Project: Anonymity Online, https://www.torproject.org/index.html.en.

5. "Support—Windows Help," Windows Help, http://windows.microsoft.com/en-us/windows /support#1TC=windows-10.

6. Julia Angwin, "The World's Email Encryption Software Relies on One Guy, Who Is Going Broke," February 5, 2015, ProPublica, https://www.propublica.org/article/the-worlds -email-encryption-software-relies-on-one-guy-who-is-going-broke.

7. "The GNU Privacy Guard," The GNU Privacy Guard, https://gnupg.org/.

8. "GPGTools," GPGTools, https://gpgtools.org/.

9. "SecureDrop," SecureDrop, https://securedrop.org/.

10. "Signal—Private Messenger on the App Store," App Store, https://itunes.apple.com/app /id874139669.

11. "Tails—Privacy for Anyone," Tails, https://tails.boum.org/.

12. "Tor."

13. "Tor Project: Bridges," Tor, https://www.torproject.org/docs/bridges.html.en.

14. Micah Lee, "Onionshare," GitHub, February 12, 2016, https://github.com/micahflee /onionshare/blob/master/README.md.

15. "Off-the-Record Messaging," Off-the-Record Messaging, https://otr.cypherpunks.ca/.

16. "Adium—Download," Adium, https://www.adium.im/.

17. "Pidgin," Pidgin, the Universal Chat Client, https://pidgin.im/.

8

BEYOND PGP

How News Organizations Can and Must Protect Reporters

and Sources at an Institutional Level

TREVOR TIMM

he story of how the Snowden revelations came to be cannot be told without also explaining how they almost didn't happen. The tale, at this point, has been told many times before (including in multiple places in this book). For many years, though, we've been looking at this event in the wrong way, and the real lessons news organizations should have learned from it have been—at least partly—discarded or ignored.

First, we should probably tell it one more time: in December 2012, an anonymous source first attempted to contact the journalist Glenn Greenwald by e-mailing him from a throw-away account and asked him to setup PGP (Pretty Good Privacy). PGP is the notoriously annoying-to-use but most secure way to encrypt e-mail. Greenwald ignored these initial requests, but this unknown person—who turned out to be Edward Snowden—persisted. He sent Greenwald how-to links; he wrote out instructions; he even made a twelve-minute video tutorial. Still, Greenwald failed to setup PGP.

Fortunately, the mysterious e-mailer did not give up. He soon contacted the filmmaker Laura Poitras, Greenwald's friend and colleague, and also one of the very few journalists at the time who was well versed in digital-security tools. Poitras quickly got Greenwald reengaged, and with a little technical help from Micah Lee, an encryption expert, the rest is history.[1]

It was this anecdote, perhaps even more than the information about the government's vast surveillance capabilities contained in the leaks themselves, that has led to a digital-security awakening among journalists in the years since the Snowden leaks. Journalists can no longer refuse to learn how to use encryption. They have been put on notice that not only will they be putting sources at risk but they may also be losing out on stories they never knew they could get in the first place.

It's unequivocally good news that many more journalists regularly use PGP than did a few years ago. Many (though certainly not all) reporters have also learned how to use OTR, or Off-the-Record, encryption for instant-messaging conversations; others have learned how to use Signal, the encrypted text-messaging application for iPhones and Android; and still others now regularly use the privacy-protective Tor web browser to protect their anonymity while browsing websites of those who they are investigating.

But when we talk about security for entire news outlets, this is just a small part of the puzzle. Many of the big news agencies do not have an organization-wide approach to security, and many of the reporters who have learned how to use these tools have done so by teaching themselves or by proactively asking outside experts to help them.

Large newsrooms may present a variety of logistical or bureaucratic barriers to adopting individual security measures across the board, even if newsroom leaders and managers are well intentioned and want to improve. As a result, journalists are often left to seek out their own solutions. But these challenges aside, encryption cannot and should not be the sole responsibility of the reporter.

Just like the act of protecting a source through refusing to testify often involves the cooperation of reporter, lawyer, editor, and publisher, taking digital security seriously involves a team of people working together. The top editors, the general counsel, and IT officers at every news organization have a responsibility to understand the basic concepts of how security works if they want to protect their reporters and sources in the future.

This is the real lesson of how Snowden first attempted to contact Glenn Greenwald: it's not the story of a failure on the part of Greenwald or any one journalist; it is instead collective failure on the part of news organizations.

—⚬⚬⚬—

The first question news organizations no doubt asked themselves after the Snowden leaks was this: How do we attract the next Snowden?

While the allure of "the next Snowden" will certainly push organizations to remove barriers that are preventing reporters from using encryption, it's equally important to realize that a Snowden-like source will always be an anomaly in the journalism world. Edward Snowden had tens of thousands of documents he was willing to hand over. He knew that his life would be changed forever, and he was willing to risk jail and his livelihood to get the story to the public. Most importantly for this discussion, he also possessed an extraordinary technical sophistication. In this case, the source was more knowledgeable about digital security than the journalists he was communicating with, not the other way around.

The real risk to sources and news organizations is not that someone else in Snowden's situation will attempt the same thing in the future but that the parties involved will have the opposite problem: that a source, with no prior knowledge, will contact them with an important story, and the news organization will have no way to offer him protection or, worse, will put him in greater peril through mistakes.

While it is essential that journalists are literate in digital security, before even getting into which encryption tools are best for which scenario, there are simple questions that editors, general counsels, and IT officers need to explore together to make sure they are doing the most they possibly can to protect their reporters and sources. For example, where is your organization's e-mail hosted? This is important in part because news organizations face a variety of threats—both foreign and domestic.

Advances in surveillance technology have made it much easier for the Justice Department to prosecute leaks and chill reporters' sources. For decades, reporters who were called to testify in court frequently refused to comply to the point of going to jail, meaning the government always faced a difficult and lengthy legal battle if it ever wanted to prosecute a source.

But in the past eight to ten years, the government figured out that it rarely has to call reporters to the stand to testify. The James Risen case that made so many headlines, where the celebrated *New York Times* reporter was initially subpoenaed to testify at a leak trial, is actually a rare event—despite the fact that the Justice Department is prosecuting a record number of sources. It's now much easier for prosecutors to just subpoena our third-party e-mail providers and get troves of information through this method. The worst part about this process is that journalists won't know their communications are in the hands of the government until it's too late to legally challenge this action.

Even in Risen's case, the Justice Department ultimately dropped the subpoena at the last minute and used electronic evidence gathered through surveillance to convict the alleged leaker, the former CIA officer Jeffrey Sterling.[2]

Twelve of the top twenty-five news organizations host their e-mail with Microsoft or Google, according to research completed in 2014 by security expert Ashkan Soltani.[3] At a lot of organizations, this is done for convenience. Having a large tech company host your e-mail removes a lot of costs and burdens from your IT department, but you're also doing your reporters who may be subpoenaed by the U.S. government a huge disservice.

Take, for example, the case of Fox News's James Rosen, who was notoriously referred to as a "coconspirator" in a 2010 leak case by the Justice Department.[4] Fox News didn't find out that the Justice Department had gotten a warrant for the contents of Rosen's e-mail until years later, precisely because he was using a Gmail account. The government was able to go to Google in secret, serve it with a warrant that forced it to hand over the content that likely included a gag order, and by the time Fox found out it was too late to challenge the order in court.

Similarly when the Justice Department subpoenaed the phone records from twenty phone lines at the Associated Press in the hunt for another leaker.[5] Because the phone company held them, the AP wasn't alerted until the government already had them, so the AP had no chance to bring a legal challenge.

And it's not only national security journalists who have to worry about this. In 2012, Microsoft unilaterally snooped on the content of a blogger's Hotmail account without a warrant[6]—or any legal process whatsoever—in an attempt to root out an employee within Microsoft who was allegedly leaking the source code of Windows 8.

Many Internet users found out—for the first time, thanks to this scandal—that Microsoft's terms of service allow for the company to read your e-mail in a host of situations. Those terms allowed Microsoft to do so not only to "protect their rights and property" but also if you violate their "code of conduct," which includes using profanity or sending pictures containing nudity. Microsoft is not unique here: Google, Apple, and Yahoo all have clauses in their terms of service that allow them to read your e-mail with no legal process if they are protecting their "rights or property" as well.[7]

Microsoft was forced to change its policy after this episode, but a similar scenario was reported in 2015, when Vodafone in Australia sifted through a journalist's phone records to root out a whistleblower inside Vodafone.[8]

Unfortunately, the solutions for news organizations isn't cut-and-dried. Securing e-mail systems is a complicated and expensive process. Many use Google because the Silicon Valley company has a team of hundreds of people working to keep hackers associated with the Chinese government and other foreign intelligence agencies out of their e-mail system. Google also has a variety of additional phishing preventions and alert systems that news IT teams may not have the capacity to handle themselves. And there's good reason they would want to outsource this service: the nation's biggest papers, including the *New York Times*, the *Washington Post*, and the *Wall Street Journal*, have all had their entire networks allegedly compromised by hackers in China.

"News orgs are stuck between a rock and a hard place. Arguably cloud services like Google provide better against outside attackers than small IT departments," Ashkan Soltani said about this problem in 2014.[9] However, these services offer far less privacy than do self-hosted solutions, especially when the terms of services allow snooping of user's e-mails. There's a significant tension between privacy and security—with very few options for these companies."

After a media backlash following the Risen case and others, the Justice Department announced in 2015 that it had tightened its restrictions on when and how the U.S. government can conduct surveillance on journalists. Critically, though, these rules completely exempted national security surveillance tools, such as National Security Letters and FISA (Foreign Intelligence Surveillance Act) court orders, which can still be used in complete secrecy and without journalists' knowledge.[10]

So what's the solution? Like so many of these security problems, it's probably different for every organization given that there are so many factors to consider. But the key is having a top-down discussion where editors, lawyers, and technologists are in the same room, and where they lay out exactly what the threats are and what types of tools news organizations already have to respond to these threats. Newsrooms need to address the questions: How are you protecting your reporters most at risk from the Chinese government? How are you protecting the reporters most at risk from the U.S. government? And how are you dealing with everything in between?

It's unclear if news outlets have had sufficient internal discussions about these types of issues, even years after the Snowden leaks. A 2015 Pew survey found that 50 percent of journalists feel that their employers are not doing enough to protect them against surveillance and hacking.[11]

Now let's go back and look at the Greenwald–Snowden story for a second and talk about PGP e-mail encryption.

Yes, Greenwald failed to set up PGP. This is generally considered a failure on his part that almost cost him the story of a generation. But can we blame him? The program is complicated to understand and hard to set up, and even security experts make mistakes while using it. Should we have really expected Greenwald to drop everything and take hours to teach himself concepts that were foreign to him, all to speak to a person he didn't know who might be not be credible? Why was there no one for Greenwald to turn to for help at the news organization that he was affiliated with?

But again, this doesn't get at the larger problem. The vast majority of sources will be nothing like Snowden. In most cases, it's likely that the journalist will have more knowledge about security than the source. And that can be a scary thought—even for journalists who know how to use e-mail encryption.

If you're an editor, ask yourself: If a source wanted to contact your reporters securely right now, how would she go about it? You may have e-mail addresses posted on your website, but is there a PGP key posted next to each of those names? Is the contact form on your website encrypted? Do sources have the option to call a phone number on Signal so the call will be more protected? The vast majority of newsrooms still don't even give reporters the option to do this (though, commendably, organizations like Gawker and BuzzFeed started posting their PGP keys at the bottom of every article in 2015).

On *every* news organization's contact page, there should be a list of every way sources can more securely contact a reporter, whether that's a PGP key, an encrypted phone or text-messaging service like Signal, a link to a SecureDrop whistleblower submission system, or whatever next-generation tool may exist in the future. It wouldn't hurt to also write a one-sentence explainer with a link for those wondering what these tools are and how to use them.

This would enable teaching sources to use these tools *before* they ever contact you in the first place. While there is increasing knowledge about encryption and anonymity tools—especially among a younger, more tech-savvy generation—there is also simultaneously a huge disparity in technological literacy and a large digital divide, which means that news organizations should actively be providing resources to those with no knowledge of encryption.

Thankfully, encryption is getting easier for everyday people to use. Apple now end-to-end encrypts its iMessages and FaceTime calls. Facebook's WhatApp, the most popular messaging app in the world, announced in 2016 all it texts and phone calls are end-to-end encrypted as well.

But this doesn't change the fact that some of the most important stories may exist in disenfranchised communities or may involve people who have little access to expensive devices like iPhones: this includes incidents occurring in local police departments or outside the bounds of large cosmopolitan cities. And this is why making clear the best way to contact a reporter safely and securely to all potential sources—and to the general public—is critical.

Unfortunately, no matter how many precautions news organizations take, there will always be sources with low knowledge of security who cold-call or cold e-mail reporters with potentially juicy information without using any type of encryption. What do you do in those situations? Chances are that right now, journalists make it up on the fly. But this is something news organizations should be prepared for even before a significant source-event happens.

Organizations should have checklists and instructions that all journalists can reference and use to make sure they follow the correct procedures every time, similar to the *New Yorker* writer and surgeon Atul Gawande's now-famous "Checklist Manifesto." Security is much like surgery: you can do things right 95 percent of the time, but if you mess up the other

5 percent, it could have catastrophic consequences for those involved. Having established protocols to follow can be incredibly important.

So, for example, say a source contacts you on your regular work e-mail address. The person says he has something sensitive to tell the journalist but does not know anything about security. What do you do? Do you try to tell the source how to encrypt his e-mail, or do you tell him to get off e-mail entirely? It's tough to set up a meeting with the source because he may have e-mailed you from a work address.

As a reporter, you also may face another problem: as James Risen said at a 2014 conference on journalism and digital security, often sources don't even know they *are* sources and would not risk their lives for a story.[12] Telling them to immediately get onto a complicated system that sounds like spycraft may scare them off before they ever tell you anything. The investigative privacy reporter Julia Angwin said at the same conference: "Asking a source to use encryption is like asking for sex on a first date; it's off-putting. But if you wait to ask for it down the road, it may already be too late."

If news organizations develop a standard checklist a reporter should follow for responses to inquiries like these, it will go a long way at putting both the reporter and the source at ease. First, the reporter won't panic and either give the source wrong advice or make it up on the fly. She could merely refer to documents already created, pick the best course of action, and respond with prewritten language that's easy to understand. She would also know the correct person to consult with if she wanted a second opinion.

If you work in a large news organization, it's very likely you have a large IT department. These departments are critical for newsrooms to function in the twenty-first century, and often their goals are many and varied: they are engineers, designers, coders, and graphic artists and most important, have become the dominant publishing arm of most news organizations.

But they are also in charge of security—and in the past, this has often been an afterthought. These IT departments often spend significant resources on new products sold by various IT vendors. Some of the products are good, some can be bad, but in many cases these products may not take security into account—at least at the level required by reporters.

Having a director of security or a Chief Information Security Officer (CISO), who oversees security across the entire organization and who reports directly to the editor in chief, is critical in making sure that security is taken into account with every major decision a newspapers makes.

There are many security-enhancing measures that CISOs can implement at the newsroom level and that are standard practice at a lot of tech companies, yet are sadly far less common in the journalism world. For example, an employee at a large U.S. news organization told me in 2014 that the organization had spent a fortune on two separate instant-messaging chat programs that their reporters ended up complaining about because they were incompatible with OTR, the most common way to encrypt your chats. The reporters then started asking IT to set them up with OTR, which is free, despite the fact that the IT department was spending resources on proprietary products that they did not see any benefit from. Having a CISO is crucial to help avoid such situations.

Since 2015, some news organizations have started to move in this direction. In 2016, the *New York Times* hired a security expert, Runa Sandvik, as its director of security. Unfortunately, this is nowhere close to industry best-practice yet.

Perhaps the most disappointing reaction to the Snowden revelations (or lack thereof) is that the vast majority of news organizations—at the beginning of 2016—still fail to encrypt their websites with HTTPS, one of the most important steps in protecting reader privacy and security. Kevin Gallagher, my colleague at Freedom of the Press Foundation, succinctly described HTTPS:

> An HTTPS connection is easily recognized by the most novice of Internet users for the lock icon it displays in your web browser's address bar. It signifies that the connection between you and the website you are reading is encrypted, so a malicious actor—whether a criminal trying to eavesdrop on you through public Wi-Fi or a government that has access to raw Internet traffic—cannot see the information that you are transmitting or requesting from a particular website.[13]

The Snowden revelations laid bare just how much the NSA preys on all sorts of websites that have insecure HTTPS connections. One leaked document, for instance, lists a variety of websites—among them Facebook, Yahoo, Twitter, Myspace, CNN.com, Wikipedia, @mail.ru, Google Earth, and Gmail—that the NSA can easily spy on because they are not protecting their users with HTTPS. (Many of these companies have since switched over, but most news organizations have not.)

Other NSA documents also showed how the spy agency can vacuum up the traffic of entire Internet streams to spy on users.[14] They were able to spoof insecure HTTP websites to deliver malware to unsuspecting visitors.[15] One Government Communications Headquarters (GCHQ) document even showed that the British spy agency was monitoring readers of news and documents on WikiLeaks's website—exactly what every news organization should fear most.[16] All these attacks could largely be prevented by using HTTPS.

In November 2014, the *New York Times*'s CTO Rajiv Pant (who has now left the company) laid out nine reasons why HTTPS is important for newspapers and called on all news organizations to pledge to switch over to HTTPS by the end of 2015.[17] Commendably, the *Washington Post* became one of the biggest newspapers to do so—by December 2015, 99 percent of its traffic was redirected to HTTPS. Neither the *New York Times* nor any other major paper followed the *Washington Post*'s lead. By early 2016, only a handful of news organizations had switched to HTTPS by default in the years since the Snowden revelations.[18] The vast majority still leave their websites susceptible to run-of-the-mill spying. Hopefully, the tide will eventually turn.

To be sure, switching over a legacy website to HTTPS is much harder than just flipping a switch, and a large part of the problem lies with the advertising agencies that serve ads on news organizations' websites (both the news organization itself and the ad company has to be HTTPS compliant for it to work). But the *Washington Post* has shown that it's entirely possible to do and can have huge benefits for sources, journalists, and readers.

Whether major news organizations will heed the call for a security-first mind-set is yet to be seen, but one thing is for sure: those who are willing to commit resources and time into building an organization-wide approach to security will win in the long run. As sources become more technologically sophisticated and surveillance threats become more dangerous, there's only one solution: adapt or be willing to put your sources, your journalists, and even your readers at more risk.

NOTES

1. Glenn Greenwald, Laura Poitras, and Micah Lee are all board members of Freedom of the Press Foundation, where this author works. Edward Snowden joined the board as well in February 2014.

2. Matt Apuzzo, "Times Reporter Will Not Be Called to Testify in Leak Case," *New York Times*, January 12, 2015, http://www.nytimes.com/2015/01/13/us/times-reporter-james -risen-will-not-be-called-to-testify-in-leak-case-lawyers-say.html?_r=0.

3. Trevor Timm, "Lessons for Journalists and Sources from the Microsoft/Blogger Privacy Fiasco," March 25, 2014, Freedom of the Press Foundation, https://freedom.press/blog /2014/03/lessons-journalists-and-sources-microsoftblogger-privacy-fiasco.

4. Ann E. Marimow, "Justice Department's Scrutiny of Fox News Reporter James Rosen in Leak Case Draws Fire," *Washington Post*, May 20, 2013, https://www.washingtonpost .com/local/justice-departments-scrutiny-of-fox-news-reporter-james-rosen-in-leak -case-draws-fire/2013/05/20/c6289eba-c162–11e2–8bd8–2788030e6b44_story.html.

5. Sari Horwitz, "Under Sweeping Subpoenas, Justice Department Obtained AP Phone Records in Leak Investigation," *Washington Post*, May 13, 2013, https://www.washingtonpost .com/world/national-security/under-sweeping-subpoenas-justice-department-obtained -ap-phone-records-in-leak-investigation/2013/05/13/11d1bb82-bc11–11e2–89c9–3be8095fe767 _story.html.

6. Andrew Crocker, "Microsoft Says: Come Back with a Warrant, Unless You're Microsoft," March 21, 2014, Electronic Frontier Foundation, https://www.eff.org/deeplinks/2014/03 /microsoft-says-come-back-warrant-unless-youre-microsoft.

7. Alex Hern, "Yahoo, Google and Apple Also Claim Right to Read User Emails," *Guardian*, March 21, 2014, http://www.theguardian.com/technology/2014/mar/21/yahoo-google -and-apple-claim-right-to-read-user-emails.

8. Ben Doherty, "Vodafone Australia Admits Hacking Fairfax Journalist's Phone," *Guardian*, September 12, 2015, http://www.theguardian.com/business/2015/sep/13/vodafone-australia -admits-hacking-fairfax-journalists-phone.

9. Quoted in Timm, "Lessons for Journalists."

10. Trevor Timm, "When Can the FBI Use National Security Letters to Spy on Journalists? That's Classified," *Columbia Journalism Review*, January 11, 2016, http://www.cjr.org /criticism/national_security_letters.php.

11. Pew Research Center, "Journalists Split on How Well Their Organizations Protect Them Against Surveillance and Hacking," February 4, 2015, http://www.journalism.org /2015/02/05/investigative-journalists-and-digital-security/pj_2015–02–05_investigative -journalists_04/.

12. Kevin Gallagher, "Watch Many of the Nation's Best Reporters and Technologists Discuss Post-Snowden Journalism Security," November 11, 2014, Freedom of the Press Foundation, https://freedom.press/blog/2014/11/watch-many-nations-best-reporters-and -technologists-discuss-post-snowden-journalism.

13. Kevin Gallagher, "Fifteen Months After the NSA Revelations, Why Aren't More News Organizations Using HTTPS?" September 12, 2014, Freedom of the Press Foundation, https://freedom.press/blog/2014/09/after-nsa-revelations-why-arent-more-news -organizations-using-https.

14. Julia Angwin, Charlie Savage, Jeff Larson, Henrik Moltke, Laura Poitras, and James Risen, "AT&T Helped U.S. Spy on Internet on a Vast Scale," New York Times, August 15, 2015, http://www.nytimes.com/2015/08/16/us/politics/att-helped-nsa-spy-on-an-array-of -internet-traffic.html?_r=0.

15. Ryan Gallagher, "The Inside Story of How British Spies Hacked Belgium's Largest Telco," Intercept, December 1, 2014, https://theintercept.com/2014/12/13/belgacom-hack-gchq -inside-story/.

16. Glenn Greenwald and Ryan Gallagher, "Snowden Documents Reveal Covert Surveillance and Pressure Tactics Aimed at WikiLeaks and Its Supporters," Intercept, February 18, 2014, https://theintercept.com/2014/02/18/snowden-docs-reveal-covert-surveillance-and -pressure-tactics-aimed-at-wikileaks-and-its-supporters/.

17. Will Van Wazer, "Moving the Washington Post to HTTPS," Washington Post, December 10, 2015, https://developer.washingtonpost.com/pb/blog/post/2015/12/10/moving-the -washington-post-to-https/.

18. Eitan Konigsburg, Rajiv Pant, and Elena Kvochko, "Embracing HTTPS," New York Times, November 13, 2014, Open Blog, http://open.blogs.nytimes.com/2014/11/13/embracing -https/.

9

FREEDOM OF INFORMATION AND INFORMATION ASYMMETRY

NABIHA SYED

How do investigative reporters know what they know? As a media lawyer, I am frequently asked to "bulletproof" investigative stories, and I subject reporters to excruciating questions about the claims in their stories. (To the BuzzFeed editorial staff: I offer no apology.) It seems like a straightforward question. But the institutions that control our society in critical ways—sprawling government bureaucracies and powerful private companies alike—are increasingly opaque, particularly so when it comes to privacy and national security. How does one report with certainty when these labyrinthine and closed organizations possess far, far more information than an individual reporter? In this post-Snowden era, while legal scholars and advocates reevaluate concepts like transparency and secrecy, I suggest we understand the current reporting state through the lens of information ecology.

There has always been some information asymmetry between reporters acting in the public interest and powerful organizations—like government agencies—that possess critical information. Increasingly, that imbalance is tilting against the interests of two critical groups: national security reporters and independent journalists. Most surprising is the role of technology in exacerbating the asymmetry. Let us examine this information asymmetry in three different ways.

1. What issues do reporters confront when obtaining information from unauthorized channels, through leaks of information by third-party sources?

2. How does increasing technological facility of many investigative reporters affect that practice?

3. How do technological advances change how the government communicates information directly to reporters?

Taking these three questions together, I hope to offer a snapshot of the information ecology that reporters grapple with in the post-Snowden universe.

───── ∞ ─────

Leaks are mundane. As I have learned working in a newsroom, leaks are hardly the territory of the Edward Snowdens or Chelsea Mannings of the world. They form the backbone of so many stories about celebrities, political campaigns, corporate malfeasance, and yes, national security. All rely on sources who have been promised some sort of confidentiality.[1] It makes sense: without some sort of protection, the incentives for leaking are low while the repercussions can remain extraordinarily high. And yet, given their commonplace nature, the post-Snowden world provides uncertain terrain for those who engage in this type of newsgathering and wish to grant their source some protection.

That should come as no surprise. The patchwork of federal, state, constitutional, and common-law approaches to source protection have long been uneven. In particular, the past decade and a half has revealed uncertainty around two questions: Who should be able to claim confidentiality for their communications? And can or should these protections trump national security concerns? Both the conversations about the federal reporter's privilege and the contemporary debates over encryption for source privilege exhibit these parallel and often intertwined concerns, and they are often exacerbated by democratized technological advances and political tumult.

While the precise contours of the reporter's privilege are covered elsewhere in this book, I would like to focus mainly on the hurdles that have troubled the formation of a federal testimonial privilege.

The erosion of the reporter's privilege has coincided with the expansion of who might claim its protection. Defining who is a journalist has long been puzzling: even thirty years ago, in the Supreme Court case often credited with establishing a qualified reporter's privilege, the court noted that trying to define who was a "newsman" deserving of the privilege "would present practical and conceptual difficulties of a high order."[2] Part of the trouble is that other recognized testimonial privileges—like doctor–patient or attorney–client confidentiality—involve the protection of private information transferred to members of an accredited profession. This bounds the privilege in predictable ways.

As countless others have noted, journalism does not fit the pattern of a bounded, accredited profession. Affiliation with institutional press can act as a proxy for accreditation, and indeed the strong overlap of "journalist" with "employed by media organization" made that proxy reasonable for quite some time. But now that publishing requires neither access to a printing press nor institutional support, the proxy makes less sense. Anyone with an Internet connection can engage in what Andy Carvin has called "random acts of journalism." While this seems to be an anomaly introduced by technological advancement, in theory it is actually more in keeping with the guarantees of the First Amendment, which affords no special privileges to institutional press over the general public.

This latest development has not escaped judicial attention. Since *Branzburg*, courts have consistently disagreed on the full scope of the privilege and who can gather its protection—but notably, almost all recognized there was a privilege. In 2003—just as blogs began to rise in their ascendancy—Judge Richard Posner of the Seventh Circuit took that assumption to task in *McKevitt v. Pallasch*,[3] warning that courts recognizing a privilege "may be skating on thin ice." In arguing that journalists had no right, qualified or absolute, to withhold testimony when subpoenaed, Posner opened the door for other judges to challenge both the existence of the privilege and its extension to emerging practitioners like bloggers. No one did this more candidly than Judge Sentelle of the D.C. Circuit Court:

> Perhaps more to the point today, does the privilege also protect the proprietor of a web blog: the stereotypical "blogger" sitting in his pajamas at his personal computer posting on the World Wide Web his best product to inform whoever happens to browse his way? If not, why not?

How could one draw a distinction consistent with the court's vision of a broadly granted personal right? If so, then would it not be possible for a government official wishing to engage in the sort of unlawful leaking under investigation in the present controversy to call a trusted friend or a political ally, advise him to set up a web blog (which I understand takes about three minutes) and then leak to him under a promise of confidentiality the information which the law forbids the official to disclose?[4]

The questions around how the shield law may apply to a blogger were not hypothetical. Only six months after Judge Sentelle's opinion, the freelance cameraman Josh Wolf covered an anarchist protest in San Francisco during which a city police officer suffered injuries. Wolf posted the video to his blog, selling a portion to a local television studio as well. Six months later, Wolf was subpoenaed before a federal grand jury for all documents and recordings related to the protest activities; federal prosecutors sought the footage, thinking that it contained evidence related to a crime they wished to investigate. Wolf refused. He moved to quash the subpoena under the reporter's privilege in *Branzburg* among other arguments, which the court denied. Wolf still refused to disclose the materials, earning a finding of civil contempt. Wolf lost his subsequent appeals.[5] He still refused to disclose the materials, a decision made in contempt of court, and consequently Wolf became the longest-jailed journalist in the United States after spending 226 days in jail.

The Wolf example illustrates another technological disruption, one that goes beyond the ease of modern distribution. The simplicity with which one—anyone—can observe, record, store, and access information severely reduces centralized control over information. Wolf's ability to record inexpensively and unobtrusively (that is, without a camera crew) is one part of that. Yet another is the ease of access: spiriting away sensitive information no longer requires access to a filing cabinet or hours of clandestine photocopying, thanks to technological advances. All it takes is momentary access to the right files. Perhaps nothing was a more a sensational reminder of this than WikiLeaks's Cablegate disclosures (2010–2011), resulting from a single actor's access to immense troves of information. Countless words have been spilled analyzing what WikiLeaks meant, but I want to underscore that it only illustrated a possible frontier of just how decentralized acts of journalism may be.

The response to WikiLeaks also highlighted another anxiety around the reporter's privilege: Can it or should it trump national security interests? This is a long-standing question but came to the fore quite prominently during the Bush administration (which, in turn, coincided with the rise of digital journalism in the early 2000s). From 2000 on, the number of federal court subpoenas sent to journalists reporting on terrorism-related matters jumped dramatically.[6] In 2002, federal prosecutors sought a videotaped interview with John Walker Lindh from the CNN reporter Robert Pelton, who was ordered to testify by a judge. Two years later, the Reuters reporter Esmat Salaheddin was similarly ordered to testify on matters related to how Sheik Omar Abdel-Rahman communicated with his followers. Perhaps most high-profile instance was the subpoena of Judith Miller, the *New York Times* reporter who refused to answer federal grand jury questions related to the public identification of the undercover CIA officer Valerie Plame. Miller refused to testify and reveal her source and was found in contempt of court by the federal district court and then federal appeals court in Washington, D.C. The Supreme Court declined to hear her appeal. Miller then spent eight-five days in jail before her release and decision to testify in front of the grand jury. The Supreme Court's choice was noteworthy: it refrained from clarifying both its opinion in *Branzburg* and the patchwork of uneven protections that had cropped up across the country. By refusing to wade in, the Supreme Court appeared to punt the question to Congress.

Congress responded to the call immediately. The Senate and the House each ushered in bipartisan proposals for the federal shield law in 2005.[7] The Free Flow of Information Act (FFIA), as the similar proposals were called, sought to prevent government officials from compelling a reporter to reveal a source unless "clear and convincing evidence" indicated that "disclosure of the person is necessary to prevent imminent and actual harm to national security." (Ironically enough, Judith Miller's disclosures in the Plame affair would not have been protected under this legislation.) The FFIA proposals appeared broad in their applicability: the language would cover "any entity that disseminates information by print, broadcast, cable, mechanical, photographic, electronic or other means" and "any employee, contractor, or other person who gathers, edits, photographs, records, prepares, or disseminates news or information for such an entity." But Senator Richard Lugar, the sponsor of the Senate bill, indicated that bloggers would "probably not" be subject to the bill's protection. Amid debate over the focus and the scope of the privilege, both acts languished. Interest in a federal reporter's privilege was rekindled in 2008, when the attorneys general from forty-one states warned that the lack of a federal shield law is "producing inconsistency and uncertainty" for journalists and sources and "frustrates the purposes" of state shield laws. A new round of proposals again went nowhere.

In 2013, the federal shield law seemed to have the most promise—and, not coincidentally, the most restrictions. This version of the FFIA, proposed by Senator Dianne Feinstein, included a number of requirements for any journalist seeking its protection, including a demonstration of how long he had spent working in a journalistic capacity and that he was paid by a media organization for his work. Feinstein minced no words in explaining why such limitations were needed: no support could go to a bill "if everyone who has a blog has a special privilege. . . . Or if Edward Snowden were to sit down and write this stuff, he would have a privilege. I'm not going to go there." The bill also contained a broad national security exemption. Ultimately, despite broad bipartisan support, approval of the Senate Judiciary Committee, the endorsement of President Obama, and backing from major news organizations and industry groups, the FFIA still failed. A year later, in 2014, the Supreme Court was given another opportunity to resolve the mess in the case of the New York Times reporter James Risen, and the Court declined again.

And so reporters, institutionally affiliated and independent alike, remain in the lurch when it comes to federal source privilege. To be certain, there are still state-based reporters' privileges—based on state law, state statutes, and state common law, court rules in thirty-nine states plus the District of Columbia that provide some authority for protection, though uneven. But there are serious questions as to whether a federal privilege would wholly solve the issue of source protection. For one thing, and as David Pozen has theorized, a privilege may normalize the process of subpoenaing records rather than framing them as extraordinary occurrences, and thus shift responsibility from the executive branch to the judiciary and the legislature.[8] Critically, no version of the reporter's privilege—as discussed in courts or in Congress—confronts the issue of acquiring reporters' records through third-party service providers, ignoring a major vulnerability for source protection.[9]

What I find most striking, however, and most instructive for the future, is how so much of the debate around legal source protection focused on two poles: expanded definitions of who can be protected and whether national security is a frontier that deserves any protection whatsoever. These happen to be the two areas in which access to information is the most difficult.

For example, take the national security journalist. The national security journalist operates in a landscape with the greatest information asymmetry: The information she seeks is often deemed classified or secret, and the cost of prying it out carries extraordinary risk for all involved. Yet national security stories are highly valuable to the public interest, as they cast light on activity where otherwise there is almost total opacity. Still, opponents of the federal shield law and even many of its proponents alike agree that protection cannot be extended to the national security journalist. Few underscore the public-interest value of national security reporting and its obvious reliance on leaks, ostensibly in order to curry enough support to pass the bill. And so to the national security journalist, the fight for source protection through the law is understandably disheartening: there are few proposals that speak to her particular needs.

Independent journalists also suffer from a lack of adequate protection in part because they, too, have been abandoned by federal proposals. Such nonestablishment journalists might cover alternative vantage points or topics that do not suit more mainstream publications—that is, topics that are underserved in the information economy. Still other notable independent journalists—like Marcy Wheeler, Laura Poitras, and Glenn Greenwald—also report on national security, and their independent affiliation can evidently attract sources that are otherwise disheartened by "traditional" or "establishment" reporting outlets.

And yet, as explained earlier, they remain a likely casualty of a definitional crisis that at its heart is about the decentralization of control over information flow. Even if a legislative proposal shifts its focus to "acts of journalism," as so many wise commentators have suggested, that only defers uncertainty. The question of whether the "act" is properly protected will be decided by a court, in a resource-intensive and lengthy process that few without institutional affiliations may have the appetite or ability to take on. This disadvantages the independent journalist, who rarely has the resources to take a case of source protection to court. The fear of burdensome and costly litigation may well have an understandable chilling effect on riskier stories. Even more worrisome, both the Miller and Risen examples show that resources, institutional support, and a willingness to fight is still no guarantee of success.

Against this background—one of uncertainty about what the protections are and even outright exclusion for some categories—it is no surprise that there has been an active search for alternative modes of source protection: something that does not require resources to hire a lawyer or navigate courts, and offers enough accessible and immediate protection to stave off the uncertainty. Could there be a more decentralized way that suits the decentralized nature of journalistic acts?

A technology-based answer appears to fit the bill. There is no shortage of reporters who now include PGP keys in their Twitter profiles and refer sources to their SecureDrop. This makes sense in the post-Snowden landscape, where Pew reports that almost half of reporters have changed the way they store or share sensitive documents, and about one-third say the same of how they communicate with other colleagues.[10] The dramatic uptick in use can be credited in large part to the Electronic Frontier Foundation, Freedom of the Press Foundation, and other groups supporting encryption for source protection. Encryption, when used properly, certainly does secure communications against unwanted viewers via direct or third-party access. But this mode of source protection is still subject to the same pressures noted in the reporter's privilege struggle: national security and questions of who can use the tool for what end.

Take the example of Lavabit. Starting in 2004, Ladar Levison set out to create an encrypted e-mail service called Lavabit as an alternative to services like Gmail, which generates advertisements and marketing data based on users' e-mail. By August 2013, Lavabit served approximately 410,000 paid and free accounts with various levels of storage and was widely recognized for providing significant privacy protection for its clients. In the aftermath of the Snowden disclosures, Lavabit received three different court orders—a pen-register order, a subpoena, and a search warrant—compelling him to disclose the master encryption key for his service. Levison refused. Undeterred, law enforcement sought and received a civil contempt order imposing a $5,000 per day fine against Levison until he handed over the key. Levison turned over a paper copy of the key, eleven pages long. When that did not work, Levison chose to shutter his service and hand over the key after closing down. He then sought to appeal all three flavors of court order requiring him to turn over the key, arguing that none of the three methods were proper. Ultimately, in April 2014, Levison lost.[11] The entire interlude had a discernibly chilling effect on privacy-protective third-party providers; in its aftermath, another e-mail service called Silent Circle shut its doors out of concerns that it, too, would be legally compelled to violate its own mandate.

The example of Lavabit is not the first time courts have grappled with encryption. While the Lavabit example illustrates the vulnerabilities with third-party providers (such as cloud e-mail and chat), the protections for individually held encrypted materials may be tentatively more promising.

Questions about forced decryption turn on the protections of the Fifth Amendment privilege against self-incriminating testimony. At its heart, the Fifth Amendment protects one from disclosing the contents of one's mind or providing testimony about the existence, possession, or control of incriminating evidence. In keeping with this principle, the Supreme Court has ruled that the Fifth Amendment protects against having to provide a combination to a safe, because conjuring those numbers would be the "expression of the contents of an individual's mind."[12] But the Supreme Court does not extend the Fifth Amendment protection to physical things—because they are not testimonial—and accordingly ruled that the Fifth Amendment did not prevent a suspect from providing a key to a lockbox.[13] Should an encryption key or a password be likened to a combination (which is protected) or to a key (which is not)? Or is it something else all together?

This is usually the point where journalists ask whether these questions relate to them, too—whether a journalist's keys or combinations are considered inherently special. There is no judicial precedent for that, at the moment. The trend of the case law also veers toward another tactic: rather than requesting passwords or encryption keys, law-enforcement officials increasingly ask individuals to directly produce decrypted records or ask individuals to input directly their pass code. This bypasses any existential questions about how a key should be treated under the law and implicates an exception to the Fifth Amendment called the "foregone conclusion" doctrine. This doctrine applies only to the government's request for production—not testimony—and turns on what the government *already* knows about what it seeks. What exactly the government must know for the foregone conclusion to apply has been the source of much judicial attention in the past few years. The answers tend to fall in two camps.

On one hand, courts have required only limited facts, such as the fact that files exist on the computer and that a defendant knows the password. For example, the Supreme Court of Massachusetts in *Commonwealth v. Gelfgatt* found that where a defendant admitted his ownership of and control over seized computers, his knowledge of their encrypted files, and his knowledge of the password, the court concluded that compelling him to provide that password "is only telling the government what it already knows."[14] Providing the password under such circumstances therefore was held not to violate the defendant's privilege against self-incrimination under either the federal or the state constitution. *In re Boucher* came out the same way, though ruling on a technicality that Sebastien Boucher had already given the government access to his computer once, and thus being forced to access the files again, did not violate his Fifth Amendment rights.[15] (This underscores why journalists should seek counsel immediately before responding to law-enforcement requests, a complicated matter for resource-strapped independent journalists.) Even there, however, the court focused on the fact that the government could link the computer to Boucher without his testimony and its awareness of files. Most recently, in *United States v. Fricosu*, the court ordered a defendant charged with mortgage fraud to decrypt her hard drive where the government already had a recording of the defendant admitting that the laptop was hers and that she knew the password.[16]

But I would argue that the more recent trend—including the judgment of an appellate court—requires much more detail before finding that the foregone-conclusion exception may apply. The standard levied by courts in these cases is the "reasonable particularity" standard, requiring that law enforcement already know things like specific file names and precise location of the files.

In *United States v. Kirschner*, the court found that requiring that defendant to give up his computer password "communicates that factual assertion to the government, and thus, is testimonial—it requires Defendant to communicate 'knowledge,' unlike the production of a handwriting sample or a voice exemplar."[17] A federal court in New York followed this logic in *United States v. Rogozin*, holding that providing a laptop password in response to a question from federal agents was "incriminating testimony" protected by the Fifth Amendment.[18] Only a few years later, an appellate court endorsed this logic, *In Re: Grand Jury Subpoena Duces Tecum Dated March 25, 2011*, determining that an individual has a valid Fifth Amendment privilege against self-incrimination that would protect him from being compelled to produce unencrypted contents of his hard drive.[19] At the time of writing, that is the highest court to embrace this logic. Subsequent courts have continued in this vein, as in *Commonwealth v. Baust*, where the court grappled with a defendant believed to possess a videotape of an assault he committed on his password-protected telephone.[20] The government sought either his passcode or his fingerprint to access the videotape. The court ruled that while there was no Fifth Amendment problem with the defendant providing his fingerprint, he could not be compelled to disclose his passcode as that would be a self-incriminating, testimonial disclosure. The foregone conclusion is no help, said the court, because the police did not *already* know the passcode. In a similar vein, in *SEC v. Huang*, the court found that the foregone conclusion could not allow for the disclosure of a password on a company-owned smartphone where the government did not already know the existence and location of incriminating records with reasonable certainty.[21]

None of these cases involve reporters. And that is a by-product of using tools that have been popularized by the general public: members of the general public, perhaps the worst examples of it, will end up the subject of case law. In any event, even on the law as it stands, there is some reason for optimism. Should the "limited facts" version of the foregone-conclusion doctrine take precedence, then it appears that compelled decryption can take place where law enforcement possesses knowledge of who owns the device and what files are contained on it. It seems unlikely that a published investigative report would disclose those details, but I would ask reporters to exercise care in what they disclose in interviews, in GitHub accounts, or elsewhere. Of course, in the line of cases that appear both more persuasive and privacy-protective, compelled decryption would require much more certainty, and would better protect information-savvy journalists as a result. The precise contours of these protections (or lack thereof) will probably be resolved by the Supreme Court eventually, but I strongly doubt that the case ascending to that level will include a reporter rather than an unfortunately unsympathetic plaintiff. All of this is to say that while the mathematics behind encryption may be a sure bet, whether its use is equally legally infallible still remains to be seen.

Similarly uncertain is the political landscape. The political battle over encryption dates back to the "Crypto Wars" of the 1990s. Originally, encryption technology in the United States was classified as a munition or military weapon and accordingly subject to regulation. Concerns over government intrusion into privacy, particularly ill-conceived "backdoors" into computers and phones, made the government abandon this approach in the mid-1990s. In the aftermath of more recent terrorist attacks, law-enforcement officials have revived their criticism of encryption technology: most prominently, the FBI director, James Comey, argues that encryption is making the world "go dark," or difficult for agents to extract evidence from computers, phones, wiretaps, or other communication platforms. (A digression, but query whether this "difficulty" only restores the privacy balance that predates the record-generating capabilities of modern communications technology.) This is particularly perilous, as Comey and others argue, because encryption is now "at the center of terrorist tradecraft."

This belief spurred a year-long campaign by Comey to convince Congress to solve the problem. His preferred solution suggested that any encrypted transaction be designed with special backdoor-access features that would permit the relevant company to bypass user protections and hand over decrypted data pursuant to a law-enforcement investigation. This is particularly pressing, Comey argues, because of a move made by two prominent third-party providers: Apple and Google announced default end-to-end encryption services for users, meaning that neither company can unlock or provide access to those communications without a user's password. Even when armed with a warrant to the third-party provider, law enforcement would not be able to acquire the relevant investigatory material from Apple or Google without having to go directly to the individual.

The clash between law enforcement and third-party provider Apple erupted in early 2016.[22] The FBI sought to access a county-issued Apple iPhone used by a mass shooter in San Bernardino, California. Because the phone was in county law enforcement's possession, after the shooter's death, and a warrant was properly obtained, this would have been a relatively simple endeavor. (Also worth noting: Apple had previously complied with at least seventy unlocking orders from courts, all for older versions of its software.) But here, a mistake by the county teed up Comey's "going dark" concern. The county IT department had reset the password for the device, which was running Apple's latest software, and obtaining the FBI's desired information would require the previous password, which was known only to the deceased. The FBI sought to brute-force guess the password, and to do so, it asked the judge to order Apple to create and cryptographically sign a weakened version of its software that would roll back features designed for enhanced security and privacy. The court granted the order. Unsurprisingly, Apple appealed the order. Tim Cook of Apple decried the order as "dangerous precedent that threatens everyone's civil liberties," with implications far beyond a single investigation in the United States. The order conscripts Apple into carrying out law enforcement's bidding, weakening its own security protocols in doing so.

Against the backdrop of a national conversation, however, the FBI abruptly announced that it no longer needed Apple's assistance in accessing the iPhone in question. A third party had demonstrated a way to unlock the iPhone, and the Department of Justice accordingly vacated the case.

This does not resolve the issue. There are numerous simultaneous phone-unlocking cases throughout the country, any of which may set up conflicting outcomes ultimately destined for the Supreme Court. And at the time of writing, the encryption debate entered a frontier beyond cell phones: WhatsApp, the online messaging service used by more than a billion people, announced end-to-end encryption to every communication on its service. The 2016 presidential election also stands to influence the course of this debate, given great uncertainty as to whether the successful candidate will support compelling third-party providers to grant access to encrypted communications services. Legislative battles on the decryption frontier are surely guaranteed.

The larger significance of this political wrangling is how the use of encrypted communications may be delimited by its worst possible users. Protection for this technological tool is determined at the margins, just as the reporter's privilege debates stalled over those viewed as "fringe" reporters. If journalists rely on the same tools as everyone else, then the rules dictating those tools may equally govern them—with no special treatment in sight.

———⊶⊷———

So, what's a reporter to do? Uncertain legal protections and an unknown political landscape for some technological protections is certainly disconcerting, to say the least. As a media lawyer, I certainly can't (and won't) advise reporters to abandon what I know to be a mainstay of their public-interest newsgathering. It is true that technology has affected the information landscape, and at least in the source-protection landscape whether it encourages more asymmetry between the government and the citizen remains to be seen.

That said, it seems relevant to note here that technology has improved information asymmetry most clearly in one arena: the information that government agencies are willing and able to voluntarily disclose. Independent and institutional journalists alike have equal access to the 130,000 data sets available on Data.gov, including data on consumer complaints filed against banks or health indicators of heart disease in a given county. Critically, however, the benefits of volunteered data are neither universal, comprehensive, nor guaranteed. Relying on what agencies volunteer will underserve topics deemed secret—the Central Intelligence Agency has no incentive to share drone-strike data—and so national security reporters can expect to glean less relevant or timely data than other investigative reporters. There is also no guarantee that data provided by government agencies provides the full story. Finally, a steady supply of data is not a reliable promise. Contemporary open-data policy is built on only executive actions and is prone to political whims and circumstance. For example, Data.gov went offline during the October 2013 budgetary wrangling and resulting government shutdown, eclipsing data on infectious disease from the Centers for Disease Control and insurance data from FEMA, among other things. A future administration could easily abdicate any commitment to providing data, and so I would encourage those who care about information flow to remain vigilant on this front.

Otherwise, the Freedom of Information Act should—theoretically, at least—be the best mediator of information flow between the government and the citizen. This, like the data just mentioned, is designed to be equally available to institutional and independent journalists alike. This channel of disclosure is altered by technology at its most basic level: a sprawling bureaucracy can generate memoranda, communications, and metadata at breakneck speed and, with the help of inexpensive storage, store them. This might appear to be a boon for the savvy FOIA requester. But how does one navigate such a trove of potentially illuminating records? Broad requests can be dismissed out of hand as vague, unduly burdensome, voluminous, or otherwise unreasonable.[23] Should a FOIA requester seek more targeted records, she must identify the correct key words, individuals of interest, or even subcomponent agencies, all of which, paradoxically, requires some existing knowledge about what the records might contain. This underscores one critical problem with FOIA and other requester-driven access initiatives: it does not work unless there is some underlying thread to pull on. To borrow the Rumsfeldian terminology, FOIA can be effective for "known unknowns" but not "unknown unknowns," whose secrecy is so shrouded that the public and those advocating on their behalf have no clue. Even when requests are well targeted, the processing time for voluminous responsive requests may take far longer than is feasible for the news cycle. Too often, FOIA requires the type of litigation most readily available to those with institutional resources, again potentially a disadvantage to the independent journalist.

The Freedom of Information Act is an especially frustrating avenue for those, like national security journalists, who seek official confirmation of sensitive matters. Take the ACLU's FOIA requests in the aftermath of WikiLeaks's disclosure of State Department cables. The ACLU asked for precisely the same documents that had *already* been disclosed and posted online, and yet still had them denied through FOIA for national security reasons.[24] Even before litigation, agencies are permitted to respond to requests with what is called a "Glomar" response, according to which they can neither confirm nor deny the existence of records. And, finally, agencies may lob the "mosaic theory" at a requester, described as "the concept that apparently harmless pieces of information when assembled together could reveal a damaging picture."[25] Courts have been deferential to this theory in the post–September 11 environment,[26] setting up what could be a difficult precedent for data journalists in particular. That said, at least one journalist—Jason Leopold, dubbed the "FOIA terrorist"—has been able to extract valuable national security information from government agencies, employing a battery of requests and frequent litigation.[27]

While often complicated and frustrating, FOIA is one of the few means of proactively asserting a right of access to information . . . and is a frontier worth fighting as a result.

And yet, neither the FOIA nor data volunteered by the government is best suited for getting at information that is at the heart of oversight, meaning information whose disclosure is not easy or favorable to the powers that be. There will be no replacement for information-gathering via leaking, in that regard. And so for those who want to continue on the source-protection fight, there are a number of frontiers worth focusing on. The most straightforward is to ensure that active participation in the still-raging encryption debate is a priority for those who seek to support national security reporters and independent journalists. The number of excellent advocacy organizations focused on this topic should make that easy. Slightly more complicated is working to ensure that legal support is available to independent journalists, for the simple reason that so much of the uncertainty around source protection appears to be resolved in courts. And should the judicial arena be the main one where these protections are fought out, I would encourage researchers and activists to examine whether the right to anonymity—that is, anonymity for any citizen—is more productive than specific testimonial privileges that attach only to "journalists" or "acts of journalism," whoever or whatever that might be. If we can frame the right to secure, confidential communications as a subset of the right of anonymity, as part of a larger conversation about privacy, that may be the best way forward.

NOTES

1. David Pozen, "The Leaky Leviathan: Why the Government Condemns and Condones Unlawful Disclosures of Information," *Harvard Law Review* 127 (2013): 512–635, http://ssrn.com/abstract=2223703.

2. *Branzburg v. Hayes*, 408 U.S. 665 (1972).

3. *McKevitt v. Pallasch*, 339 F.3d 530 (7th Cir. 2003).

4. *In re Grand Jury Subpoena*, 397 F.3d 964 (D.C. Cir. 2005).

5. *In re Grand Jury Subpoena* (Joshua Wolf), 201 Fed. Appx. 430 (9th Cir. 2006).

6. RonNell Anderson Jones, "Media Subpoenaes: Impact, Perception, and Legal Protection in the Changing World of American Journalism," May 19, 2009, Social Science Research Network, http://papers.ssrn.com/sol3/papers.cfm?abstract_id=1407105.

7. Free Flow of Information Act of 2005, S. 1419, 109th Cong. (2005); Free Flow of Information Act of 2005, H.R. 3323, 109th Cong. (2005).

8. Pozen, "Leaky Leviathan."

9. Brad A. Greenberg, "The Federal Media Shield Folly," *Washington Law Review* 91 (2013): 437, http://openscholarship.wustl.edu/law_lawreview/vol91/iss2/5.

10. Pew Research Center, "Investigative Journalists and Digital Security: Perceptions of Vulnerability and Changes in Behavior," February 5, 2015, http://www.journalism.org /files/2015/02/PJ_InvestigativeJournalists_0205152.pdf.

11. *In re Under Seal*, 749 F.3d 276, 293 (4th Cir. 2014).

12. *Doe v. U.S.* (1988).

13. *Schmerber v. California*, 384 U.S. 757 (1966).

14. *Commonwealth v. Gelfgatt*, No. SJC-11358 (Mass. June 25, 2014).

15. *In re Boucher*, 2009 WL 424718, *1 (D. Vt. 2009).

16. *United States v. Fricosu*, 841 F. Supp. 2d 1232 (D. Colo. 2012).

17. *United States v. Kirschner*, 2010 WL 1257355 (E.D. Mich. March 30, 2010).

18. *United States v. Rogozin*, 2010 WL 4628520 (W.D.N.Y. Nov. 16, 2010).

19. *In Re: Grand Jury Subpoena Duces Tecum Dated March 25, 2011*, No. 11–12268 (11th Cir. 2012)

20. *Commonwealth v. Baust* (Virginia State Court 2014).

21. *SEC v. Huang* (E.D. Pa. 2015).

22. At the time of publication, the litigation is still unfolding.

23. *Hudgins v. Internal Revenue Serv.*, 620 F. Supp. 19, 21 (D.D.C. 1985) (dismissing requests that appear to be "a general fishing expedition for answers to questions"); *Ruotolo v. Dep't of Justice*, 53 F.3d 4, 9–11 (2d Cir. 1995) (denial where the request was unduly burdensome); *People for the Am. Way Found. v. U.S. Dep't of Justice*, 451 F. Supp. 2d. 6, 12 (D.D.C. 2006) (examining "reasonableness" of the search based on the volume of documents that must be searched to identify responsive records).

24. Nathan Freed Wessler, "Government Wins Right to Pretend That Cables Released by WikiLeaks Are Still Secret," July 23, 2012, American Civil Liberties Union, ttps://www .aclu.org/blog/free-future/government-wins-right-pretend-cables-released-wikileaks -are-still-secret?redirect=blog/national-security-free-speech/government-wins-right -pretend-cables-released-wikileaks-are-still secret?

25. *Daily Orange Corp. v. CIA*, 532 F. Supp. 122, 126 (N.D.N.Y. 1982); *Ingle v. U.S. Dep't of Justice*, 698 F.2d 259, 268 (6th Cir. 1983); *Am. Friends Serv. Comm. v. U.S. Dep't of Defense*, 831 F.2d 441, 445–46 (3d Cir. 1987); *Lawyers Comm. for Human Rights v. INS*, 721 F. Supp. 552, 564 (S.D.N.Y. 1989); *Knight v. CIA*, 872 F.2d 660, 663–64 (5th Cir. 1989); *Hunt v. CIA*, 981 F.2d 1116, 1118–20 (9th Cir. 1992).

26. *Center for National Security Studies v. U.S. Department of Justice* (applying the mosaic theory to uphold the Justice Department's categorical denial of FOIA requests for information about more than seven hundred people detained in the wake of the September 11 attacks); *North Jersey Media Group v. Ashcroft* (applying the theory to uphold the government's decision to close September 11–related "special interest" deportation hearings to the public and the press); *ACLU v. U.S. Department of Justice*, 321 F. Supp. 2d 24 (D.D.C. 2004).

27. Jason Fagone, "The Secret to Getting Secrets," *Medium*, June 16, 2014, https://medium. com/matter/the-secret-to-getting-top-secret-secrets-1f693eaf609a#.nrxf5fqof.

III

GOVERNING SURVEILLANCE

10

POLITICAL JOURNALISM
IN A NETWORKED AGE

CLAY SHIRKY

E dward Snowden's revelations about the conduct of the NSA don't just tell us about the past conduct of the government. They tell us something about the future of political journalism. In light of the extraordinary pressure on the *New York Times* reporter James Risen to reveal his sources,[1] and significant movements to restrict journalistic reporting of leaks by the Obama administration, it's clear the stories that arose from Snowden's leak have moved journalistic coverage of the world's governments, already a fraught endeavor, into a new and more contentious phase.

Before Snowden, we saw the distribution of video titled *Collateral Murder*, which depicted the killing of several civilians and journalists and cables from the State Department, leaked by Chelsea (then Bradley) Manning. That was an extraordinary occurrence, but one of such strangeness— the scale, the involvement of Julian Assange, Manning's own military history—that it was impossible to know which aspects of that leak were singular occurrences and which indicated larger patterns.

Snowden, a far more knowledgeable and confident source than Manning, and holding far more significant material, has made some of those patterns visible. The leak of the NSA documents provides much information about political journalism in a networked age. The most important patterns are these: individual sources have improved leverage, transnational news networks are becoming both essential and normal, and digital data is undermining older patterns of journalistic reputation.

Taken together, these changes disrupt the unstated bargain between governments and news outlets. In all but the most extraordinary cases, national news has been published in national outlets, with the borders of reporting, national interest, and national jurisdiction all lining up. After Snowden, that pattern is shredded. As journalistic outlets become more networked, the familiar geographic link between sources, reporters, publications, and subjects will weaken.

The open issue for the world's investigative journalists is how far the world's governments will go to restrict these networks. The threat of relatively unconstrained reporting of secrets has prompted extrajudicial attacks on publishing outlets, as with suspension of credit card payments to WikiLeaks following congressional complaint. (Full disclosure: I am a supporter of WikiLeaks, both as a philosophical matter and as a donor during the period in which its finances were first under attack. I am also a donor to ProPublica and the *Guardian*, in large part because of their role in preventing the United States from limiting publication of the Snowden revelations.)

We are quite accustomed to autocratic governments like those of Saudi Arabia and Egypt hampering journalism,[2] but with the rising threat of real transnational reporting, we are seeing authoritarian leaders in South Korea and Turkey push for control of media. Even governments with a constitutional commitment to freedom of speech and of the press, such as the United Kingdom and the United States, have attempted to create de facto restrictions on publishing where the law allows them no direct relief. The essential question is how journalists and publications can strengthen their ability to report important news in an age of increasing interference.

There have always been leaks and leakers. Any discussion of journalism in the United States will eventually come around to Watergate and Deep Throat, the code name for Mark Felt, then the acting associate director of the FBI and leaker-in-chief. Likewise, digital data made leaking easier long before Snowden; the site Cryptome.org was set up in 1996 to do much of what WikiLeaks also does, and WikiLeaks itself was roiling national politics long before Manning ever showed up, as with its accusations of corruption by Daniel arap Moi in 2007.[3]

The Manning case, though, was unusual: a massive leak from inside a secured network run by the richest country on earth, one seemingly well equipped to guard its own secrets. It concerned the United States, the world's sole superpower and most important global actor. And Manning was allowed continued access only because the wars in Iraq and Afghanistan increased the need for technical talent while decreasing the supply.

The cumulative effect was to make the revelations of 2010 seem as if they might be a one-off, rather than a new pattern. Many people commenting on the Manning leak believed that nothing of that magnitude would happen again. This assumption rested on the conviction that national governments and large firms would quickly find ways to limit access to their secrets by insiders who might be willing to leak that information.

The Snowden leak shows us that this organizational adaptation did not happen. The National Security Agency is among the best funded and most competent group of electronic spies in the world.[4] It had three years after the example set by Manning to limit possible leaks, and it failed, spectacularly. Not only did the agency lose a huge trove of data, but officials could not initially identify who had leaked it and, if they are to be believed, still cannot use their own internal controls to discover which documents Snowden had in his possession when he left.

If the NSA cannot secure its own documents, what hope is there for less competent institutions? All large institutions with secrets now face a serious threat to their current practices in making use of digital data (exactly as Assange predicted they would back in 2006). The value of freeing information from physical containers is that more people can see and use it simultaneously, at lower cost. This is a boon for almost every possible use of this data, but it is in tension with any desire to keep it secret.

This tension is fundamental. Sharing data widely is the principal source of risk to its secrecy, but making secret data harder to share also makes it harder to use and thus less valuable. This dilemma grows more severe the more is to be kept secret, because large stores of data require increasingly automated processes of indexing and linking, which in turn require reducing barriers between data stores, so as to "connect the dots." And all this hoped-for dot-connecting requires scores of junior analysts and administrators just to manage basic operations.

From a bureaucratic point of view, there are three obvious solutions to this problem: immediate restrictions on system access for anyone skeptical about the mission, dramatic limits on the number of junior employees given access, and total internal surveillance. Acting on these solutions would indeed lower the number of leaks but would leave an organization trying to use vast data sets with a skeleton crew of paranoid yes-men, hardly a recipe for effective organizational action.

Some bureaucracies will indeed subject themselves to dramatically increased degrees of internal paranoia over who is to have access to which pieces of data, but most won't, and the ones that do will find that it hampers their effectiveness. Just as people write down their nominally secret passwords on Post-its, organizations will reopen their databases to competent administrators and entry-level analysts, because they will have to if they want to make use of the information.

Bureaucracies are permanently vulnerable to a revolt of the clerks. The increased value of digital data comes almost entirely from its improved shareability, and if data is more shareable, there is a greater risk that it will be shared. In a digital world, it no longer takes a senior figure like Mark Felt to leak; it can be anyone who has access to the data. For all Snowden's genius, he operated far from the levers of power within his organization.

What Snowden (and Manning) show is that in large bureaucracies, the scarcest resource is not access to data but individual bravery. Brave sources are rare but not vanishingly so; a brave source can accomplish the delivery of information on a scale unimaginable even a decade ago.

One curiosity of the half-millennium since Gutenberg, and especially of those hundred years in which the telegraph, photograph, phonograph, telephone, cinema, radio, and television all appeared, is that for all the innovation, media remained relentlessly national, constrained by local economics and politics.

For physical media—books and newspapers, letters and photographs—international tariffs priced out much border crossing. The cost of building out the infrastructure for the telegraph and later the telephone had the same effect. Even radio and television, transported as pure energy, first appeared when broadcast engineering was barely adequate to cover a whole city, much less cross national boundaries. Even border-spanning news organizations such as the BBC had to set themselves up country by country.

Through the end of the twentieth century, leaks of any importance would be leaked to, and published by, the press in that nation. Profumo was reported in England, Watergate in the United States, and so on.

Even as entertainment became more global, the news (especially political news) remained nationally sourced, nationally published, and nationally consumed.

Here, too, there are historical precedents before Snowden. It is no exaggeration to say that the current pope got his miter in part because of the *Boston Globe*'s coverage of child sexual abuse by priests.[5] The *Globe* published its series on the horror of Father John Geoghan's crimes in 2002, just far enough into the Internet's existence for the story to spread outside the United States, sparking international scrutiny. Similarly, the *Guardian*'s correspondent in South Africa told me later in that decade that he had regarded his job as reporting on South Africa to the United Kingdom, but had recently discovered that his South African audience was now larger than his British one. The *Guardian* website had become a platform that allowed South Africans to read about themselves.

Those were twenty-first-century equivalents of the first English Bibles being printed in Antwerp: a way of placing a single publisher out of the reach of the target nation's government. What's different today is the "multiple publishers" strategy that Assange improvised and Snowden extended, akin to insisting that every synagogue have two Torahs or every database store information in multiple locations. Having more than one copy of the leaked data and more than one publication working on the story makes the leak more effective.

After Manning, it was easy to believe that organizations like WikiLeaks were the hinge on which any such leak would depend. In the aftermath of the State Department leak, Assange rather than Manning was presented as the central figure, not least because he was charismatic, brilliant, and odd—catnip for the press. Given his outsized presence, it was easy to believe that there had to be some organization between the leaker and the press to make any system of international distribution work.

After Snowden, we see how much power now lies with the leaker. Snowden demonstrated that the principle value WikiLeaks had provided was not in receiving the source materials but in coordinating a multinational network of publishers. Snowden himself took on this function, contacting Laura Poitras and Glenn Greenwald directly.

The potential for a global news network has existed for a few decades, but its practical implementation is unfolding in ours. This normalization of transnational reporting networks reduces the risk of what engineers call a "single point of failure." As we saw with Bill Keller's craven decision not to publish James Risen's work on the NSA in 2004, neither the importance of a piece of political news nor its existence as a scoop is enough to guarantee that that it will actually see the light of day. The global part is driven by the need for leakers to move their materials outside national jurisdictions. The network part is driven by the advantages of having more than one organization with a stake in publication.

The geographic spread of the information means that there is no one legal regime in which injunctions on publication can be served, while the balance of competition and collaboration between organizations removes the risk of an editor unilaterally killing newsworthy coverage. Now and for the foreseeable future, the likelihood that a leak will appear in a single publication, in the country in which it is most relevant, will be in inverse proportion to the leak's importance.

These two changes—the heightened leverage of sources and the normalization of transnational news networks—are threatening even to democratic states with constitutional protections for the press (whether de jure, as in the United States, or de facto, as in the United Kingdom). Those governments always had significant extralegal mechanisms for controlling leaks at their disposal, but empowered sources and transnational networks threaten those mechanisms.

This containment of journalistic outlets inside national borders resembled a version of the prisoner's dilemma, a social science thought experiment in which each of two people is given a strong incentive to pursue significant short-term gain at the other's expense. At the same time, each participant has a weaker but longer-lasting incentive to create small but mutual, longer-term value. The key to the prisoner's dilemma is what Robert Axelrod, its original theorist, calls "the shadow of the future." The shadow of the future is what keeps people cooperating over the long term—in friendships, businesses, marriages, and other relationships—despite the temptations of short-term defection of all sorts.

News outlets and governments exist in a version of the prisoner's dilemma. Publications have a short-term incentive to publish everything they know, but a long-term incentive to retain access to sources inside the government. Governments have a short-term incentive to prevent news outlets from discovering or publishing anything, but a long-term incentive to be able to bargain for softening, delaying, or killing the stories they really don't want to see in public (as happened with Keller.)

As long as both institutions have an extended time horizon, neither side gets all of what it wants, but neither side suffers the worst of what it fears, and so the relationship bumps along, year after year. (There have been a few counterexamples: I. F. Stone did all his work for his weekly newsletter by researching government data, never interviewing politicians or civil servants. He reasoned that the quid pro quo of increased access but reduced ability to publish would end up creating more restrictions than it was worth.)

The shadow of the future has meant that even in nations with significant legal protections for free speech, the press's behavior is considerably constrained by mutual long-term bargains with the government. Empowered leakers and transnational publication networks disrupt this relationship. A leaker with a single issue—the world should see what the State Department or the NSA is doing, to take the two obvious examples—has no regard for the shadow of the future, while publications outside the United States will be not be constrained by legal challenges, threatened loss of insider access, or appeals to patriotism.

There is one final pattern that the Snowden leaks make visible. In the middle of the twentieth century, mainstream news both relied on and produced cultural consensus. With the erosion of the belief that mainstream media speaks to and for the general public in an unbiased way, the presumed lack of objectivity of any given news organization has become a central concern. Alongside this change, however, we are witnessing the spread of a new form of objective reporting: reporting done by objects.

There are, of course, precedents to object-based reporting; tape-recorded conversations in Nixon's White House ended his presidency, as his foulmouthed, petty vindictiveness became obvious to all. The heroic work of the *Washington Post* is the stuff of journalistic lore, but the mechanical nature of the tape recorders actually made them the most trusted reporters on the story.

As the quality and range of reporting by objects has increased, it has had the curious effect of making the partisan nature of both reporters and publications a less serious issue. If *Mother Jones*, predictably liberal, had been able to report Mitt Romney's remarks about the 47 percent only because a bartender heard and repeated them,[6] the story would have circulated among the magazine's left-leaning readers but no farther (as with most stories in that publication). That bartender recorded the conversation, however, and the fact of the recording meant *Mother Jones's* reputation didn't become a serious point of contention. Because people had to trust only the *recording*, not the publication, the veracity of the remarks was never seriously challenged.

This pattern of objective recording trumping partisan reputation is relatively new. Indeed, in the 47 percent story, otherwise sophisticated political observers like Jonathan Chait predicted that Romney's remarks would have little real effect,[7] because they didn't understand that the existence of a recording simply neutralized much of the "out of context" and "he said, she said" posturing that usually follows. *Mother Jones* no longer had to be mainstream to create a mainstream story, provided that its accuracy was vouched for by the bartender's camera.

In Snowden's case, many of the early revelations about the NSA, and especially the wholesale copying of data flowing through various telecom networks, had already been reported, but that reporting had surprisingly little effect. The facts of the matter weren't enough to alter the public conversation. What did have an effect was seeing the documents themselves.

All inter-office PowerPoint decks are bad, but no one does them as poorly as the federal government. The slides describing the PRISM program were unfakeably ugly, visibly made by insiders talking to insiders. As with Romney's remark about the 47 percent, the NSA never made a serious attempt to deny the accuracy of the leak or to cast aspersions on the source, the reporters, or the publications.

Like the Nixon tapes and the Romney video, the existence of the Snowden documents also gave Glenn Greenwald, one of the most liberal journalists working today, a bulwark against charges of partisan fabrication. Indeed, he didn't just publish his work in the *Guardian*, a liberal U.K.-based paper; he took the data with him to an Internet startup, the *Intercept*, believing (correctly) that the documents themselves would act as a kind of portable and surrogate reputation, disarming attempts by the government or partisans elsewhere to deny the accuracy of present or future stories generated from those documents.

In past leaks—the Pentagon Papers, Watergate—it took the combined force of leaked information and a mainstream publication to get the public's attention, and mainstream publications were, almost by definition, the publications most invested in the shadow of the future. Meanwhile, more partisan publications of the twentieth century were regarded with suspicion; even accurate reporting that appeared in them rarely went beyond niche audiences. After Snowden, the world's governments are often denied even this defense. This creates a novel set of actors: an international partisan press that will be trusted by the broad public, as long as it traffics in documents that announce their own authenticity.

There will be more Snowden-style leaks, because the number of people with access to vital information has proliferated and cannot easily be reduced. Even one-in-a-million odds of a leak start to look likely if a million people have access, as was the case with the State Department's cables. So what should journalists and publications do to maximize their ability to report newsworthy stories and minimize government interference? Three broad skills are required.

First and most important, reporters have to get good at encrypted communication. (It would be useful if news organizations began encrypting even routine communication to avoid not just signaling to the governments they cover when something particularly important is happening but also to provide cover to sensitive sources.) Encryption is not an IT function; individual reporters have to become comfortable sending and receiving encrypted e-mail, at a minimum. And, as was the case with both Manning and Snowden, it's important to recognize—and to get the source to recognize—that encryption is no guarantee that a source won't eventually be identified. It is a tool for buying time, not guaranteeing anonymity.

Second, journalists and institutions in contact with leakers need to have a plan for involving other journalists or institutions located in a different jurisdiction. While the leaks that get the most attention are national scale, we can expect additional leaks from inside businesses and local governments. It may be valuable to have a New Jersey newspaper holding vital documents about a sheriff in Colorado to make sure the Colorado paper can't be successfully pressured to withhold them. (This "doomsday switch" scenario seems to have been used by John McAfee, in his fight with the government of Belize, an indication that the pattern extends beyond journalism.)

And third, both journalists and publications should figure out to whom they might be useful as a third-party recipient of some other journalist's or publication's secrets. In moments of crisis (and important leaks tend to precipitate crises), those in need of backup will turn to people they already trust. If you are a journalist, an editor, or a publisher, ask yourself which other publications, anywhere in the world, would turn to you if they needed backup?

These leaks are far more threatening to secretive organizations when perpetrated by clerks instead of chiefs and distributed outside the bounds of local jurisdiction; they are also harder to question or deny. We are already seeing the world's democracies behave like autocratic governments in the face of this threat; the Obama administration has become the greatest enemy of press freedom in a generation (a judgment made by James Risen, the man whose NSA story Bill Keller quashed).

Leaks will still be relatively rare. But because they can happen at large scale, across transnational networks, and provide documents the public finds trustworthy, they allow publications some relief from extralegal constraints on publishing material in the public interest.

Brave sources are going to require brave journalists and brave publications. They are also going to require lots of technical expertise on encryption among reporters and lots of cooperation among sometime competitors. The job of publications is to air information of public concern, and that is increasingly going to mean taking steps to ensure that no one government can prevent publication. Nothing says "We won't back down" like burning your boats on the beach.

NOTES

1. Matt Apuzzo, "Times Reporter Will Not Be Called to Testify in Leak Case," *New York Times*, January 12, 2015, http://www.nytimes.com/2015/01/13/us/times-reporter-james -risen-will-not-be-called-to-testify-in-leak-case-lawyers-say.html.

2. Phillip Bennett and Moises Naim, "21st-Century Censorship," *Columbia Journalism Review*, January 2015, http://www.cjr.org/cover_story/21st_century_censorship.php?page=all.

3. Xan Rice, "The Looting of Kenya," *Guardian*, August 31, 2007, http://www.theguardian .com/world/2007/aug/31/kenya.topstories3.

4. Barton Gellman and Greg Miller, "'Black Budget' Summary Details U.S. Spy Network's Successes, Failures and Objectives," *Washington Post*, August 29, 2013, https://www .washingtonpost.com/world/national-security/black-budget-summary-details-us-spy -networks-successes-failures-and-objectives/2013/08/29/7e57bb78-10ab-11e3-8cdd -bcdc09410972_story.html.

5. "The Story Behind the 'Spotlight' Movie," *Boston Globe*," January 3, 2015, http://www
.bostonglobe.com/arts/movies/spotlight-movie.

6. David Corn, "SECRET VIDEO: Romney Tells Millionaire Donors What He REALLY
Thinks of Obama Voters," *Mother Jones*, September 17, 2012, http://www.motherjones
.com/politics/2012/09/secret-video-romney-private-fundraiser.

7. Jonathan Chait, "The Real Romney Captured on Tape Turns Out to Be a Sneering
Plutocrat," *New York*, September 17, 2012, http://nymag.com/daily/intelligencer/2012/09
/real-romney-is-a-sneering-plutocrat.html.

11

NATIONAL SECURITY AND THE "NEW YELLOW PRESS"

STEVEN G. BRADBURY

Professional news organizations are critical to the health of a mature democratic republic. But the professionalism of news reporting today is under great stress in this age of the Internet. Established media outlets compete for attention against social networks, weblogs, and Wiki sites—sometimes by rushing to publish sensationalist news articles that skirt the important ethical and editorial standards developed over decades by traditional journalism.

One of the most worrisome examples of this trend is found in mainstream news coverage of classified national security programs, particularly following the unlawful leaks of U.S. government secrets by Edward Snowden and Bradley Manning. (In all other instances in this book, Chelsea is used to reflect Manning's chosen name and gender. In this case, the author has chosen to use Bradley on the basis that she was Bradley at the time of the leaks that are referred to.) Reporters and editors at reputable newspapers have been quick to print sensationalized descriptions and titillating operational details of some of America's most sensitive national security activities, even though the reporters may not have any concrete basis to assert that the activities are unauthorized or violate the law. These dramatic stories may garner significant attention for the newspaper, and in today's upside-down environment they often attract prestigious journalism awards like the Pulitzer Prize. But in choosing to publish them, editors lend the reputations of major news organizations to advance what some may view as the agendas of provocateurs like Glenn Greenwald and Julian Assange, who appear intent on using leaked information to undermine U.S. government policies.

There is much at stake in preserving high journalistic standards in press coverage of national security matters. The derogation of these standards in the sensitive area of national security will inevitably contribute to a further breakdown in the essential function of government accountability that the press can and should perform.

THE INDISPENSABLE ROLE OF JOURNALISM AND IMPORTANCE OF STRONG JOURNALISTIC ETHICS

The Framers of our Constitution understood that effective political representation rests on the informed consent of the governed and that the surest guarantee of an informed citizenry is an uncensored press. Thus the First Amendment protects the editorial integrity of journalism from governmental interference by prohibiting the federal government (and by extension state and local governments) from "abridging the freedom . . . of the press."[1] Though very few journalists in America are employed by the state, it is appropriate to think of the free press as the fourth branch of our political system. Among other things, the press serves to give public exposure to the corruption and incompetence of government officials, abuses of power, the waste of taxpayers' money, and the failures or unexpected pitfalls of government policies. Through the skepticism and insistent digging of good investigative reporting, voters, legislators, and policy makers learn valuable information that can lead them to make important course changes in the policy direction of government at a local or national level.

Of course, investigative journalists are only human. They sometimes make mistakes in their reporting and may jump to illogical or unsupported conclusions. And they may be tempted to distort or exaggerate the facts to attract more attention to their articles. Sometimes, reporters pursue their own personal agendas or the agendas of movements or groups, and they do not always disclose to their readers that the source of some key information reported in an investigative article is an interested person or group or that a point of view presented in the article serves the agenda of some interested party.

If a modern day Ida Tarbell or Lincoln Steffens writes an overheated piece of investigative journalism purporting to expose the nefarious actions of a private company or an individual, the target of the exposé may have recourse to defamation law if there are grounds to believe the article includes false and harmful factual assertions. When the libel suit is brought by a government official or another "public figure," the claim may proceed under the First Amendment doctrine announced in *New York Times v. Sullivan*, if (but only if) the plaintiff can plausibly allege the journalists acted with "actual malice"—meaning that they knew the factual assertions in the article were false or made the assertions with reckless disregard for their truth or falsity.[2]

Even beyond the protections of *New York Times v. Sullivan*, journalists have no fear of libel suits brought directly by federal agencies seeking to challenge inaccurate, misleading, or sensationalized news articles about the agencies' programs since Congress does not authorize agencies to pursue libel claims. In most cases, an agency's best defense is further public disclosure, usually through speeches or statements by the head of the agency, letters to Congress, or testimony at congressional oversight hearings. The best antidote to unfair or unfounded criticism of a government agency is the open square of public debate, where truth should prevail.

But sunlight and transparency are usually not feasible or advisable when it comes to national security programs. Making more facts public in response to news reports about secret intelligence activities will often be inconsistent with the national interest and may, in fact, put the nation at serious risk. In the not-so-distant past, when faced with a leak of sensitive information about a classified intelligence program, the government could rely with some confidence on the editorial discretion and professionalism of the traditional press. Major news organizations were inclined to put the national interest above the narrow pecuniary goal of selling more newspapers, and they often refrained from disclosing sensitive activities at all or from publishing unnecessary details that could compromise the safety of the nation or of U.S. citizens, allies, or troops.

The news business has not always adhered to high standards. Historically, there have been times when prominent news organizations competed to publish news stories with more regard for entertainment value and the bottom line than for the accuracy of their reporting, let alone for higher principles of journalistic integrity or the public interest. In the era of "yellow journalism" in the late nineteenth century, for example, the Pulitzer and Hearst papers battled for readers with hyperbolic reporting that often exaggerated and sensationalized news events and relied on anonymous or questionable sources.[3]

In the decades since the heyday of the yellow press, leading news organizations strived to rise above the practices of the past in hopes of gaining more trust from the public. Toward that end, journalists have developed a code of ethics and standards of professionalism in the reporting of news. In a series of distilled principles of conduct, the "Code of Ethics" promulgated by the Society of Professional Journalists admonishes reporters and editors to

> Take responsibility for the accuracy of their work. Verify information before releasing it. . . .
>
> Provide context. Take special care not to misrepresent or oversimplify in promoting, previewing or summarizing a story. . . .
>
> Identify sources clearly. The public is entitled to as much information as possible to judge the reliability and motivations of sources.
>
> Consider sources' motives before promising anonymity. . . . Explain why anonymity was granted. . . .
>
> Never deliberately distort facts or context. . . .
>
> Balance the public's need for information against potential harm. . . . "
>
> Pursuit of the news is not a license for arrogance. . . .
>
> Recognize that legal access to information differs from an ethical justification to publish. . . .
>
> [Remain objective and independent, free of associations and activities] "that may compromise integrity or impartiality, or . . . damage credibility.[4]

A further tenet of journalistic ethics is the understanding that news organizations will "obey the law in the pursuit of news."[5] In the context of news stories about national security matters, there are a number of federal criminal statutes imposing legal injunctions that bear directly on the decisions made by reporters and editors. They include the basic proscription in the Espionage Act against "willfully communicat[ing]" any classified document or information "relating to the national defense" with knowledge that the information "could be used to the injury of the United States or to the advantage of any foreign nation."[6] More specifically, Congress has also enacted an express criminal prohibition on "knowingly and willfully . . . publish[ing] . . . any classified information . . . concerning" the "cryptographic" systems or "communication intelligence activities" of the United States or any information "obtained by" the communications intelligence operations of the United States.[7]

The potential application of these criminal laws to journalists cannot be dismissed as beyond the bounds of the First Amendment.

In his concurring opinion in the Supreme Court's Pentagon Papers case, Justice Byron White joined in the Court's holding that the government was not entitled to a court order preventing the *New York Times* from publishing the sensitive Defense Department documents leaked by Daniel Ellsberg.[8] But in agreeing that the government could not enlist the courts to suppress publication of the Pentagon Papers, Justice White stressed that this holding did not mean that newspapers "will be immune from criminal action" once they proceed to publish sensitive classified information, since the heavy burden the First Amendment places on any effort to justify a prior restraint "does not measure [the government's] constitutional entitlement to a conviction for criminal publication."[9] In other words, even if the First Amendment prohibits the government from blocking publication of leaked national security secrets except in the most compelling cases, the First Amendment does not prohibit the government from pursuing an after-the-fact criminal prosecution of news organizations and journalists for publishing the leaked information in violation of federal law.

Justice White enumerated the various statutes that make it a federal crime to publish classified information, including information about the communications intelligence programs of the United States. He declared that news organizations "must face the consequences if they publish" material in violation of these criminal statutes, and he added that he "would have no difficulty in sustaining convictions under these sections on facts that would not justify the intervention of equity and the imposition of a prior restraint."[10]

The attorney general and federal prosecutors are always appropriately reluctant to press charges against news organizations for publishing classified information. It is politically perilous for any administration to pursue criminal penalties against the media for their editorial decisions. But even if such prosecutions are hardly ever pursued, professional journalists still have an ethical responsibility to abide by federal law and to refrain from disseminating sensitive government secrets that have been leaked without authorization and whose publication will clearly threaten significant harm to the interests of the United States.

THE BREAKDOWN OF JOURNALISTIC STANDARDS IN THE AGE OF SNOWDEN

Unfortunately, in my opinion, in the media frenzy triggered by the stream of leaked documents originating with Snowden and Manning and propagated by Greenwald and Assange, the code of journalistic standards seems to have broken down. We see a new kind of "yellow journalism" in the willingness of major news organizations to rush to press with leaked information about national security matters, to sensationalize the coverage of intelligence programs, and to publish the operational details of intelligence activities with seemingly prurient relish and with little apparent regard for the harm that could result. In short, news outlets today compete for readers and viewers with one another and with the blogosphere by racing to go live with the most sensitive national security information. And in this day of celebrity journalists, the news desk at a major newspaper is sometimes in competition its own publicity-hungry reporters, who may threaten to bypass balky editors and publish the information directly, either in book form or through the reporters' own websites or Twitter feeds, which often serve as one-person news outlets.[11]

In the wake of the Snowden leaks, leading newspapers published sweeping claims that in the view of those familiar with the classified programs at issue, significantly mischaracterized critical communications intelligence activities of the U.S. government. The programs disclosed by Snowden included what has come to be known as the "section 215" telephone metadata program and the "section 702" program of foreign intelligence surveillance targeted at the international communications of non-U.S. persons located outside the United States. The history and details of both of these important programs are now largely public because the federal government has been forced to reveal them in order to clarify and rebut the mistaken assumptions and misunderstandings created by the press coverage of the Snowden leaks.[12]

Section 215 of the USA Patriot Act allows the FBI, with approval from the federal judges assigned to hear applications under the Foreign Intelligence Surveillance Act (FISA), to obtain business records "relevant" to an ongoing counterterrorism investigation.[13] As Snowden revealed, the government obtained section 215 court orders authorizing the bulk collection of business records from telephone companies. The collection involved the "metadata" of phone calls—simple numerical tables showing which phone numbers called which numbers and the time and duration of the calls. The program did not involve geolocational data or any other subscriber information, and it did not enable the government to listen to anyone's phone calls. Furthermore, while broad in scope (in terms of the bulk nature of the metadata collected), the program was quite narrow in application: the court orders approving the collection strictly prohibited the government from conducting random searches or data mining in the database or from using the metadata collection for any purpose other than supporting the FBI's ongoing investigations of specific, identified foreign terrorist organizations, like Al Qaeda. Under the FISA court orders governing the section 215 metadata program, the government was permitted to access and use the database only when it had identified a particular phone number that the government had reasonable grounds to believe was being used by one of the specified foreign terrorist organizations under investigation; in that event, the court orders permitted the government to "query" only the metadata collection to see what other phone numbers had been in communication with the known terrorist phone number. And the only permissible purpose of this very limited "contact chaining" analysis was to identify previously unidentified phone numbers with potential connections to terrorist plots—in other words, to "connect the dots" as part of the government's continuing efforts post–September 11 to discover and thwart terrorist threats to the United States. The section 215 telephone metadata program was approved by federal judges every ninety days, with intense court oversight for more than seven years before the Snowden disclosures.[14]

Press coverage of the section 215 program has inaccurately characterized it as "a domestic surveillance program,"[15] "indiscriminate government surveillance of Americans," "mass surveillance," and "dragnet surveillance."[16]

The reality is that the metadata collection did not involve "surveillance" at all. "Surveillance" is a well-understood concept in national security law; it is expressly defined in FISA to mean acquiring "the contents" of private communications or using a "surveillance device" "for monitoring to acquire information" in which an individual has an expectation of privacy protected by the warrant requirement of the Fourth Amendment.[17] Metadata collection does not reveal the contents of any communications and does not entail the monitoring of any private information. News articles also incorrectly implied that the program involved "data mining," or random searching and sifting through the database looking for suspicious patterns, and, most sinister of all, that it could enable the government to assemble comprehensive profiles of the private behavior of ordinary Americans, including their personal associations and political inclinations.[18] The truth is that any such use of the metadata collected in the section 215 program was expressly prohibited by the court orders that governed the program, and there was never any reason to suspect that these restrictions were violated or abused.

Nevertheless, despite the narrow purpose and tight, court-overseen restrictions on the section 215 program and the lack of any intentional misuse, the program has now been shut down by Congress, largely because of perceptions created by the press coverage that the program might someday, in some speculative way, be abused.[19]

The Snowden leaks also generated breathless and misleading news coverage of the so-called PRISM collection of Internet communications, also known as the "section 702" program. This program targets the international communications of non-U.S. persons reasonably believed to be outside the United States, and it is conducted entirely under court-approved procedures expressly authorized by Congress in amendments made to FISA in 2008.[20] The surveillance authorized under section 702 may not (1) intentionally target any person, of any nationality, known to be located in the United States, (2) target a person outside the United States if the purpose is to reverse target any particular person believed to be in the United States, (3) intentionally target a U.S. person anywhere in the world, or (4) intentionally acquire any communication as to which the sender and all recipients are known to be in the United States.[21] The statute requires the attorney general to adopt, and the FISA court to approve, targeting procedures reasonably designed to ensure compliance with these limitations, as well as detailed restrictions known as "minimization procedures," designed to ensure that any information about U.S. persons captured through this surveillance will not be retained or disseminated in intelligence reports unless the information is necessary to understand the intelligence significance of the report.[22] The surveillance is focused on specific e-mail addresses or other identifiers associated with individual foreign targets.[23] The bottom line is that the section 702 program is aimed at particular foreign targets outside the United States; section 702 may not be used for any electronic surveillance targeted at a U.S. person or at any person believed to be in the United States, and under FISA, electronic surveillance designed to intercept the communications of U.S. persons anywhere in the world requires an individualized court order supported by probable cause.[24]

The news coverage of the PRISM collection painted a very different picture. One major newspaper reported that the "National Security Agency and the FBI are tapping directly into the central servers of nine leading U.S. Internet companies" and "reaching deep inside the machinery of American companies that host hundreds of millions of American-held accounts on American soil," and the article implied that section 702 included a "backdoor search loophole" that enabled the government to collect "the content of innocent Americans who were swept up in a search for someone else."[25] Such reports generated enormous business pressures on U.S. Internet companies, in part because of the inaccurate perception that all non-U.S. data content (and much of the content of American users) is subject to unlimited access by U.S. spy agencies.[26] In addition, these news articles totally ignored the protective "minimization procedures" that are required to be applied to any content of U.S. persons that may be indirectly captured through the foreign-targeted section 702 program. The requirement to apply such minimization protections is set forth expressly in the text of section 702 itself, and the general procedural requirements for minimization are well known and are fleshed out in other sections of the FISA statute.[27] In the author's view, any responsible article discussing the section 702 program should have acknowledged the narrow focus on particular foreign targets located outside the United States and the requirements for protecting and "minimizing" any information about U.S. persons or U.S. communications that might be captured by the program.

The breakdown in journalistic standards in the reporting of national security matters is not limited to inaccurate or misleading characterizations of classified programs. Today, in the author's opinion, the new norm is for major newspapers to exercise little self-restraint in needlessly trumpeting details about the most sensitive U.S. government intelligence activities, even when there is no suggestion in the news coverage that the activities disclosed exceed legal bounds. In these cases, there seems to be no apparent reason for publishing the specifics, other than attracting attention to the newspaper by catering to the kind of voyeurism that exists for national security secrets.

As an example, one article published by the *Washington Post* in August 2013 exposed "top-secret documents" describing an extensive "clandestine campaign" involving "surreptitious U.S. control" of foreign computer networks, and it detailed the "231 offensive cyber-operations" conducted by the U.S. government in 2011, as enumerated "in a classified intelligence budget provided by NSA leaker Edward Snowden."[28] An article published in the *New York Times* in September 2013 described how the National Security Agency "circumvented or cracked much of the encryption . . . that guards global" computer systems, "deployed custom-built, superfast computers to break codes, and began collaborating with technology companies in the United States and abroad to build entry points into their products." To stress the importance of the information disclosed in the article (and thus the potential harm that the revelations could do to national security interests), the *Times* went out of its way to emphasize that the NSA considered these activities "among its most closely guarded secrets, restricted to those cleared for a highly classified program," according to documents "provided by Edward J. Snowden."[29] The next week, the *Times* published a follow-up article touting one of the consequences of its own reporting: that the National Institute of Standards and Technology was reopening the public vetting process for encryption standards because of the *Times* report that the NSA had written the standard.[30]

There is no doubt that the revelation of such highly sensitive details through the publication of news stories has a serious impact on U.S. intelligence methods and capabilities.[31] The editorial decisions of major news organizations can compromise and degrade the effectiveness of national security programs and can diminish the willingness of foreign intelligence services to collaborate with the United States. In producing such effects, leading news organizations are advancing the very objectives that motivated the illegal leaks committed by Edward Snowden and Bradley Manning, as well as the mission of those supporters and abettors who organized the widespread dissemination of the leaked materials to major news outlets.

———— ❀ ————

The most profound, long-term fallout from this new brand of aggressive sensationalism in mainstream news coverage of national security matters will involve the role of the press itself. The unrestrained urge to compete with the blogs and publish every leaked secret about critical intelligence programs will inevitably lead to a further loss of faith in the mainstream press as a conscientious guardian of the public interest. And when the faith of the public is squandered, journalists will have less influence, and journalism will be a less effective check on the true excesses and abuses of government. There are countless benefits made possible by the free flow of ideas and information on the Internet, including an explosion in the number of news sources and an unbelievable diversity of voices and viewpoints. In serving the essential function of political accountability, however, this informational free-for-all cannot substitute for mature editorial discretion and professional standards of journalism.

NOTES

1.   U.S. Const. Amdmt. I.
2.   *New York Times Co. v. Sullivan*, 376 U.S. 254 (1964).
3.   Department of State, Office of the Historian, *U.S. Diplomacy and Yellow Journalism, 1895–1898*, https://history.state.gov/milestones/1866–1898/yellow-journalism; Frank Luther Mott, *American Journalism: A History of Newspapers in the United States Through 250 Years, 1690–1940* (New York: Macmillan, 1941), 539.
4.   Society of Professional Journalists, "SPJ Code of Ethics" (revised September 6, 2014), http://www.spj.org/ethicscode.asp. See also *New York Times*, "Guidelines on Integrity," (revised September 25, 2008), http://www.nytco.com/wp-content/uploads/Guidelines-on -Integrity-updated-2008.pdf, and *Ethical Journalism: A Handbook of Values and Practices for the News and Editorial Departments* (revised September 2004), http://www.nytco .com/wp-content/uploads/NYT_Ethical_Journalism_0904–1.pdf.

5. *New York Times, Ethical Journalism,* 9, paragraph 25.

6. Espionage Act of 1917, 18 U.S.C. § 793(e) (1917).

7. Ibid., § 798(a).

8. *New York Times Co. v. United States,* 403 U.S. 713, 730–31 (1971) (J. White, concurring).

9. Ibid., at 733.

10. Ibid., at 735–37.

11. Michael Calderone, "James Risen Recalls 'Game of Chicken' with *New York Times* Editors to Reveal NSA Spying," *Huffington Post,* May 14, 2014, http://www.huffingtonpost. com/2014/05/14/james-risen-new-york-times_n_5324303.html (reporting that *New York Times* reporter James Risen's plan to disclose information about the NSA's warrantless surveillance program in a book scheduled to be published in January 2006 played a role in forcing *New York Times* editors to publish an article by Risen revealing the existence of the program on December 16, 2005, after the *Times* had previously held the story for thirteen months because of national security concerns raised by the Bush administration and the intelligence community).

12. The Director of National Intelligence (DNI) has declassified and released extensive information about both programs in response to the misleading press coverage of the documents leaked by Snowden. See, for example, press releases of the Office of the DNI for 2013, http://www.odni.gov/index.php/newsroom/press-releases/191-press-releases-2013; and NSA, "The National Security Agency: Missions, Authorities, Oversight and Partnerships," August 9, 2013, https://www.nsa.gov/news-features/press-room/statements/2013 -08-09-the-nsa-story.shtml (describing the NSA's participation in the section 702 and section 215 programs). For a detailed description of the two programs based on declassified information, including the specific court-overseen requirements and limitations that govern them and the legal authorities that support them, see Steven G. Bradbury, "Understanding the NSA Programs: Bulk Acquisition of Telephone Metadata Under Section 215 and Foreign-Targeted Collection Under Section 702," *Lawfare Research Paper Series* 1, no. 3 (2013): 1–18, https://lawfare.s3-us-west-2.amazonaws.com/staging /s3fs-public/uploads/2013/08/Bradbury-Vol-1-No-3.pdf.

13. Section 215 of the Patriot Act amended section 501 of FISA, 50 U.S.C. § 1861.

14. Bradbury, "Understanding the NSA Programs." The critical need to "connect the dots" in counterterrorism investigations, including through analyses like that enabled by the telephone metadata program, was a central point emphasized by the Report of the 9/11 Commission.

15. Charlie Savage and Edward Wyatt, "U.S. Secretly Collecting Logs of Business Calls," *New York Times,* A16, June 6, 2013 ("a domestic surveillance program"); Glenn Greenwald, "NSA Collecting Records of Millions of Verizon Customers Daily," *Guardian,* June 6, 2013 ("domestic surveillance" and "domestic spying").

16. Timothy B. Lee, "Everything You Need to Know About the NSA's Phone Records Scandal," *Washington Post,* June 6, 2013. See also Jonathan Weisman, "Congress Pursues Deal on Phone Data Collection in Rare Talks During Recess," *New York Times,* May 25, 2015 (referring to the section 215 program as "the National Security Agency's dragnet of phone records").

17. FISA, 50 U.S.C. § 1801(f) (defining "Electronic surveillance").

18. Greenwald, "NSA Collecting Records" (referring to the section 215 program as a "data-mining program" and asserting that the collection "would allow the NSA to build easily a comprehensive picture of who any individual contacted, how and when, and possibly from where," in order "to discover an individual's network of associations and communication patterns"); Lee, "Everything You Need to Know" (stating that "the NSA is probably using a software technique called data mining to look for patterns that could be a sign of terrorist activity," and asserting that "having the calling records of every member of Congress would likely reveal which members kept mistresses, which could be used to blackmail members of Congress into supporting a future president's agenda" and "could also provide valuable political intelligence, such as how frequently members of Congress were talking to various interest groups").

19. USA Freedom Act of 2015, Pub. L. No. 114–23, 129 Stat. 268 (2015). "It was never the intent of Congress in passing Section 215 and Section 702 to allow a dragnet surveillance program that captures the communications of all Americans," according to Congress-woman Anna G. Eshoo, who expressed support for legislation "to ensure Section 215 of the Patriot Act will no longer be used to justify blanket surveillance programs" (http://eshoo.house.gov/legislative-priorities/foreign-affairs/intelligence/).

20. Bradbury, "Understanding the NSA Programs." Congress added section 702 to FISA in the FISA Amendments Act of 2008, Pub. L. No. 110–261, 122 Stat. 2436 (codified at 50 U.S.C. § 1881a). Similar foreign-targeted, programmatic surveillance authority was initially provided on a temporary basis in the Protect America Act of 2007, Pub. L. No. 110–55, 121 Stat. 552. Congress reauthorized and extended the authority enacted in the FISA Amendments Act in 2012.

21. FISA, 50 U.S.C. § 1881a(b).

22. Ibid., § 1881a(c)–(g).

23. NSA, "National Security Agency."

24. Bradley, "Understanding the NSA Programs." See also FISA, 50 U.S.C. § 1804 (setting forth the requirements for individualized FISA court orders authorizing electronic surveillance), and § 1802 (providing a limited exception authorizing electronic surveillance without a court order of communications wholly between or controlled by foreign governments or nations where "there is no substantial likelihood that the surveillance will acquire the contents of any communication to which a United States person is a party").

25. Barton Gellman and Laura Poitras, "U.S., British Intelligence Mining Data from Nine U.S. Internet Companies in Broad Secret Program," Washington Post, June 7, 2013.

26. According to Mark Zuckerberg, CEO of Facebook, "I want to respond personally to the outrageous press reports about PRISM: Facebook is not and has never been part of any program to give the U.S. or any other government direct access to our servers. We have never received a blanket request or court order from any government agency asking for information or metadata in bulk" (June 7, 2013, https://www.facebook.com/zuck/posts/10100828955847631). In response to company denials, Gellman and Poitras acknowledged, "It is possible that the conflict between the PRISM slides and

the company spokesmen is the result of imprecision on the part of the NSA author. In another classified report obtained by the *Post*, the arrangement is described as allowing 'collection managers [to send] content tasking instructions directly to equipment installed at company-controlled locations,' rather than directly to company servers" ("U.S., British Intelligence Mining Data"); nevertheless, they chose to begin the article with the unambiguous declaration that the U.S. government is "tapping directly into the central servers" of the Internet companies.

27. See, for example, 50 U.S.C. § 1801(h) (describing FISA "Minimization procedures"), and § 1881a(e) & (i) (requiring court-approved minimization procedures for section 702 surveillance).

28. Barton Gellman and Ellen Nakashima, "U.S. Spy Agencies Mounted 231 Offensive Cyber-operations in 2011, Documents Show," *Washington Post*, August 30, 2013.

29. Nicole Perlroth, Jeff Larson, and Scott Shane, "N.S.A. Able to Foil Basic Safeguards of Privacy on Web," *New York Times*, September 5, 2013. The *Times* published excerpts from the top-secret documents leaked by Snowden. See "Secret Documents Reveal N.S.A. Campaign Against Encryption," *New York Times*, September 5, 2013.

30. Nicole Perlroth, "Government Announces Steps to Restore Confidence on Encryption Standards," *New York Times*, September 10, 2013.

31. Such revelations also have collateral consequences for the commercial interests of American companies, which can have a significant indirect effect on U.S. national security interests. For example, following the press coverage of NSA involvement in computer systems architecture and commercial encryption standards, there was an immediate drop-off in the purchase of U.S. technology by foreign customers, particularly in China. See Spencer E. Ante, Paul Mozur, and Shira Ovide, "NSA Fallout: Tech Firms Feel a Chill Inside China," *Wall Street Journal*, November 15, 2013; and Eva Dou and Don Clark, "Struggles in China Push Cisco to Strike a Deal," *Wall Street Journal*, September 23, 2015.

12

A NEW AGE OF CYBERWARFARE

DAVID E. SANGER

I n the end, what kind of change did Edward J. Snowden bring about?

In the realm of privacy protection, not much—at least so far. For all the talk on Capitol Hill in the summer of 2013—immediately after the Snowden leaks—about a reassessment of the balance between security and privacy rights, no significant legal changes to the authorities of the National Security Agency or the Foreign Intelligence Surveillance Court have passed Congress since the Snowden leaks.

The biggest change in NSA practice ordered by President Barack Obama—his announcement in January 2014 that the government would get out of the business of amassing a vast database of metadata for all the telephone calls made into or out of the United States—finally went into effect at the end of 2015. It gets the government out of the business of retaining the call records of Americans and puts that responsibility on the telecommunications firms. They were reluctant and had to be compelled (and paid) by the government to play this role. Some intelligence officials (and a few candidates for president) have complained that the change will make it harder for the United States to track terrorist communications. But they forget that the NSA itself had considered, at various points, giving up the metadata collection because it was yielding so little.

But beyond that, years after the Snowden revelations, there has been very little government compulsion of the private sector to take on roles in surveillance. Apple and others have resisted the calls to allow "backdoors" for encrypted communications—and the Obama administration, at this writing, has been unwilling to take them on. It is another sign of how the tensions between Silicon Valley and the government, born of the Snowden revelations about the government's exploitation of data collected by American companies, has poisoned a once-vital relationship.

———— ∞ ————

Inside the NSA, Snowden's influence has been more profound—but perhaps not in the ways he imagined. Unlike the CIA, which has had many insiders clean out the family jewels, the NSA. never really imagined the damage that could be done by a single disgruntled, or ideological, officer or contractor. So Snowden had the run of the agency's computer systems. Today, systems administrators like him, with access to vast numbers of documents, can no longer download or move them alone; there is now a "two-man rule" reminiscent of the keepers of the keys for launching nuclear weapons, to protect against lone actors. New detection technology, the agency says, would make it impossible for someone to launch a "web crawler," as Snowden did, that could sweep up hundreds of thousands of documents without setting off alarms.

But all this suggests that Snowden's biggest impact on the NSA was not a reconsideration of its activities but a reconfirmation of its fear of leaks, largely to the news media. Oddly enough, the internal committee at the NSA that assessed the damage done by Snowden and recommended internal changes was titled the "Media Leaks Task Force," as if the problem here had been newspapers or broadcasters or new web publishers who spread the Snowden documents around the globe once they were in the public domain. The problem, of course, was not the media; it was a poorly supervised insider who was given far more access to sensitive material than he needed. (A more appropriate name for the committee might have been the "Insider Threat and Internal Mismanagement Task Force.) As some NSA officials acknowledge privately, there was a lack of imagination about how vulnerable the agency was to an insider who defeated the NSA's protections to exfiltrate huge amounts of data. And perhaps because the NSA had never before suffered such an embarrassing loss, it did not regularly conduct a review to weigh the intelligence value of what it was collecting against the political cost should its activities ever become known. That kind of review is held annually at the CIA, as it evaluates the cost of covert actions. Yet as one longtime intelligence official said soon after the Snowden disclosures: "The CIA is used to leaks—and usually weighs the possibility of disclosure when it acts. The NSA did not." Today, of course, it no longer has that luxury—every week, more of its documents are still dribbling out into the public realm.

Now, with the benefit of hindsight, Snowden's impact turned out to be greatest in those areas he appears to have thought little about when he was planning his disclosures. While he was hoping to awaken American citizens, the far bigger reaction came in the way allies see the United States, in the way other nations around the world have seized on the evidence of American spying for their own economic and trade benefit, and in the way he revealed the size and scope of the American offensive cyberactivities. He created an opening for countries around the world that were looking for ways to stymie American technological dominance in their markets—and suddenly found in the argument that to "buy American" is to let the NSA into local networks.

Moreover, in revealing the depths that the NSA and other intelligence agencies went to pierce the encryption and transmission systems of American firms, Snowden drove a wedge between the U.S. government and the companies, from Apple to Google to Microsoft and Silicon Valley startups, that need those markets to grow. He ended the era, which ran from the cracking of the Enigma codes in World War II to the long years of post–September 11 counterterrorism, in which corporations based in the United States felt a national obligation to help the government in its surveillance activities and in the development of new ways to counter cyberthreats. Now many of those companies are declaring that they must be international firms first, even if that means working against American interests, in an effort to preserve their business abroad.

Whether these are good developments or bad, whether they were inevitable even without Snowden's disclosures, is up for debate. But they are far less discussed in Washington than are the tensions between privacy and security or the question of what kind of oversight should exist over the NSA. Over time, however, they could well prove to be the lasting legacy of Snowden—a divide between the government and the technology firms that are the sources of America's economic power. It is an argument playing out every week now, as Silicon Valley and the likes of Apple,

Google, and Microsoft engage in an arms race. The government is racing to preserve its access to the communications systems of the digital age. And the companies are determined to stop the NSA and other intelligence agencies in their tracks.

—— ∞∞∞ ——

To start with the most obvious, the world now knows a lot more about how the NSA operates. And collecting a vast database of metadata about the calls placed or received inside the United States is the least of it.

The agency's biggest challenge in the past decade has been to stay ahead, or at least abreast, of a world of connected computers. Much of that job requires traditional espionage, updated for the digital age: Tapping into the computer communications of suspected terrorists, the Skype calls made by foreign adversaries and even many allies, the spreadsheets and photos and apps of anyone that the U.S. government needs to know about. The agency became what Scott Shane of the *New York Times* called "an electronic omnivore of staggering capabilities," not just for its ability to eavesdrop but for its ability to use its abilities to design offensive cyberweapons.

It is the development of those weapons that is probably the biggest and most secret governmental technology effort since the Manhattan Project, the effort to build the atomic bomb. No American president has ever talked about the country's cybercapabilities, other than to refer to them in the most oblique way—President Obama mentioned our "capabilities" in an interview early in 2015—and then quickly move on. But while billions of dollars are being spent on those systems each year, both at the NSA and in U.S. Cyber Command, the sister organization also run by the NSA's director, the government has squelched virtually all of the debate about how those powerful new tools should be used.

The government's fear of those revelations predated Snowden. The largest and most sophisticated cyberattack of modern times, conducted jointly by the United States and Israel, was the "Stuxnet" attack on Iran's nuclear facilities. It was part of a far larger program called "Olympic Games," the code name for an ambitious program to use a cyberweapon to accomplish a task that previously could be conducted only by bombing a nuclear facility or sending in saboteurs. Instead, working together, the

United States and Israel developed computer code that was inserted in the controllers that ran Iran's huge nuclear-enrichment complex at Natanz. Suddenly, nuclear centrifuges spun out of control and often blew up. The Iranians were mystified. At the NSA and Cybercommand, it was the proof of concept: a software "implant" could be, in the NSA's parlance, "weaponized." President Obama oversaw the program closely but also expressed fears that once it was exposed, as he knew it eventually would be, other countries would feel free to head down that road as well.

The "Stuxnet" worm exposed itself, because of a flaw in the software, in the summer of 2010. Two years later, the *New York Times* revealed the broader program, triggering a major leak investigation. Though the stories revealed extensive evidence of the central role that Washington, and the Bush and Obama administrations, had played in the program, the decision was made not to acknowledge the role of the United States. It seemed too fraught, at a moment the United States was negotiating with Iran over the future of its nuclear program and was often at odds with its Israeli allies. Then came the Snowden revelations, which described a vast infrastructure of which "Olympic Games" was just a part—a huge investment in a new kind of warfare. The Obama administration again could have chosen to acknowledge the effort, capitalizing on the revelations to deter other countries—from China to Russia to North Korea and Iran—that have attacked the United States with cyberweapons of their own. Instead, they decided to retain whatever secrecy around the programs they could salvage.

That secrecy appears based on three fears. One is that to talk in anything beyond the most banal generalities about America's offensive cyber capabilities is to risk exposure of scores, if not hundreds, of still-sensitive programs. The second is that no one in the U.S. government can agree on what kinds of limits should be put on the American development of cyberweapons, or how to use the capability to negotiate something akin to arms control. So, just as the United States avoided nuclear treaties until two decades after Hiroshima and Nagasaki, it wants more time to enjoy its nuclear technological lead. And the third fear is that the mere acknowledgment of American capabilities might seem to justify the development of similar weapons by American adversaries. The result was a huge gap between the government's words and the evidence: the Snowden revelations had revealed a Manhattan Project–size effort that had stretched over two presidencies. But no one could figure out how to talk about it.

That effort had started small: President Bush had made use of some primitive weapons during the Iraq War, using NSA capabilities to get inside the laptops or networks of individual terrorists, sometimes manipulating data to make sure that specific individuals showed up at a specific time or place for a meeting or supposed operation; there, a team of Special Forces or a drone, might be waiting for them. But by the end of his presidency, he had ordered the far more ambitious effort against Iran.

News of that effort leaked out in the last days of the Bush presidency. Obama, who at the time was just learning about America's offensive cyber capabilities, was outraged and told his defense secretary, Robert Gates, that there should be a major leak investigation, something Gates reported years later in his memoir *Duty*. Curiously, Obama was not alone in his anger at the disclosure. Edward Snowden, writing under a thinly created pseudonym in a weblog, also denounced the disclosures as a breach of national security, a view he apparently revised later.

But in retrospect, that moment was an important one: it marked the beginning of a series of decisions by the new president to keep the American cyber capability among the country's deepest held secrets. That was wishful thinking. No government can team up with allies to blow up centrifuges in Iran, get inside North Korea's systems for both espionage and potential destructive attacks, or infiltrate China's fast-expanding networks without leaving footprints. And now, we see those footprints far more clearly.

What we have learned from the Snowden disclosures is that the attack on Iran, while customized to fit the target, was part of a much larger effort, reaching back a decade, to develop a far more comprehensive way to get inside the computer networks and computer systems of both allies and adversaries. It is a program far larger than the domestic-surveillance effort that seized the initial headlines that Snowden sought. And in many respects far more technically and politically challenging. The idea was to mark every major thoroughfare and intersection of global networks with an "implant" that can act as an early-warning system for cyberattacks— the equivalent of the undersea microphones the United States placed strategically in oceans to track Soviet boomers during the Cold War. But these implants were designed to do more than just passive surveillance:

once in place, they can be used to exploit a network—changing data, for instance—or to destroy it.

Two years after the Snowden revelations, the NSA still fights efforts by news organizations to report even basic facts about this effort. Its concern about revealing sources and methods is understandable, but its opposition to publishing the basic facts gets more mystifying over time. Early in the Snowden inquiry, American officials contended that Russia and China almost certainly had full copies of his trove of data, obtaining it during his time in Hong Kong and then Moscow. Snowden denies this. But whether they have the full trove or not, they now know far more about the implant program, in part because of documents Snowden released that have nothing to do with personal privacy but that shed tremendous light on the NSA's activities.

They described, for example, the ANT program (an open-source build tool from Apache), which enabled the United States to leap into computers that are walled off from the Internet, something that many countries and companies now do routinely in an effort to secure their systems. Segregating computer systems offers a false sense of security: Iran, for example, had walled off the computers that operated its nuclear centrifuges as the ultimate defense against cyberintrusions. But the United States and Israel were able to leap the "air gap" fairly easily, using an array of new and old technologies. In fact, Snowden's documents included a catalog of products that can be used to get USB cards or electronic boards into a target's computer, making it possible to beam in code from seven miles away, using a low-frequency radio transmission.

Similar techniques pierced Huawei, the telecommunications and network-switching giant that many American officials believe is a front for the Chinese People's Liberation Army. The operation against Huawei apparently found no evidence that was true. Nonetheless, the United States placed "implants" in the Chinese systems that would enable them to get inside though servers once they were shipped to American adversaries— in Latin America, for example, or in Europe. In one of the great ironies, for years Huawei was all but banned from the U.S. market for fear it would do something similar in American networks.

We know this strange history because the Snowden documents that have leaked out bit by bit long after the initial disclosures have provided documentary evidence. No doubt readers found their eyes glazing over:

it was hard sometimes to remember what programs had previously been revealed, what programs were incremental improvements over others, and what represented truly new capabilities. Everyone knew, for example, that the NSA was looking for ways to get into foreign telephone systems—but it was still a surprise that the NSA attacked the European firm that makes SIM cards for smartphones, hoping to place an implant directly into the circuitry. Everyone knew that the NSA was worried about the encryption on the iPhone, but it was still surprising to discover its willingness to implant secret "backdoors" into the products of American companies, without telling the firms.

Journalistically, the steady drip of new Snowden documents, combined with reporting that the old trove of documents has launched, creates a running debate between the government and a few news organizations that plays out every month. Government officials ask, "What is the public good in revealing a program like this?" After all, they argue, the NSA is a foreign intelligence service—breaking into foreign cell phones, or companies like Huawei, or disrupting the Iranian nuclear program to buy more time for negotiations is what Congress organized the agency to do six decades ago. So why publish?

The answer is not always simple, and sometimes operational details are removed from the reportage. But the case for publication boils down to this: in the digital age, Americans are the most vulnerable society on earth to hacking. We are targets, from our Home Depot credit cards to our bank accounts at JPMorgan Chase to the health information stored in Anthem's computer systems, which contains private medical data for Blue Cross/Blue Shield claims. When the NSA routinely breaks into computer systems around the world, for either espionage or destructive activity, it creates pathways that other powers can follow. As one executive who challenged Admiral Michael Rogers, the head of the NSA, at a forum in Washington in early 2015, said, every NSA effort to weaken encrypted systems is like "drilling a hole in your windshield." It is not only the NSA that will fly in. The People's Liberation Army hacking operation, Unit 61398, will be right behind it, along with the Iranian cybercorps.

Moreover, the most extreme of the American actions—the cyberattacks on foreign computer systems—raise questions about what kinds of rules the United States wants to negotiate with other nations around the world to create some sense of arms control in the cyberworld. To use the example most cited by American officials, President Obama frequently talks about creating some cyber "norms" so that countries do not steal one another's intellectual property. But we are not going to get to set those norms alone, even on American terms. China views American efforts to break into Huawei with the same alarm that the United States views the theft of plans for the F-35 Joint Strike Fighter. Yet in the American telling of events, targeting Huawei is a legitimate national security operation, yet targeting the jet's blueprints is illegal corporate theft. The rest of the world doesn't see it that way.

All these issues need to be aired, just as the issues of nuclear deterrence were debated in public throughout the Cold War. While the analogy is imperfect, it is also instructive. Like cyberweapons, nuclear weapons are highly classified, yet we understood their terrible destructive capability and managed to have a public, unclassified debate about how and when to use them. We can do the same with cyber, even though its effects are quite different and often far harder to discern. (At the same time, we have to acknowledge that nuclear weapons are in the hands of very few players, making the conversation about controlling them far easier; cyberweapons are in the hands of states, terror groups, criminal organizations, and teenagers. And most of *those* groups don't sign treaties.)

It may turn out that the Snowden disclosures, like the revelation of the attacks on Iran that preceded Snowden, were a catalyst for that debate—forcing the U.S. government to acknowledge its capabilities. That is the first step in discussing how to control those weapons. If so, the Snowden affair will have contributed significantly to a critical American discourse—though intelligence officials argue that there must be a better way to do that than the wholesale release of America's secrets.

There was a second surprising effect of the Snowden revelations: it triggered a war between Silicon Valley and Washington that will not end for years, if not decades.

From the end of World War II to recent times, many American technology firms had an unspoken deal with the government. With Washington as one of their biggest purchasers, they would become partners in many classified programs and often help out with surveillance: IBM's giant federal systems division built mainframes for the federal government and put the computers aboard the space shuttle; AT&T wired the country but also the government's classified systems, and when help was needed with call records or other surveillance, it often quietly provided the information—sometimes without benefit of a court order. The firms viewed themselves as Americans first and global enterprises second.

Today that is the exception, not the rule. Robert Litt, the general counsel for the Director of National Intelligence, acknowledged as much in early 2015 in an appearance at the Brookings Institution: "One of the many ways in which Snowden's leaks have damaged our national security is by driving a wedge between the government and providers and technology companies, so that some companies that formerly recognized that protecting our nation was a valuable and important public service now feel compelled to stand in opposition." Those providers feel compelled to be in opposition because buyers around the world learned the extent to which American products had been pierced by American intelligence agencies—and seized on that news to justify shunning American products. Many countries passed "data localization" laws to require firms to put servers in their own territories, rather than in the United States. (Why these countries think that practice will slow the NSA's ability to burrow into their networks is mystifying.) India, Nigeria, China, and Russia have all insisted that American firms place the servers on *their* soil, presumably to ensure sovereignty over the data stored there. China has issued new regulations to require firms to turn over source code for their products—essentially giving the Chinese their most valuable intellectual property.

All these regulations are costly to American companies, and some, especially those imposed by China, would have likely been imposed even if the Snowden revelations never happened. But the cost is being borne by companies and ultimately their consumers; at no point did the NSA consider the potential economic impact on America's technology sector if its programs ever be revealed. In other words, it was unconsciously counting on the companies to take the downside economic risk for the NSA's intelligence programs.

The companies are fighting back in ways that today have the intelligence agencies deeply worried. Tim Cook, the chief executive of Apple, has made it clear that he will spend whatever it takes to demonstrate to the world that the company's products cannot be pierced by the NSA.

So far the most vivid example has been the introduction of a new operating system for the iPhone in which users, not Apple, hold the encryption keys. Even if served with a court order to turn over data from an iPhone—contact lists or pictures or e-mail—Apple has no way to decipher the contents; it hands over gibberish. The director of the FBI, James Comey, protested this change, as did the heads of the intelligence agencies. Litt appealed to corporations to embrace "a solution that does not compromise the integrity of encryption technology but that enables both encryption to protect privacy and decryption under lawful authority to protect national security." Technology executives insist that compromise might sound nice, but it is impossible; to create a backdoor for the NSA is to create a hole through which others will find a way to squeeze through.

In the end, Snowden's legacy will be mixed. He wanted to be known for the changes he would bring about in altering the government's monitoring of American citizens. That seems unlikely. But he opened the world's eyes to a new world of surveillance and cyberwarfare. There, what he revealed cannot be stuffed back into a black box—and will change the way we view American power over the next decade.

13

THE SNOWDEN EFFECT ON
THE NSA AND REPORTING

SIOBHAN GORMAN

George W. Bush was coming to visit the National Security Agency's Fort Meade headquarters. It was 2008, and the staff members preparing for the visit gathered around a table and introduced themselves to the director, General Keith Alexander, who was then three years into his job.

"I'm from NSA public affairs," one aide said, according to a person familiar with the meeting.

"NSA public affairs? We have a press shop?" General Alexander responded.

When asked about the exchange in an interview, Alexander said he was joking. But some officials around the table didn't take it as a joke. "I don't think he was joking," said the person familiar with the meeting.

Current and former intelligence officials say that the NSA's arm's-length approach to the press has stemmed largely from its insular culture reinforced by decades of secrecy and few requirements to explain or justify their spy activities to the public. When the 9/11 Commission studied the NSA's intelligence failures, its NSA findings remained—and still remain—classified, while the rest of the findings were immediately made public.

Edward Snowden, the former NSA contractor, upended reporting on NSA operations like nothing I have witnessed in more than a decade of covering spy agencies. The key difference was that Snowden provided documents to reporters who then made them available to the public. Official documents cannot be ignored or challenged the way anonymous sources can. And the NSA then became the focus of global media investigations. In some cases, news reports exposed activities beyond what Snowden disclosed.

Shaken, the NSA slowly began parceling out additional information on some of the key programs at the center of the Snowden leaks. Even then, much of the press relations were handled by the Office of the Director of National Intelligence (ODNI), rather than the NSA. Some of the NSA's largest privacy violations were disclosed by the government, which in response to Freedom of Information Act (FOIA) requests declassified reams of Top Secret rulings from the secret Foreign Intelligence Surveillance Court (FISC).

As the initial impact of the Snowden leaks fade, the NSA could press ahead with the mantra of "transparency" now voiced by top U.S. intelligence officials, including its director, Admiral Michael Rogers. The agency could also decide to revert to its pre-Snowden posture and engage less with the press.

The approach adopted by the NSA at the height of the Snowden leaks is likely to prove the exception and not the rule. "That's the tendency inside NSA culture, so there's a real risk of that happening," a former intelligence official said of the likelihood that the NSA will withdraw from the public eye when the immediate public pressure eases.

A key test will be whether the NSA provides information on surveillance programs that haven't already been disclosed in documents leaked to the media. So far, it hasn't.

Earlier reporting on NSA operations relied largely on shoe-leather information gathering. Those reports, particularly the *New York Times* reports on warrantless surveillance, revealed new details of NSA operations. But Snowden's decision to provide documents—and so many of them—made it impossible for the government to refuse to comment on the disclosures or play down their significance.

The Snowden documents, for example, showed an undeniable breadth of the NSA's surveillance. The U.S. government had previously refused to acknowledge such a wide scope of intelligence collection in the wake of earlier reports by the *New York Times*, *USA Today*, the *Baltimore Sun*, and the *Wall Street Journal*.

The agency maintains that its collection is focused on communications of specific foreign intelligence targets, but officials have acknowledged having broader, indirect access to data both inside and outside the United States.

The Snowden leaks occurred against a backdrop of a renewed government push to prosecute media leaks. The administration had been heavily criticized for the seizure of phone records of Associated Press reporters. The Snowden leaks showed, however, that the prosecution of leakers had not deterred all government employees from revealing government secrets.

The Snowden disclosures affected other reporting efforts, as well. No doubt some sources were scared off from seeking out reporters to reveal what they saw as government misdeeds, but there were a number of sources who spoke with reporters about additional NSA-related concerns.

THE NSA'S APPROACH TO THE PRESS

Reporting on any U.S. spy agency is different from covering other agencies. A spy-agency press office, for example, will almost never be a source for a story. But on a good day, a reporter can persuade a spy-agency press officer to provide off-record guidance about the accuracy of information the reporter has learned from other sources. On an even better day, a reporter can tease out an unattributed comment or two that flesh out a story. The NSA didn't engage in providing that type of guidance.

General Alexander said the NSA's focus on secrecy is rooted in its World War II history, when keeping the secret that it had broken the German communications codes was critical to winning the war. "Anybody who starts out at NSA knows that if we are to be successful, the adversary can't know what we're doing in this area," he said. "That's almost the opposite of where the press is."

American spy-agency press offices tend to mirror the culture of that agency. The NSA is largely composed of engineers and mathematicians, and has developed an insular culture focused on the collection of huge volumes of data from its systems.

There's a joke that circulates regularly in among U.S. intelligence officers: How do you tell an introvert from an extrovert at the NSA? The extrovert is the one staring at the other guy's shoes; the introvert is staring at his own shoes.

Perhaps contrary to the recent public depiction of the NSA, the agency is also largely populated by employees who follow rules and laws religiously. They don't usually color outside the lines, including when the message from the top is to not engage with the press. That ethos is, in part, why the Snowden leaks caught NSA officials so off-guard. NSA leaders, including General Alexander, repeatedly said they felt betrayed by one of their own.

The NSA's press office has a reputation for not engaging much with colleagues at other agencies, either. Officers in other spy agencies complained that the NSA's press officers wouldn't share information with them. "They share as little as possible, and it's highly formal," one former intelligence official recalled. "They don't reach out to build relationships."

At the NSA, an assignment to the press office was not a prized posting, as evidenced by the churn among chief spokespeople at the agency, a position that has turned over frequently throughout the past decade.

General Alexander praised the NSA press office's work. "I think the press office had a tough time," he said, noting that the NSA debated at length whether to speak publicly about capabilities in war zones like Iraq and Afghanistan: "By and large ours was a 'no comment, stay quiet'" response.

By comparison, the press officers at the Central Intelligence Agency, whose culture is geared toward understanding and influencing world events, tend to develop relationships with reporters. The CIA places officers in its press operation who have expertise in areas like counterterrorism or the Middle East.

The CIA press office's efforts to build relationships with the press have been uneven, and at times that office has resorted to demanding that most queries be handled by e-mail. During that time frame around 2012, I had the privilege of having six months of my correspondence with the CIA requested under the FOIA. The CIA obliged and released 250 pages of e-mail. It then blacked out the vast majority of the CIA side of the exchanges, effectively removing much of the context of the e-mails— leaving the reader wondering why I spent months making inquiries about the dilapidated CIA gym.

But over the past decade, CIA press officers have more often than not sought to develop relationships with the reporters who cover the agency regularly. Those relationships don't change the news that is reported, but they increase the likelihood that the CIA's perspective will be reflected in the stories.

Knowing the coverage of the 2014 Senate report detailing misman-agement and torture of detainees in the CIA's interrogation program was going to cast the agency in a very ugly light, CIA director John Bren-nan scheduled a rare press conference at agency headquarters. That move ensured that his comments would, at least for a day, be at the center of the coverage of that program. Somewhat unexpectedly, the introspective tone and vague stance he took on the effectiveness of "enhanced interrogation techniques" was well received by the author of the highly critical report, Senator Dianne Feinstein.

Officials who have worked at the NSA and other spy agencies say the sensitivity of NSA operations makes it uniquely difficult for the agency to speak publicly about what it does.

Matthew Olsen moved from his post as general counsel at the NSA to become head of the National Counterterrorism Center (NCTC), which analyzes terrorist-threat information. At the NCTC, he said, he had "con-tinuing relationships and conversations with members of the press to talk about the threat," which "compared really drastically with when I was at NSA, where there is not an unclassified aspect to the mission." He added that "it was pretty striking to see how cautious and careful NSA was about the mission. Everything they did was dependent on protecting the secrecy of what they did."

The NSA's distancing itself from the press is also unusual for a military organization. The NSA is a hybrid military–civilian organization, led by a military officer but usually with a civilian deputy and a civilian press office. But at the Pentagon, public affairs is a high priority for a military aware that warfare requires public support. Press officers who know how to build relationships with reporters are promoted. While far from per-fect, military public-affairs offices have a reservoir of experienced officers who know how to handle classified information but are committed to a general goal of public disclosure.

At the NSA, not all officials agreed with the agency's distant treatment of the press. Some resorted to a variation of spycraft—cutouts—to convey messages reporters by using intermediaries outside the NSA to relay the information.

Some NSA officials did the same inside the U.S. government. One U.S. official recalled top NSA leaders waiting until General Alexander was out of town to seek guidance on how the NSA should handle a press story. But those officials would consult with press officers at other agencies, not the NSA's press shop; the concern, the official said, was that the NSA's press shop would report back to General Alexander.

REPORTING ON THE NSA BEFORE SNOWDEN

I first began covering the NSA in 2005, when I took a job reporting on U.S. spy agencies for the *Baltimore Sun*. The paper had a unique and intense interest in the agency, because the NSA is in the *Sun's* readership area. The press officers in the agency made initial efforts at outreach to the new reporter at their hometown paper, inviting me to meet and have a tour of the NSA's National Cryptologic Museum.

The museum itself was an immediate indicator that the NSA had not invested heavily in public outreach. While the NSA did have a museum open to the public, it was housed in a rundown space that was formerly a motel. Despite the NSA's high-tech bent, my tour focused largely on Cold War history.

My joining the *Sun* coincided with the arrival of a new NSA director, Army General Keith B. Alexander. Repeated requests to both U.S. Army and NSA press officers finally yielded one of three back-to-back interviews they were arranging with the press on a single day.

My on-the-record interview with General Alexander in his office at the NSA's Fort Meade headquarters was straightforward and focused on his plans for the agency. It produced a medium-length story inside the paper. After the interview, however, I was told by the NSA's spokesman that General Alexander wouldn't be engaging with the press again anytime soon.

I was mystified, because my interview had been so innocuous, and the stories that appeared in the other two outlets—National Public Radio and the *New York Times*—were similar.

At that time, the *New York Times* was also working on what would be the most explosive story on NSA activities in decades. The *Times*'s December 16, 2005, report revealing that NSA was intercepting phone calls of Americans without a warrant provided the first window into a previously unknown post–September 11 NSA surveillance program in the United States. The explosive nature of the story forced government officials to acknowledge a key piece of the NSA's surveillance efforts, but officials made clear they were confirming only part of the NSA's activities and refused to acknowledge other related programs.

I began reporting my first investigative NSA article shortly after my interview with General Alexander. It was a lengthy effort to find people who knew about a long-failing NSA program known as Trailblazer.

By the time the story ran in January 2006, I'd pieced together details from twenty-five sources. Because so much of what the NSA does is classified, the only document I was able to unearth was an internal report from 2003, which I obtained under the FOIA just days before the story went to print. I had to drive to the NSA's headquarters to pick it up at the Cryptologic Museum to get it in time.

The NSA's spokesman declined to comment for that story.

As I began to write more articles focused on NSA spy programs that were grossly mismanaged, over budget, and not producing results, the agency engaged only minimally. For example, NSA press officers would accept press inquiries only via e-mail, and I was instructed to copy the entire NSA press office on any request. This is an unusually depersonalized way to manage a relationship with a reporter.

The NSA did respond internally to some of those stories after they ran, when General Alexander wrote all-agency e-mails, known as "DIRGRAMS" in agency parlance, that criticized a story and reminded employees that they were not to communicate with the press.

A pattern emerged in which I would collect the details for an investigative story and then e-mail the NSA a few days before the story was expected to run. A few days later, I would receive a "no comment" response. Even an attempt to report on an uncontroversial topic—an NSA employee killed in the line of duty who was being honored on Memorial Day—got no traction.

But the NSA did ramp up its internal response by launching a wide-ranging leak investigation as the media disclosures mounted. It eventually lead to the prosecution under the 1917 Espionage Act of an NSA employee, Thomas Drake. If found guilty, he faced a potential thirty-five years in jail.

Since the resolution of his legal case in 2012, in which he ultimately pleaded guilty to a misdemeanor, Drake has said he was fired for providing unclassified information on NSA mismanagement and surveillance to the *Baltimore Sun*. He has gone on to become a proponent of Snowden and other whistleblowers.

Shortly after I moved to the *Wall Street Journal* in late 2007, I pursued a story about the NSA's wide-ranging collection of data on U.S. Internet communications. The government wouldn't acknowledge that program before or after the article published, and the story got little notice. I lacked documents that would force an acknowledgment.

Among the documents disclosed by Snowden was extensive discussion of the NSA's program to collect so-called Internet metadata, like the sender and the recipient of an e-mail and the time when that e-mail was sent.

REPORTING ON THE NSA AFTER SNOWDEN

June 5, 2013, transformed intelligence reporting. That night, I was preparing dinner when my editor forwarded me an article from the *Guardian* with the headline NSA COLLECTING PHONE RECORDS OF MILLIONS OF VERIZON CUSTOMERS DAILY.

Hoping to get on with my evening, I responded that the report didn't strike me as new and noted that *USA Today* had reported in 2006 that the NSA was collecting tens of millions of Americans' call records, including from Verizon. But when I read the story, I discovered why this report was different. It directly cited—and published—a top-secret court order from the U.S. national security court known as the Foreign Intelligence Surveillance Court.

That story—and the many, many that followed—was fundamentally different from earlier reporting on the NSA's surveillance activities because it included primary source material. As the reports based on the Snowden documents mounted, they filled in many of the gaps in the understanding of the NSA's surveillance programs inside the United States and highlighted some new ones.

Reporting over the years had revealed components of the NSA's post–September 11 surveillance program—which was called Stellar Wind, as the Snowden documents confirmed—and the Snowden documents knitted together earlier reports of warrantless surveillance, phone-record collection, and Internet-data collection. They also added new revelations, particularly about U.S. companies providing large amounts of data to the NSA under very broad court orders.

The public release of troves of classified documents forced the NSA and other intelligence agencies to respond to press inquiries far more concretely than earlier reporting that relied on information provided by sources word of mouth. Documents presented the NSA with a new dilemma: it could not comment and let the documents speak for themselves, or it could try to explain the programs.

The NSA spokeswoman Vanee Vines, who joined the NSA's press office in 2010, said that NSA had made a continuing effort to engage with the media since she arrived, adding that the Snowden disclosures prompted more press outreach. "Being proactive is the new normal," she said.

For the first several months after the Snowden revelations, the ODNI handled most press announcements. Inside the NSA, officials appeared to be focused more on leaks than on the debate over the programs that had been revealed. The agency established a task force to address the Snowden disclosures, which in a nod to greater engagement with the press, had its own designated spokeswoman. General Alexander called the group "the Media Leaks Task Force," which showed how he viewed the problem the NSA was addressing. He also called legislation to reform NSA surveillance "media leaks" legislation.

General Alexander said some of the press reports about NSA programs omitted the fact that they were overseen by Congress, the executive branch, and the courts.

The degree to which those branches of government fully understood the programs they were approving is still unclear. Meanwhile, the DNI and the NSA also began reevaluating whether they could or should continue to withhold information about the programs in the Snowden documents, especially when a number of FOIA requests were pending.

General Alexander said he discussed the issue with his deputy, and they concluded that they should continue to be very cautious with public statements because they feared risking operations and lives. "It was our joint agreement that if we were to go out starting to defend NSA, and we revealed something that started to cost lives, we were just as guilty as everyone else," he said. "We would rather be vilified than do something that would hurt any lives."

Starting in August 2013, the ODNI began to respond to those FOIA requests by releasing redacted versions of documents about the NSA programs that Snowden had disclosed.

Those documents revealed the NSA's repeated violations of court orders and were significant because they showed continued misman-agement of highly invasive surveillance programs. They showed that the program that taps the U.S. Internet backbone was collecting tens of thousands of wholly domestic communications in clear violation of the court order. They also revealed that the NSA's program to collect Americans' phone records violated the privacy protections in the court's order for three years, and the NSA didn't in fact understand how its own program worked.

The reporting on the Snowden documents also shifted the balance that media outlets contend with when reporting on sensitive security matters: how and when to report on classified programs in the face of govern-ment arguments that the programs are legal and revealing them will harm national security.

The Snowden revelations and ensuing debate over the wisdom of pol-icies, and the laws used to justify them, led media outlets to weigh the potential for prompting public debate much more heavily in the face of arguments from the government that their programs were legal and needed to remain secret to protect U.S. national security. Media outlets began publishing stories far more frequently than before on intelligence sources and methods, such as efforts to circumvent or break encryption.

The impact of the Snowden documents was also amplified because they were published by media outlets internationally. Beyond the *Guard-ian*, documents were provided to other foreign news outlets in countries like Germany and Brazil.

Those reports served as a reminder to the U.S. press, the U.S. govern-ment, and the American public that U.S. spy activities look more menacing through the lens of the country being spied upon. Revelations about spying on foreign leaders, including German chancellor Angela Merkel, riled the U.S.–German relationship at a critical time for foreign policy making on a range of issues like Syria and Ukraine.

The ferocity of the foreign reaction showed a tone deafness on the part of U.S. officials, whose initial response was to say that all countries spy on one another. Yet the Obama administration reevaluated U.S. surveillance of foreign leaders and cancelled many of those efforts. Intelligence leaders began speaking publicly about the need to factor diplomatic considerations into surveillance programs.

Snowden also inspired other sources to make public their concerns about NSA activities. While there are surely sources who said less or didn't engage with reporters for fear that the government was enhancing its hunt for leakers, there were also a number of sources who felt emboldened to raise other issues related to NSA spying that they were concerned about. That reporting led to a set of additional revelations outside the Snowden documents.

For example, the *Wall Street Journal* reported on the NSA's programs to tap the United States' telecommunications backbone—an effort that gave the government indirect surveillance coverage of roughly 75 percent of the American telecommunications infrastructure. It also reported about electrical problems that were delaying the completion of the NSA's much-vaunted and -criticized data center in Utah. The *New York Times* reported on an NSA pilot program that collected American cell-phone location data.

The declassification of top-secret NSA documents by the government has since become so voluminous as to become commonplace. Reporters came to dread the document dumps because they frequently came late on a Friday and required considerable time to wade through for information that incrementally added details to information disclosed in the thousands of documents already released.

As the Snowden documents continued to generate news reports throughout 2013, the NSA did begin to engage quietly with the press to provide some background information for certain stories and on-the-record interviews for others. NSA officials also began to provide more detailed information to the public when they believed stories were being reported incorrectly by some news outlets.

The NSA also got a new director in March 2014, after General Alexander served an unusually long nine-year tenure. His successor, Admiral Michael Rogers, had good relations with the press in his prior post as the U.S. Navy's cybersecurity chief.

He arrived at the NSA and sought to take on a more public profile and spoke of the need for transparency. "I am a firm believer that public dialogue and transparency is an important part of securing our mission today and in the future," he said in August 2014 in remarks at a dinner broadcast on C-SPAN.

Admiral Rogers has begun some limited, restricted engagement with the press and a fairly robust—for an NSA director—public-speaking schedule. But it remains to be seen whether he will change the culture of the agency, or the culture of the agency will change him.

Realizing that it has a branding problem, the NSA has sought to beef up its public-affairs office. It announced a search for a top public-affairs officer, promising a salary of up to $175,000. In early 2015, the NSA filled the job with a former CNN correspondent and New York Federal Reserve spokesman, Jonathan Freed. He reports directly to Admiral Rogers.

The Snowden disclosures have forced usually insular spy agencies to engage more with the press and the public, but the commitment to transparency has so far been limited to those programs that Snowden disclosed. The test of that stated commitment to greater openness in discussing U.S. spy programs will be the next set of major spy-program disclosures post–Edward Snowden—particularly if they don't involve the publishing of documents that force a government response.

14

EDWARD SNOWDEN, HIS PASSPORT, AND THE LEGAL IDENTITY OF AMERICANS

PATRICK WEIL

O n June 22, 2013, Edward J. Snowden, a Hawaii-based computer specialist and contractor for the National Security Agency (NSA), had his passport revoked by the U.S. State Department.[1] Snowden had secretly downloaded classified documents detailing NSA surveillance operations. By May 20, 2013, Snowden had left Hawaii for Hong Kong, where he started releasing the top-secret material in his possession to the press.[2] On June 14, the U.S. Justice Department filed criminal charges against him in federal district court.[3] The following day, the Justice Department formally requested that Hong Kong authorities issue a provisional arrest warrant for Snowden.[4] Eight days later, on the very morning that his passport was revoked, Snowden was able to board a flight to Moscow. He remained in Moscow Sheremetyevo Airport's transit zone until August 1, 2013, when Russian authorities granted him a one-year temporary asylum, which was renewed for three years last August.[5] Snowden found himself living a paradox. He remains an American citizen, but the only identity document affirming and certifying his American citizenship is Russian.[6]

Having worked on comparative history of immigration and citizenship, I became interested in Snowden's situation. Like many others, Snowden provided significant amounts of secret information to the general public. However, unlike those before him, Snowden revealed to us that we have entered a new era, an era of systemic surveillance, that puts at risk some of our fundamental liberties, and this is what enhanced my interest. I wrote an article showing that the constitutional asylum inscribed in the preamble of the French Constitution was available to Snowden.[7] The question should the State Department have behaved as it did when it revoked Snowden's passport remains unanswered.[8]

At the cost of being transformed into a de facto stateless person, Edward Snowden demonstrated that new technologies infringe upon civil liberties. However, new technologies also offer a novel avenue to protect the essential right of Americans to maintain a legal identity. An understanding of the history of denaturalization and denationalization and technological developments reveals that Snowden's situation presents an ideal opportunity for United States courts to recognize the link between U.S. citizenship and the right to carry proof of one's legal identity, through their passport, when abroad.[9]

THE TWO PURPOSES OF A PASSPORT

It is Saturday evening: a wonderful week of rest, culture, and food in Italy is ending. You are ready to fly back to work in the United States. As your hand reaches into your pocket for your hotel key, you have a premonition that is quickly confirmed: your wallet and passport are lost.

There is no way you will replace your passport over the weekend—you will have to delay your return home. But this is only the beginning of your troubles. Returning to the reception desk, you tell the clerk that your wallet was stolen. You need a new room key. The clerk answers, "Do you have an ID? No ID—no key." What began as an annoyance has become a nightmare.

Your passport's loss highlights the two functions it plays when you are abroad. First, it permits travel across international borders. Second, it attests to your legal identity—including your first and last name, place of birth, and citizenship.[10]

The Supreme Court has consistently recognized these two functions of the American passport. As early as the Supreme Court case *Urtetiqui v. D'Arcy* (1935),[11] the Court clearly distinguished and recognized these two functions of the passport. The Court in *Urtetiqui* stated:

[1] [A passport] is a document, which, from its nature and object, is addressed to foreign powers; purporting only to be a request, that the bearer of it may pass safely and freely; and [2] is to be considered rather in the character of a political document, by which the bearer is recognised, in foreign countries, as an American citizen; and which, by usage and the law of nations, is received as evidence of the fact.[12]

In *Haig v. Agee* (1981), addressing the revocation of former CIA agent Philip Agee's passport, the Court reaffirmed the dual role of passports by quoting the entirety of this paragraph.[13] The executive branch itself noted the dual function of a passport. Responding to a question raised by Justice Rehnquist during the oral argument, U.S. Solicitor General Wade McCree asserted that a passport "serves two purposes. First, the purpose of identifying the bearer as a citizen or a national of the issuing nation; and second, to request free passage for him from a foreign nation as well as the efforts of the foreign nation to facilitate his travel."[14] Yet, in reasoning that the freedom to travel abroad was subordinate to national security and foreign policy considerations[15] and therefore the secretary of state could revoke a passport when the holder's activities in foreign countries were causing serious damage to national security,[16] the Court dealt with only one dimension of the American passport: the one that guarantees American citizens the freedom to travel.

LEGAL RIGHTS AND OPPORTUNITIES

Following the Court, if it is constitutional to restrict freedom of travel across borders for security reasons (first function), it does not follow that a U.S. citizen could be deprived of her right to legal identity as a citizen (second function). Pleading against the revocation of his passport, Agee did not invoke this right, and Chief Justice Burger—who included answers to Agee's constitutional claims only in the final stages of writing the majority opinion[17]—did not raise the issue *sua sponte*.[18] However, if asked today by Edward Snowden, the Court would have to confirm that it is his absolute right not to be deprived of his legal identity as an American citizen.

THE FOURTEENTH AMENDMENT
AND A RIGHT TO IDENTIFICATION

The right to be provided identity papers when abroad is expressed by the fact that when a human being does not possess a nationality or the protection of a state that can provide identity papers, the international community has agreed to enter into an absolute obligation to provide them. The 1951 Geneva convention Relating to the Status of Refugees provides in Article 27 that "the Contracting States shall issue identity papers to any refugee in their territory who does not possess a valid travel document."[19] Under the convention, all signatory states have to provide refugees travel documents that are also identity documents. There is an exception to the required travel provision—security reasons. There is no exception to the obligation to provide identity documents. This means that the United States, which has signed the Protocol Relating to the Status of Refugees,[20] is obliged to deliver identity documents to foreign refugees who are in its jurisdiction and lack them.[21] This is an absolute obligation.[22] Should not this obligation fulfilled toward noncitizens be considered *a fortiori* imposed on the signatory states—including the United States—for their own citizens?

In fact, this right to legal identity as an American citizen can be deduced from the Fourteenth Amendment. Adopted in 1868, the Fourteenth Amendment states first that all persons born or naturalized in the United States are citizens of the United States. It then continues: "No state shall make or enforce any law which shall abridge the privileges or immunities of citizens of the United States."[23] The Supreme Court in *Afroyim v. Rusk* (1967) interpreted the first sentence of the Fourteenth Amendment as providing an absolute protection to citizenship.[24] Under *Afroyim*, a citizen of the United States is protected absolutely against any deprivation of her citizenship, independently of any crime or illegal act committed. In the *Slaughter-House Cases* (1872),[25] the Court interpreted the privileges and immunities clause narrowly. Nevertheless, Justice Miller, writing for the majority, stated a "privilege of a citizen of the United States is to demand the care and protection of the Federal government over his life, liberty, and property when on the high seas or within the jurisdiction of a foreign government. Of this there can be no doubt, nor that the right depends upon his character as a citizen of the United States."[26]

Thus under the *Slaughter-House Cases*, one of the privileges of being a citizen of the United States "is to demand the care and protection of the Federal government . . . when on the high seas or within the jurisdiction of a foreign government."[27]

At the time of the *Slaughter-Houses Cases* and in the following decades, the question of the protection of the citizen living abroad had been addressed in a very classical way. Edwin Borchard—drawing on the eighteenth-century legal thinker Emmerich de Vattel's *The Law of Nations*—believed that states had the right, but not the obligation, to protect the interests of their citizens while abroad. This right seemed to be derived from the nature of national sovereignty; because the interests of a citizen were also the interests of the state, the state had the right to vindicate those interests abroad whenever it thought doing so was necessary.[28] Yet *Afroyim* reversed this classical conception of sovereignty. In his majority opinion, Justice Black—after conceding that all nations possess an implied attribute of sovereignty—stated that in the United States, "the people are sovereign and the Government cannot sever its relationship to the people by taking away their citizenship."[29]

The Supreme Court has not yet ruled on a case that allowed the justices to bring the privileges and immunities of the U.S. citizen up-to-date with this new understanding of citizenship. It is on the basis of the sovereignty of the citizen—a sovereignty limited to the status of citizenship itself and to certain privileges and immunities stemming from it—that American citizenship has become absolutely secured.[30] It is now time, and Snowden's situation presents an opportunity, for the Court to read the Privileges or Immunities Clause and the *Slaughter-House* jurisprudence in the spirit of *Afroyim* and declare as an absolute right the possession by all Americans abroad of a document attesting to their legal identity.

DEVELOPMENTS IN TECHNOLOGY SUPPORT THE PROTECTION OF THE LEGAL IDENTITY OF AMERICANS

In 1835, when the Supreme Court in *Urtetiqui* clearly recognized the two functions of a passport, the State Department could claim that it was difficult to separate a passport's function as a document allowing for freedom to travel and a document that fulfills the right to an identity. In 1981, at the time of *Haig v. Agee*, it was also difficult to revoke the freedom to travel without seizing the passport. This is no longer the case. The technology of the passport has significantly progressed and now permits one to distinguish easily between the freedom to travel and the right to bear a legal identity.

The biometric passport emerged as a global standard following the implementation of stricter border-security measures after the September 11 attacks.[31] More and more states have developed versions of this technology. The passport is equipped with a Radio Frequency Identification (RFID) chip that contains the biometric information of the passport holder. Biometric data are physiological and behavioral characteristics of the individual—including fingerprints, voice, and typing patterns—that serve to identify her within a certain population.[32]

Even when not issuing biometric passports, all member states of the International Civil Aviation Organization (ICAO), a United Nations specialized agency, have achieved their goal of "global interoperability," understood as the capability of inspection systems (whether manual or automated) in different states throughout the world to exchange data, to process data received from systems in other states, and to utilize that data in inspection operations in their respective states on Machine Readable Travel Documents (MRTDs).[33]

If a fundamental right is being violated, the Court has sufficient reason to pay heed. With technology now easily allowing the two functions of the passport to be separated, it makes even more sense for the court to revisit the issue. If no technical or legal issue can be raised as an obstacle for the fulfillment of this right, the time has come for the courts to affirm it.

By issuing Edward Snowden a passport, the United States would fulfill the normal obligation of all states toward their own citizens. Furthermore, technology makes feasible what was arguably impossible in the past. The two functions of a passport are now separable. This capability opens possibilities that could not be considered by previous justices. Thus the ability of an American citizen to keep a legal identity should be recognized as one of the privileges and immunities of American citizens as defined in the *Slaughter-House Cases*. By affirming both that a passport belongs among the privileges and immunities of an American abroad and that the secretary of state cannot revoke a passport as a matter of administrative routine, courts could make the passport an almost inalienable auxiliary of the American citizen abroad: the symbol and substance of an irreducible citizenship, which the Supreme Court has already proclaimed.

NOTES

A first version of this article has published under the title "Citizenship, Passports, and the Legal Identity of Americans: Edward Snowden and Others Have a Case in the Courts," 123 *Yale Law Journal* (2014): 565, http://yalelawjournal.org/forum/citizenship-passports-and-the-legal-identity-of-americans. For this version, Patrick Weil wants to thank Adam Saltzman for his very professional assistance.

1. Peter Baker and Ellen Barry, "Snowden, in Russia, Seeks Asylum in Ecuador," *New York Times*, June 23, 2013, http://www.nytimes.com/2013 /06/24/world/asia/nsa-leaker-leaves-hong-kong-localofficials-say.html.

2. Ibid. On June 6, 2013, the *Guardian* and the *Washington Post* published the first articles revealing the secret NSA operations. See Roy Greenslade, "How Edward Snowden Led Journalist and Film-Maker to Reveal NSA Secrets," *Guardian*, August 19, 2013, http://www.theguardian.com/world/2013/aug/19/edward-snowden-nsa-secrets-glenn-greenwald-laura-poitras; and Barton Gellman and Laura Poitras, "U.S., British Intelligence Mining Data from Nine U.S. Internet Companies in Broad Secret Program," *Washington Post*, June 6, 2013, https://www.washingtonpost.com/investigations/us-intelligence-mining-data-from-nine-us-internet-companies-in-broad-secret-program/2013/06/06/3a0c0da8-cebf-11e2-8845-d970ccb04497_story.html.

3. Baker and Barry, "Snowden, in Russia, Seeks Asylum in Ecuador." The charges contained allegations of theft of government property and two violations of the Espionage Act. Sari Horwitz, Jia Lynn Yang, and Peter Finn, "Legal, Political Maneuvering Let Snowden Flee," *Washington Post*, June 24, 2013, http://www.washingtonpost.com /world/national-security/legal-political-maneuvering-let-snowden-flee/2013/06/23/5643e0b6-dc36-11e2-bd83-e99e43c336ed_story.html.

4. Horwitz et al., "Legal, Political Maneuvering Let Snowden Flee."

5. Kevin Rawlinson, "Russia Grants NSA PRISM Whistleblower Edward Snowden a Year's Asylum," *Independent* (London), August 1, 2013, http://www.independent.co.uk/news/world/europe /russia-grants-nsa-prism-whistleblower-edward-snowden-a-years-asylum-8741940.html; Alec Luhn and Mark Tran, "Edward Snowden Given Permission to Stay in Russia for Three More Years," *Guardian*, August 7, 2014, http://www.theguardian.com/world/2014/aug/07/edward-snowden-permission-stay-in-russia-three-years.

6. A copy of Snowden's Russian-issued identity document is available at Steven Lee Myers and Andrew E. Kramer, "Defiant Russia Grants Snowden Year's Asylum," *New York Times*,

August 1, 2013, http://www.nytimes.com/2013 /08/02/world/ europe/edward-snowden
-russia.html (featuring an image of the identity document).

7. Patrick Weil, "Edward Snowden Has a Right to Asylum in France," *Le Monde*, June 5,
2014, http://combatsdroitshomme.blog. lemonde.fr/2014/06/05/edward-snowden-has-a
-right-to-asylum-in-france-le-monde-patrick-weil/.

8. Snowden is abroad and remains a citizen of the United States, and only of the United
States, which highlights a passport as the only valuable identification document. It dis-
tinguishes his case from Americans in the United States who can use other means of
legal identification and of individual Americans abroad with dual nationalities who may
possess foreign legal means of identification. Snowden is eligible, according to former
U.S. Attorney General Eric Holder, for only a "limited validity passport good for direct
return to the United States." Furthermore, the State Department will not grant Snowden
a passport of the common kind, which allows a U.S. citizen to remain abroad. See Eric
H. Holder Jr., Attorney General, U.S., to Alexander Vladimirovich Konovalov, Minister
of Justice, Russian Federation, July 23, 2013, http://s3.documentcloud.org/documents
/740227/attorney-genral-letter-to-russian-justice-minister.pdf; and Sari Horwitz and
Michael Birnbaum, "U.S. Won't Seek Death Penalty for Snowden, Holder Says in Letter
to Russian Official," *Washington Post*, July 26, 2013, https://www.washingtonpost.com
/world/national-security/us-will-not-seek-death-penalty-for-snowden-holder-says-in
-letter-to-russians/2013/07/26/5ab3f4da-f601-11e2-aa2e-4088616498b4_story.html; 22 C.F.R.
§ 51.60(a) (2014) states that "[t]he Department may not issue a passport, except a passport for direct return to the United States," before enumerating the cases in which the
department can act in such a way. It is this particular type of passport—available only for
a short period, solely for the purpose of permitting direct return to the United States—
that Attorney General Holder was referencing in his letter.

9. Patrick Weil, *The Sovereign Citizen: Denaturalization and the Origins of the American
Republic* (Philadelphia: University of Pennsylvania Press, 2013).

10. While other documents may be used for identification, a valid passport is the ultimate
and definitive proof of citizenship and identity under international law; other identity
documents such as driver's licenses and birth certificates are not necessarily available or
recognized abroad. See Adam I. Muchmore, "Passports and Nationality in International
Law," *UC Davis Journal of Law and Policy* 10 (2004): 301, 324, 340–41.

11. *Urtetiqui v. D'Arcy*, 34 U.S. 692 (1835).

12. Ibid., at 699.

13. *Haig v. Agee*, 453 U.S. (1981), at 292–93.

14. Transcript of Oral Argument, *Agee*, 453 U.S. 280 (No. 80–83), http://www.oyez.org
/cases/1980 1989/1980/1980_80_83.

15. *Agee*, 453 U.S., at 306.

16. Ibid., at 309–10.

17. *Agee* was decided on June 29, 1981. At the end of May 1981, Chief Justice Burger circulated
a draft opinion that did not address the constitutional claims that Agee was presenting. On May 29, Justice White informed the chief justice that "several of us, perhaps as

many as five, indicated that both statutory and constitutional issues should be dealt with" (Justice Byron White to Chief Justice Warren Burger, May 29, 1981 [Library of Congress, Brennan Papers, I 543/1]). On June 3, Chief Justice Burger circulated additional pages that would become Part III of his opinion (memorandum from Chief Justice Warren Burger to the Supreme Court [Library of Congress, Brennan Papers, I 543/1]).

18. See, generally, *Agee*, 453 U.S., at 306–10 (containing no discussion of the recognition and identification function of passports).

19. Convention Relating to the Status of Refugees, art. 27, July 28, 1951, 19 U.S.T. 6259, 189 United Nations Treaty Series (U.N.T.S.), 150 at art. 28. See also United Nations High Commissioner for Refugees, "Identity Documents for Refugees," July 20, 1984, http:// www.unhcr.org /3ae68cce4.html.

20. The United States has signed the Protocol Relating to the Status of Refugees; under Article 1 of the protocol, signatories "undertake to apply articles 2 to 34 of inclusive of the Convention [Relating to the Status of Refugees] to refugees as hereinafter defined" (Protocol Relating to the Status of Refugees, art. 1, January 31, 1967, 606 U.N.T.S. 267).

21. Convention Relating to the Status of Refugees, art. 28n.20.

22. James C. Hathaway, *The Rights of Refugees Under International Law* (Cambridge: Cambridge University Press, 2005), 237.

23. U.S. Const. amend. XIV, § 1.

24. *Afroyim v. Rusk*, 387 U.S. 253 (1967). The struggle that led Justice Black and Chief Justice Warren to find a way to declare citizenship an absolute right while in the minority of the Court in *Peres v. Brownell*, 356 U.S. 44 (1958), and to summon the majority in *Afroyim* nine years later, after many divisive cases had been decided—often in contradiction with each other—is described in Weil, *Sovereign Citizen*, 145–75.

25. *Slaughter-House Cases*, 83 U.S. 36 (1872).

26. Ibid., at 79.

27. Ibid.

28. Edwin M. Borchard, "The Protection of Citizens Abroad and Change of Original Nationality," *Yale Law Journal* 43 (1934): 359, 361, 363.

29. *Afroyim*, 387 U.S., at 253, 257.

30. Weil, *Sovereign Citizen*, 183–85n.24.

31. On May 28, 2003, the International Civil Aviation Organization (ICAO), which establishes the global standards for passports, released "a global, harmonized blueprint for the integration of biometric identification information into passports and other Machine Readable Travel Documents (MRTDs)" (ICAO, "Biometric Identification to Provide Enhanced Security and Speedier Border Clearance for Travelling Public" [press release], May 28, 2003, http://legacy.icao.int/icao/en/nr/2003/pio200309_e.pdf). In the blueprint, "[f]acial recognition was selected as the globally interoperable biometric for machine-assisted identity confirmation with MRTDs." The ICAO has since revised its blueprint to include the possibility of using fingerprint and iris recognition. See International Civil Aviation Organization, *Machine Readable Travel Documents*, 6th ed. (2006), http://www .icao.int/publications/pages/ publication.aspx?docnum= 9303.

32. ICAO, *Machine Readable Travel Documents: Supplement to ICAO Doc 9303*, October 21, 2013, http://www.icao.int/Security/mrtd/Documents/Supplement%20to %20ICAO%20 Doc%209303%20 %20Release _13.pdf.

33. ICAO, *Machine Readable Travel Documents*, iii, I-1, http://www.icao.int/publications /Documents/9303_p1_v1_cons_en.pdf.

15

SURVEILLANCE POLICY
AS RISK MANAGEMENT

CASS R. SUNSTEIN

As a member of President Obama's Review Group on Intelligence and Communications Technologies, whose report to the president was released in December 2013, I was struck by some close connections between debates over national security and debates over environmental protection. In both contexts, countless people favor some version of the precautionary principle. That principle has had special traction on the left, especially in the environmental arena, but it sometimes has unmistakable appeal on the right as well. The difference, and the question, is this: What, exactly, are we taking precautions against? Risks to national security? Risks to civil liberties? Risks to journalists? What are the worst-case scenarios that focus our attention and attract our most intense fears? When we perceive a need to take precautions, what is the precise target of our concern?

PRECAUTIONS AGAINST WHAT?

I aim to challenge the precautionary principle here, not because it leads in bad directions but because, read for all that it is worth, it leads in no direction at all. The principle threatens to be paralyzing. To explain this problem very briefly, the precautionary principle provides help only if we blind ourselves to many aspects of risk-related situations and focus on a narrow subset of what is at stake. A significant part of this essay will be devoted to showing why this is so—whether the problem involves the environment or surveillance policy. With a narrow viewscreen, it is possible to ignore, or to neglect, some of the risks that are actually at stake. To capture the full set of values, we need to abandon the precautionary principle in favor of what I call the risk management principle. The risk management principle should orient our thinking about surveillance policy, and it amounts to a challenge to some widely held views within the intelligence community, among privacy and civil liberties advocates, and among journalists as well.

THE PARALYZING PRINCIPLE

THE ENVIRONMENTAL ANALOGY

In environmental policy, the precautionary principle means that we should take aggressive action to avoid risks, even if we do not know that those risks will come to fruition. If the problem involves genetic modification of food or nuclear power, we should welcome precautions against potentially serious hazards, simply because it is prudent to be precautionary and better to be safe than sorry. In 1982, for example, the United Nations World Charter for Nature apparently gave the first international recognition to a strong version of the principle, suggesting that when "potential adverse effects are not fully understood, the activities should not proceed." The widely publicized Wingspread Declaration, from a meeting of environmentalists in 1998, is another example: "When an activity raises threats of harm to human health or the environment, precautionary measures should be taken even if some cause and effect relationships are not established scientifically. In this context the proponent of an activity, rather than the public, should bear the burden of proof."

In the environmental area, the problem with the precautionary principle is that risks are on all sides of social situations. If we take aggressive steps against genetic modification of food, we might deprive people, including poor people, of food that is low in cost and high in nutrition. If we do that, we offend the precautionary principle. If we ban nuclear power, we might end up with greater reliance on coal-fired power plants, which increase the risks of climate change. If we take aggressive steps against coal-fired power plants to reduce those risks, we increase the risk of an economic downturn, even a recession, and that offends the precautionary principle as well.

The point is general. Whenever we engage in regulation, we are likely to impose costs, which will be borne by some combination of employers, workers, and consumers. Increases in costs can create risks, including potentially catastrophic ones. It is for this reason that the precautionary principle is incoherent, even paralyzing, because it forbids the very steps that it requires. Precautions are mandated by the principle, but precautions create risks, so they simultaneously offend the principle.

None of this means that we should not be concerned about genetic modification of food, nuclear power, and climate change. None of this means that we should neglect worst-case scenarios or require definitive proof before regulating risks. The points are that we need to investigate the consequences of precautions, and that some of those consequences are unlikely to be so good. It is for this reason that the precautionary principle turns out to be unhelpful. It distracts attention from the right question (the consequences of precautions) and focuses us on the wrong one (how to be precautionary along just one dimension).

SURVEILLANCE

Now turn to the area of national security and to surveillance in particular. In that context, many members of the intelligence community, and many privacy advocates, are focused on some version of the precautionary principle. Within the intelligence community, it is tempting to adopt some version of the principle on the ground that it is important, even crucial, to counteract serious threats to the nation, including terrorist attacks, and surveillance can be helpful, even indispensable. A tempting thought is that even if some kinds of surveillance sweep up an immense amount of material, surely it is better to be safe than sorry. It is hard to rule out the possibility that if the intelligence community obtains as much information as technology permits, it will find some information that is helpful for national security purposes. In light of that fact, we might think: Why not acquire information that might save lives?

That question should not be trivialized. But there is a serious objection, which is that multiple risks are involved. Excessive surveillance creates risks to public trust, personal privacy, individual liberty, and self-government itself. If government holds a great deal of information, there is at least a risk of abuse—if not now or soon, then potentially in the future. And if government is engaged in extensive surveillance, there is a risk of a serious chilling effect on free discussion, on journalists, and on journalists' sources. To that extent, there is a risk to self-government itself. The free speech principle itself requires people to feel confident that as a general rule, the government is not listening to their conversations.

That is hardly all. As the recent period has shown, surveillance can create significant risks to our relationships with other nations. To the extent that the United States is collecting intelligence on foreign leaders and on citizens of foreign nations, our relationships might be strained, potentially risking collaborative endeavors (and thus national security itself). Economic factors matter as well. Surveillance and the acquisition of information might turn out to have—and, in fact, have turned out to have—harmful effects on commerce, certainly if it discourages people from using certain communications providers. To attract business, providers would like to be able to assure their users that their communications are secure. If they cannot do that, customers might look elsewhere. And if American companies are particularly vulnerable to a perception of subjection to surveillance, then they will lose business to companies from other nations, which is hardly in the national interest.

For privacy advocates and the civil liberties community—and for some journalists—a different form of the precautionary principle has widespread appeal. Here the risks, and the worst-case scenarios, involve targeting of political dissenters, exposure of private details, intrusions into people's personal lives, and chilling effects on those who would engage with journalists. Some of these risks are of course less speculative than others. The only point is that for many of those who invoke them, some version of the precautionary principle is in the background or even the foreground. The idea is that we should promote reforms that will create precautions against all such risks.

Here as well, the central motivations are appealing, but the idea of precaution is at best a start. If the relevant reforms would eliminate all risks to privacy and civil liberty, they would undoubtedly create real risks to national security. Even a modest surveillance program, surrounded by limitations and safeguards, creates some risks to privacy and liberty. Trade-offs are inescapable, and invocations of worst-case scenarios, with respect to privacy, threaten to divert attention from that fact. They also threaten national security itself.

In these circumstances, it is far from sufficient to defend any particular approach to surveillance as "precautionary," or as a way to reduce certain categories or real or potential risks. We need to focus on all risks, not a subset. True, precautions can be exceedingly important, and protection of national security and personal privacy must be central goals of any well-functioning government. In our report, the Review Group honors those in the intelligence community who have worked, and are working, every day to keep their fellow citizens safe. We also honor those who emphasize the need to protect privacy. For Congress and the president, the task is to manage a wide assortment of social risks, with careful attention to the likely consequences (including both costs and benefits). In short, the operating principle involves risk management. The risk management principle does not exactly have a nice ring to it, but it is the right foundation for public policy—whether the question involves environmental protection or national security.

WHY PRECAUTIONS?

If the precautionary principle, taken in a strong form, is unhelpful, how can we account for its extraordinary influence and, indeed, for the widespread belief that it can and should guide regulatory judgments? I suggest that an understanding of human cognition provides useful clues, and it helps to explain some of the political polarization on both environmental issues and surveillance. Three factors seem especially important in this domain:

1. *The availability heuristic.* It is well known that people focus on some risks simply because they are cognitively "available," whereas other risks are not. When the precautionary principle seems to require stringent

controls on one risk, even though other risks are in the vicinity, the availability heuristic is a common reason. And when the availability heuristic is at work, certain hazards will stand out, whether or not they are statistically large. The hazards associated with heat waves, for example, usually receive little public attention, while the hazards associated with air travel are often a significant source of public concern. One reason for this is that in the aftermath of a crash, the latter hazards come readily to mind.

Terrorist-related hazards stand out from the background, and no one wants to be responsible for actions or omissions that contribute to another September 11. For this reason, the availability heuristic can produce forms of surveillance that would not be easy to defend by reference to an all-things-considered judgment—but that seem quite sensible if we focus only on the risk of another terrorist attack. Because of the operation of the availability heuristic, some defenders of certain practices of the intelligence community focus on a subset of the full universe of risks—and ignore or downplay some of the risks that those practices create.

2. *Probability neglect.* When emotions are running high, people are prone to neglect the probability that a bad outcome will occur; they focus instead on the outcome itself. As it operates in the real world, the precautionary principle often embodies a form of probability neglect. At least it does so when people invoke the principle to favor stringent controls on a low-probability risk, even though the consequence of those very controls is to give rise to new risks of equal or greater probability. In the area of surveillance, some civil liberties advocates, and some journalists, focus intensely on the risk of government abuse, and perhaps not sufficiently on the magnitude of that risk. The worst-case scenarios, involving potential abuse, dominate their judgments, when they should be focusing on the size of all relevant risks.

3. *The affect heuristic.* The third point deals with emotions more generally. A great deal of social science research has recently been devoted to what psychologists call the affect heuristic. The basic idea is that people often have a rapid affective reaction to people, activities, processes, and ideas, and the affective reaction operates as a mental shortcut for a more sustained analysis. Consider nuclear power, genetically engineered foods, and climate change—in these and other cases, affective reactions play a large role in producing people's judgments. Some evidence in favor of the affect heuristic: people tend to think that activities with high

benefits have low risks; they also tend to think that activities with high risks have low benefits. (Consider nuclear power.) And under time pressure, people show a greater inclination to think that high-benefit activities have low risks and that high-risk activities have low benefits. The fact that the inclination to see high benefits/low risks and high risks/low benefits is greater under time pressure strongly suggests that a general affective reaction comes first, and helps orient judgments about both risks and benefits.

I believe that the affect heuristic plays a large role in people's reactions to surveillance—and that its power suggests the pressing need to use a risk management principle. For some people, the idea of surveillance, as it is now practiced, produces intense, immediate, and intuitive outrage and fear. For others, it does not, and the idea of weakening our ability to prevent terrorist attacks—by scaling back on surveillance—produces a comparable outrage and fear. Of course, social and cultural factors—as well as available incidents—help account for those divergent reactions. But there is no question that affect plays a large role, and that it helps to drive people's ultimate judgments. The problem is that the affect heuristic is not a sensible basis for public policy.

NINE REFORMS

What does the risk management principle specifically entail? Drawing on our report, I suggest that nine reforms, based on that principle, are particularly important:

1. The U.S. government was right to terminate its storage of "metadata," information about many millions of calls made by ordinary Americans. (This includes information about the times and dates of calls, and of the numbers involved; it does not include any content.) To be sure, the capacity to search metadata is one that should be preserved (with the standard judicial safeguards) but without government itself holding it. Under the model, we recommend that metadata would be treated like any other kind of information; the usual Fourth Amendment model would be followed. Current law adopts this approach.

Many people, including the Review Group's members, have proposed that metadata should be held by the phone companies (which have it in any case) or by a new, private entity. Our central argument is that government storage produces risks to personal privacy, civil liberties, and public trust, and it is not necessary for national security purposes (as long as government can obtain access to the information if it shows a need to do so). The phone companies aggressively resisted our proposal, which they say would impose serious economic and operational burdens on them. But those burdens are manageable; they should not be taken as a veto on a framework—private ownership, with government access under the usual Fourth Amendment standards—that has long served the nation well.

2. More generally, Americans should be assured that their government will respect strong safeguards against intrusions into their personal domain. Public officials should not have access to otherwise private information (such as bank records, credit card records, phone records, and Internet data) from third parties (such as banks, credit card companies, telephone companies, and Internet providers) without a court order.

3. Americans should be assured that when engaging in communications with non-Americans—an increasingly common practice in a world of global communications—their government will respect their privacy. The usual safeguard should not be eliminated if Americans are speaking with citizens of the United Kingdom or France. If, for example, the U.S. government incidentally captures communications of American citizens when they are communicating with non-Americans, it should generally be prohibited from using those communications in any proceeding against those American citizens.

4. New measures should be put in place to safeguard the privacy of non-Americans, including foreign leaders. When the United States collects information abroad, its goal should be to protect national security, not to monitor ordinary conversations, to intrude into people's private lives, or to track people solely on the basis of their political convictions or religious beliefs. To this end, some version of existing privacy safeguards for Americans should be extended to people overseas, limiting how long information can be held and when it can be disseminated. And without sufficient national security purposes, the United States should not monitor the communications of leaders of our close friends and allies.

Within the government, a process should be institutionalized to ensure that high-level officials, including those whose jobs are not protection of national security in particular, are involved in making decisions about such monitoring, with close reference to the wide range of risks that must be managed.

5.   Communications providers, including telephone companies, should be able to disclose more information about the orders they have received to provide data to the government. Such companies have argued strongly for this proposal, in part on the grounds that it will show that such orders are not common, and that providers are rarely turning over private information to public officials. Whatever the practice in any particular year or period, it ought not to be hidden.

6.   A public advocate should be available to represent privacy and civil liberties interests before the Foreign Intelligence Surveillance Court. In recent years, the court has been asked to assess some fundamental questions of statutory and constitutional law. Our legal system is based on the fundamental premise of the adversarial presentation of competing views. At least in significant cases, it is important to have a genuine adversary proceeding, including a team of lawyers whose mission is to protect privacy and civil liberties. There should also be an increase in declassification of the court's opinions.

7.   There should be far more transparency with respect to National Security Letters (NSLs), by which the Federal Bureau of Investigation is able, without court approval, to obtain access to people's records (such as their bank and credit card information). In addition, the FBI should not be able to obtain records without judicial authorization. The idea of NSLs should not be invoked to bypass the usual Fourth Amendment safeguards.

8.   The White House should appoint a designated official with the specific responsibility of protecting privacy. Within the federal government, officials often respond to a particular role. If that role is to reduce the risk of terrorist attacks, officials will focus on that risk. If the role is to protect privacy, they will focus on privacy. An official should be given that role, and he or she should be included in a wide range of meetings so that the interest in privacy is taken into account.

9.   Substantial steps should be taken to safeguard Internet freedom, not least to protect journalists. The United States should support international norms or agreements to increase confidence in the security of online

communications. We should make it clear that the United States will not in any way subvert, undermine, weaken, or make vulnerable generally available commercial encryption. To this end, the United States should support efforts to encourage the greater use of encryption technology for data in transit, at rest, in the Cloud, and in storage.

Many of these proposals require additional specification, and support for each of them would, of course, require a far stronger supporting argument than I have been able to provide here. The United States has already made considerable progress in the direction of the proposals. Nonetheless, my central goal is not to insist on any particular reform but to suggest that fears of worst-case scenarios tend to drive people's judgments in this domain, and that precautionary thinking and the affect heuristic play a dismayingly large role.

The problem is that public policies should not be made by reference to worst-case scenarios or the precautionary principle, whether they involve terrorist attacks or government abuse. Trade-offs are inescapable, and while precautions make a great deal of sense, they need to be defended by close reference to their costs and benefits. The risk management principle hardly answers all questions, but at least it guarantees that we pose the right ones, which is a good place to start.

IV

COMMUNICATIONS NETWORKS AND NEW MEDIA

16

SILICON VALLEY AND JOURNALISM

EMILY BELL

This chapter is an edited version of a speech Emily Bell gave as the Reuters Institute Memorial Lecture in November 2014. The following year saw a rapid development in social-media companies and platform companies developing their own publishing tools and hosting journalism directly. The revelations by Edward Snowden raised a flag on the convergence of communication technologies and why this might compromise the integrity and safety of journalists and sources. Part of the duty of the fourth estate and all of its effectiveness derives from a separation between reporting and other conflicting interests, like commerce or government. However, the financial imperative faced by many publishers to reach wider audiences at lower costs has made partnerships with Facebook, Google, and other players not just desirable but potentially imperative.

We have reached a point of transition where news spaces are no longer owned by newsmakers. The press is no longer in charge of the free press and has lost control of the main conduits through which stories reach audiences.

The "public sphere" is now effectively operated by a small number of commercial companies, based largely in Silicon Valley, and while not ill intentioned, they are subject to neither the regulation nor the simple transparency that we might want for the future of our communications infrastructure.

Largely thanks to these developing platform technologies and the role of social media in elevating new voices, professional journalism is now augmented by untold numbers of citizen journalists who break news, add context, and report through any number of new tools.

This has happened extremely quickly, at a pace where it has been difficult often to conceive of the scale of the shift, let alone to process what it means and how we as citizens ought to respond. To have our free speech standards, our reporting tools, and publishing rules set by unaccountable software companies is a defining issue not just for journalism but for every part of our society. Journalism has an important role in building and deploying new technologies, shaping noncommercial parts of a new public sphere, and holding to account these new extensive systems of power. However, it is now also reliant on these new types of third-party publishers for relevance, reach, and revenue. What makes journalism more vibrant in the converged world also makes it more challenging to sustain as a consistent institution-based independent activity.

The "two cultures" of engineering and journalism are very different. They do not share the same motivations, they have not in the past shared the same skills, they do not seek the same outcomes, and they do not in general share the same growth and revenue models. Yet, they now occupy the same space in terms of conveying news and discussion to a broad public.

There is implicit logic in distinguishing "real" news companies from platform companies. Silicon Valley technology companies don't employ journalists to report; they don't tell stories; they don't seek cultural and political impact for the furtherance of democracy; they don't have as their core purpose much outside delivering utility to users and returning money to shareholders. On the other hand, journalism's future is inextricably linked to and increasingly dependent on these communication technologies. This is an awkward new relationship in which both parties are rather surprised to find themselves. Mark Zuckerberg, the founder of Facebook, categorically stated in a 2016 interview that Facebook was "definitely a platform company." Yet, increasingly he is taking on the tasks of an editor and publisher.

In 2015, we saw a sudden and definitive shift from platform companies and social networks distancing themselves from the idea that they were in any way editorial organizations, to them embracing and beginning to shape journalism more overtly. Enabled by the very high uptake in mobile smartphone technologies, social sites and apps started to dominate our digital time. In 2015, first the ephemeral photo-sharing service SnapChat, then Facebook, Twitter, and even Apple developed internal tools enabling publishers to put their stories directly onto these platforms. Google developed a product, Accelerated Mobile Pages (AMP), that it deployed to help publishers to push their stories to the open web but at a much faster speed. Hesitancy and some reluctance on the part of publishers rapidly became a rush to participate. By the end of 2015, what had started as a small experiment by Facebook, opening its Instant Articles to only six publishers, became a new way of publishing for anyone. News organizations like the *Washington Post* decided to put everything they published onto Facebook Instant Articles. The reasoning was clear: it was better than the alternative. In April 2016, Facebook opened Instant Articles to all publishers.

The sell to publishers was straightforward: we will publish your articles so that more people can see them; we will sell advertising around them, and you keep most or sometimes all of the revenue. The anxiety, however, was that what news organizations were encouraging was an irreversible shift in power and control, which once done might never be undone. Yet by maintaining independence from these systems, publishers risk their very own survival.

The fourth estate, which liked to think that it operated in splendid isolation from other systems of money and power, has slipped suddenly and conclusively into a world where it no longer owns the means of production or controls the routes to distribution. There are few ways in which this could, or even should, have been prevented or altered.

Most journalists lacked the fundamental technological literacy to understand how these new systems of distribution and expression were going to emerge, journalism organizations often lacked the institutional will or insight to move swiftly enough in that direction, and we were slowed in transformation by large legacy systems and the revenues that came with them. Doing journalism well is a hard, resource-hungry business, and it is impossible to imagine how somewhere like the *New York Times* would have simultaneously kept up its reporting while at the same time inventing Facebook in its basement. The success of social platforms is a parallel narrative to the decline of news organizations, not dependent or changed by it.

News companies, by their nature, make it hard to publish; social media platforms make it easy to publish. Consequently, most journalism is published or shared at some point on a social platform, even if it didn't originate there. As news organizations cease to print physical newspapers, as linear television struggles to survive the buffeting of on-demand services, as services become not just digital first but digital only, journalism and free expression become part of a commercial sphere where the activities of news and journalism are marginal.

It is worth noting that while engineers have developed Facebook, YouTube, Twitter, LinkedIn, Instagram, Reddit, SnapChat, Pinterest, Ello, Medium, Kickstarter, and others, not one existing journalism or media company has conceived of or developed a widely adopted social platform. And only two, MySpace and Reddit, were acquired by media companies, by News Corp and Condé Nast, respectively. Social-media platforms have been insistent that they are not interested in the difficult and expensive business of employing actual journalists or making editorial decisions. Their culture is as alien to reporting and editing as ours is to designing social software, but this is beginning to change.

Even if the creators of social platforms believe that they are not editorial, this is in the eyes of the users and increasingly the law—an unsustainable position. Every algorithm contains editorial decisions; every piece of software design carries social implications. If the whole world connects at high speed in 140 characters, it changes the nature of discourse and events. It is thrilling and empowering, but it is also terrifying and threatening. The language of news is shaped now by engineering protocols, not by newsrooms norms, and on the whole the world is a better place for it. We would not want to unwind time and move back to an age where in order to find a public voice individuals had to squeeze through narrow channels of editing, and where another opaque and often undemocratic elite made decisions about what was, and what was not published.

However, although there is great progress it is not without some obvious challenges. Engineers who rarely think about journalism or cultural impact or democratic responsibility are making decisions every day that shape how news is created and disseminated. In developing these amazingly easy-to-use tools and encouraging the world to publish, the platform technologies now have a social purpose and responsibility far beyond their original intent.

It is possible that over the first decade of the twenty-first century, legacy media did not understand what it was losing, but equally Silicon Valley did not fully understand what it was creating. As of 2016, Facebook has 1.5 billion users, around 20 percent of the world's population. Surveys regularly conducted by the Pew Center demonstrate that at least 30 percent of adults in America see Facebook as a source of news. YouTube has a billion users, and a hundred hours of video are uploaded to the platform every minute. Twitter, the closest platform to a journalistic service, is considered a stuttering failure with a mere 300 million users. An Indiana University survey found that in the United States, 80 percent of journalists use Twitter to find out about breaking news, and 60 percent of them use it directly as a source for stories. Weibo, the main Chinese social network, is bigger than all of them. Instagram, Snapchat, WhatsApp, and WeChat are rapidly becoming default platforms for younger audiences.

There is a dilemma now for platform companies: How much do they edit and create new stories themselves? For media companies, the temptation must be to scale back investments in creative technology and advertising sales, and outsource much more of this to the new platforms with far greater skills and scale in this area. No other single branded platform in the history of journalism has had the concentration of power and attention that Facebook enjoys. Facebook uses a series of complicated formulae to decide which news stories rise to the top of your page or news feed. These mechanisms are known as algorithms. They not only dictate what we see but also provide the foundation of the business model for social platforms. They are commercially sensitive and therefore remain secret. They can change without notice, and they can alter what we see without us even noticing. A news executive described to me how the Facebook news algorithm is now the most important way readers find his journalists' stories. He added, "But we don't know much about how Facebook sorts stories, and that scares the hell out of me."

In 2014, when the *New York Times*'s late columnist David Carr interviewed Greg Marra, Facebook's product manager, Marra was quoted as saying, "We try to explicitly view ourselves as not editors." He said, "We don't want to have editorial judgment over the content that's in your feed. You've made your friends, you've connected to the pages that you want to connect to and you're the best decider for the things that you care about." However, even by making the decision that people see news based on their social circles, Marra and his colleagues have made a profound editorial decision that has a broad societal impact.

When I interviewed Dick Costolo, then chief executive of Twitter, on stage at the Online News Association annual conference in 2012, I congratulated him on running the free press of the twenty-first century. He grimaced and countered, "That's not really how I like to see it." Silicon Valley executives are not stupid—they know that editing and shaping culture is a hard, thankless, politically charged, and financially unprofitable business.

In 2014, Zeynep Tufekci, an academic and a commentator on sociology, media, and technology, was following the social unrest in the St. Louis suburb of Ferguson, Missouri, after the police shot Michael Brown, an unarmed, young, black man. She noted that although her Twitter feed was full of reports from Ferguson, nothing appeared on Facebook. Overnight, as the Facebook algorithm worked its filtering magic, stories began to appear but not until long after the first reports and discussions. Facebook's algorithm had decided that Tufekci was not as immediately interested in the unrest of a small Missouri suburb as she would be in the ice-bucket challenge. Without other social signals from less-filtered platforms, Tufekci wondered if she would have ever seen events in Ferguson on Facebook at all. In a world where we navigate our daily lives through social platforms, just how this information reaches us, what is on a "trending" list, how these algorithms work, becomes not just of marginal interest but a central democratic concern.

Even the obscure issue of equal access to the Internet, or "net neutrality," can affect how we get our news and information. Tufekci suggested that without what she called "the neutral side of the Internet" such as live streams, and also Twitter, where feeds are determined not by opaque corporate algorithms but by individual choices, people might not have been talking about Ferguson at all.

The general public has been relatively unaware of how these intimate social platforms might be used. In June 2014, the findings of an academic experiment were published in which Facebook had manipulated the news feed of 700,000 users for a week to see how exposure to different types of news might affect the users' mood. The answer was that happy posts made people more likely to be happy. It was a legitimate academic experiment, but when the findings were made public there was predictable uproar.

"How dare Facebook literally toy with our emotions?" people complained. Yet Facebook is under no obligation to disclose how it manipulates the news feed or any other type of information.

It was striking that the public expectation of how information reaches them is still relatively naive. If Facebook can nudge your emotions toward happiness or sadness by manipulating what you see, can it use obscure algorithms to influence something more sinister, such as, for instance, the way we vote? Well, yes it can, as it turns out. In 2010, Facebook conducted another experiment to see whether issuing voting prompts in certain feeds increased turnout. It did. The Harvard law professor Jonathan Zittrain asked what would happen if Mark Zuckerberg decided to tweak an algorithm so that only voters who favored a particular party or candidate were prompted to vote? Zittrain draws a parallel between this and subliminal television advertising in the 1970s, which was regulated by the FCC. Of course, television stations are licensed and open to sanction in a way that Facebook might not be. Zittrain noted: "As more and more of what shapes our views and behaviors comes from inscrutable, artificial-intelligence-driven processes, the worst-case scenarios should be placed off limits in ways that don't trip over into restrictions on free speech." Twitter, perhaps the most useful tool for journalists since the invention of the telephone, tried to stick to a "raw" feed, but this approach is at odds with what advertisers want and with what investors require. It also gave Twitter greater problems with trolling and hate speech. When ISIS circulated the first videos of the beheading of the American journalist James Foley in 2014, they did it through Twitter. In a departure from established practice, this led to Dick Costolo announcing that not only would the account distributing the video be closed but so would any account retweeting the video. An open and clearly editorial decision, Costolo's action sat uneasily with those who had thought Twitter was a "free" platform that made no distinction at all between types of posts.

To editors used to making editorial decisions, it seemed a sensible call. Citizen journalists, professional journalists, and news companies are trying to work out how to secure more attention for their work in an environment they don't control, and technologists are struggling to come to terms with the full implications of being news agencies to the world. A senior executive of a social platform admitted to me that they knew editing their platform for problematic content was a persistent and growing problem, "but we have no system for it," he said. "We scramble a small group into a war room and make decisions on an ad hoc basis. We know it is a problem."

Journalism in all its forms grapples on a daily basis with similar problems and might have things to offer in how these more explicit cultural filters can be built. The most vivid example of the friction between the new platforms and the traditional role of the press sits in the remarkable set of stories published about the NSA activities, brought to light by material obtained by the whistleblower Edward Snowden. These disclosures spelled out that the tools we use for journalism—Gmail, Skype, social media—are already fatally compromised by being part of a surveillance state. Platforms like Google were aghast, supposedly, at how their infrastructure was tapped for information by security agencies.

In order for there to ever be an exit route or alternative to platforms, those interested in independent journalism need to stop relying solely on the tools and platforms of others and build independent systems. Maybe this is a joint project, as we already have seen, that those who made fortunes in software companies are curious about journalism too. Pierre Omidyar, of eBay, has invested $250 million into First Look, a journalism start-up. Jeff Bezos, the founder of Amazon, bought the *Washington Post* from the Graham family for $250 million, and, in all fairness, the investment in publishing tools by platform companies is not insignificant. It is not really feasible for journalism to have an adversarial relationship with technology companies, but it is arguably imperative that there is a public sphere, of which journalism is a part, that is not wholly reliant on them.

There is a significant amount of intellectual capital and some monetary capital dedicated to public-service journalism. If we include the mission to make communications technologies fit for a free press, every one of us who works in that sphere should push hard on three initiatives.

The first is to build tools and services that put software in the service of journalism, rather than the other way around. We need a platform for journalism built with the values and requirements of a free press baked into it. Change in technology is constant. Journalists and editors should learn programmatic thinking and skills to enable them to understand the world they operate in. There is a significant civic and open software movement that has helped activists throughout the world use mesh networks, secure SMS (short message service) communication, and build other alternative technologies that skirt compromised or commercial technology. Larger journalism organizations should embrace and extend these types of technologies as part of their core mission. This will take both a technologically sophisticated leadership and hitherto unseen amounts of collaborative goodwill. Instead of news executives enjoying monthly visits to the Googleplex to play around on bicycles, they should convene serious forums about archiving, moderation, deletion, censorship, and submission of user information to the authorities. These are all critical social issues at the heart of both fields.

The second unfashionable and unpopular call would be for regulation. Journalism has been firing shots at companies like Google over redundant issues like copyright for years, while the more serious regulatory issues relating to monopoly, utility status, and opacity have been largely untouched. Journalism still has a powerful voice in influencing issues of regulation, and it should use both its corporate presence and its intellectual capital to surface and interrogate some of the issues we are seeing today.

And the third and most achievable is that journalists need to report the issues more consistently—they should cover technology as a human right and political issue or as if it were government. The beats of data, privacy, and algorithmic accountability either don't exist or are inadequately staffed in many organizations. We have to stop coverage of technology being about lining up for an iPhone and make it about society and power. Google is building fiber networks for American cities, which is a very laudable project; it is putting self-driving cars, which record, collect, and transport data, on the roads, again an invaluable service to humans; but with every extension of power, we need to be able to ask difficult questions. We need to explain these new systems of power to the world and hold them accountable. It is, after all, what we do best. It is impossible to imagine that journalism has a future without being closely aligned to these extensive new platforms. However, in making sure that democratic process does not lose out in this grand reordering, journalism, or at least the principles of good journalism, need to be at least an equal partner in this most modern of relationships.

17

DIGITAL THREATS AGAINST JOURNALISTS

RON DEIBERT

ournalism is essential to the public interest and core to liberal democracy. Like many other institutions, journalism is undergoing a profound transformation as a consequence of digital media. Mobile devices allow events to be captured in real time by scores of individuals, social media provides instantaneous communication regarding important developments, and vast troves of data provide significant opportunities for analysis and enhanced comprehension.

The adoption of digital media and communications has introduced not only many new conveniences for journalists but also new risks. While the ability to communicate with sources and colleagues is easier than ever, there is a growing number of ways to compromise, monitor, and otherwise inhibit those communications. Incriminating information about sensitive data, confidential sources, meeting locations, and geographic whereabouts is potentially now contained entirely in a journalist's handheld device. Newsrooms and media headquarters are obvious targets for nefarious actors, as editors and senior staff process the data and reports sent in from the field. Meanwhile, nondemocratic governments and others that seek to contain or stifle free press have at their disposal a growing arsenal of increasingly sophisticated tools to surreptitiously access, copy, modify, or even delete that information. The risks for journalists are increasing daily, as those motivated to contain and silence independent media and investigative reporting are becoming better equipped and more tech savvy.

It is widely agreed that the discipline of journalism has only begun to grapple with, let alone accommodate, the changes required to adapt to these new security threats. Journalists—some working in highly sensitive topic areas—often admit to possessing a rudimentary understanding of how to navigate these concerns and protect themselves from digital risks. Shrinking resources force many newsrooms to focus on immediate events as opposed to in-depth analyses. Undertaking non-news-related tasks, such as fortifying their computer security, can be a distant luxury.

This chapter examines some of the characteristics of the changing digital landscape for journalists, with a special focus on the risk environment that has developed as a result of Edward Snowden's stunning disclosures. We begin with an overview of the threats related to mass surveillance—in particular, the operations of the NSA and its "Five Eyes" allies. The next section turns to mass surveillance outside the Five Eyes. We then examine issues regarding a more fine-grained targeted surveillance, and in particular revelations concerning off-the-shelf lawful interception tools sold to regimes as spyware. The final section provides an overview of changing digital-media laws, policies, and practices that have a significant effect on those who research and deliver the news. We conclude with reflections on the overall state of journalism in today's digital-media environment.

MASS SURVEILLANCE (FIVE EYES)

Since June 2013, a stream of highly classified documents leaked by former United States National Security Agency (NSA) contractor Edward Snowden has provided the public with an unprecedented view of the exceptional capabilities of the world's most powerful signals intelligence agency (SIGINT), the NSA, and its allies in the United Kingdom (GCHQ), Canada (CSEC), Australia (ASD), and New Zealand (GCSB). These disclosures reveal an extraordinary effort across all layers of the global telecommunications infrastructure to infiltrate, collect, and even subvert or destroy data that passes through it. The impacts of these disclosures—many of which are still unforeseen—are felt across multiple sectors and have generated intense debates about the proper balance between security and privacy.

For journalists and journalism in general, the implications are, on one level, easy to discern: the disclosures reveal that the entire communications stream—from the newsroom to the field—is at risk of *potential exposure*, protected only by policy and law, where relevant, and if enforced. To what extent the intelligence derived from communications in specific cases has been exploited is another matter, and very difficult to verify. But inferences can be drawn from what we currently know.

For example, some of the Snowden disclosures indicate that the U.K.'s GCHQ is explicitly authorized to spy on investigative journalists and other groups covering sensitive topics. The documents reveal that agents must have "reasonable grounds to believe that they are participating in or planning activity that is against the interests of national security, the economic well-being of the U.K. or which in itself constitutes a serious crime." In other words, the justifications for such spying are very broad, and there is wide latitude given to determine who may classify as a "target." In the U.K., oversight of such operations is limited to a single senior politician in the government, usually the foreign or home secretary, who signs their approval.[1]

While the United States exercises more stringent oversight than the U.K. or the other Five Eyes partners, it is safe to assume that similar targeting is possible and potentially undertaken. Case in point: in 2012, the U.S. Justice Department seized, from wireless-telecommunications provider Verizon, the phone records of more than twenty Associated Press telephone lines.[2] Even if the United States does refrain from targeting U.S. journalists, the sharing agreements between the Five Eyes would give the NSA and other partners access to data collected by GCHQ. In the absence of explicit checks and balances to the contrary, it should be assumed that journalists working on sensitive topics of interest to any Five Eyes partner would be at risk of having their communications routinely intercepted.

These revelations have prompted a variety of reactions from the journalism profession, some of which will no doubt result in increased protection for those who investigate and deliver the news. Some media outlets, newsrooms, and individual journalists are taking immediate and extraprecautionary steps to protect their communications' security. The *New York Times* argued in a recent editorial that major news outlets should encrypt access to their websites by default, and some media outlets have followed suit. Other companies are resisting, however, because of the associated maintenance costs and the inconveniences that default encrypted access presents, especially for targeted advertising (on which media depend for revenues).

Outside the news world, companies—including Google, Yahoo!, Facebook, and, most notably, Apple—are taking steps on their own to secure their communications. While these measures are partially in response to the surveillance disclosures and intended to rebuild consumer trust lost in the wake of the scandal, the increased attention to security will likely also benefit journalists and news organizations. A landmark case in this respect is the 2016 standoff between the FBI and Apple, in which the Department of Justice and the FBI sought to compel Apple to build new software that would allow government access to its encrypted devices. Apple strongly resisted the court order and was backed up by numerous other technology companies. Eventually, the FBI withdrew its case when it received third-party support to break into the suspect device without Apple's support. For its part, Apple has stood firm by its commitment to providing all consumers with the strongest possible encryption. The iPhone 6S, for example, encrypts all the device's data so that if the phone is lost, confiscated, or stolen, the data cannot be accessed—even by the company—without the user's password. In April 2016, WhatsApp, the popular instant-messaging system owned by Facebook, announced it was turning on end-to-end encryption for its system. The more that journalists can rely on a trustworthy default security architecture on their devices, the less they need to rely on installing and employing these security measures themselves, and the better off they will be.

Steps are also being taken on a more institutional and behavioral level, focusing on the practices of editors, newsrooms, journalists, and their sources. In years since the Snowden disclosures, numerous workshops on secure communications have been held. Guides have been published and training resources made available for editors and journalists, in order to help them securely communicate and protect the confidentiality of their sources.[3] Given that the risks are a relatively new phenomenon, and the learning curve quite steep, there will be no doubt be a period of adjustment where mistakes are made. After the *Wall Street Journal* put up a secure communications "drop" for whistleblowers, security researchers found "critical security problems, including poorly chosen encryption algorithms, vulnerability to interception, and a privacy policy that reserved the right to disclose information about the source 'to law enforcement authorities or to a requesting third party, without notice.'"[4] Such inconsistencies are to be expected but should also raise alarm bells for newsrooms, editors, and journalists (and where relevant, their funders) to take the learning and evaluation process seriously. It is nearly impossible to secure oneself completely against an adversary with the resources and capabilities of the NSA or its allies, but concerted efforts to take precautions will help raise the bar and eliminate sloppy habits, thereby staving off lower-level threats. The Snowden disclosures should therefore be regarded as a wake-up call.

OUTSIDE THE FIVE EYES: MASS SURVEILLANCE CAPABILITIES IN THE GLOBAL SOUTH

It goes without saying that the Five Eyes are not alone in engaging in sophisticated signals intelligence or in employing surveillance as a way to target the efforts of journalists. Many other countries have their own well-developed surveillance capabilities, including countries that are notorious for having poor human rights practices.

For example, China (PRC) has the most notorious and active cyber-espionage operations and has a long track record of targeting dissidents, human rights groups, journalists, and others both within China and abroad. Citizen Lab research has tracked numerous cases where media organizations have been targeted by persistent China-based cyberespionage (China-based targeted surveillance is covered later in this chapter).[5] The PRC also requires social-media and other communications companies to install means for the government to monitor their communications— a form of "surveillance-by-design." For example, in 2008 and again in 2011, Citizen Lab and University of New Mexico researchers found that the Chinese version of Skype was programmed with hidden keyword surveillance: whenever a keyword is typed into the client, the user's communications are sent to a server in mainland China, presumably to share with authorities.[6] More recent Citizen Lab research has confirmed that three of the most popular mobile browser applications in China all contain "strikingly similar" privacy and security problems, including sending highly sensitive and personally identifiable user information back to corporate servers, where companies are required by law to share with the Chinese government.[7] Journalists working in China or communicating with sources inside China should be aware that the entire infrastructure of that country is vulnerable to state surveillance.

Likewise, Russia has a long track record of being one of the world's most dangerous places for investigative journalism, a risky environment that extends deep into the digital domain. The country's security services are well equipped with very sophisticated cyberespionage capabilities. Telecommunications (telcos) surveillance is comprehensive throughout Russia, as well as in neighboring countries that connect upstream through Russian telecommunications networks. Both ISPs and telcos in Russia are required to be "SORM-compliant" by law, SORM being the Russian acronym for the technical system that sends a copy of all network traffic to local security services to be archived and analyzed for an indefinite period of time. Russia also enforces media-specific surveillance laws. For example, leading up to the 2014 Sochi Winter Olympic games, President Medvedev signed a decree requiring all companies bidding on the infrastructure-development project to have in place systems with the capability to monitor and archive all the communications of visitors to Sochi—including foreign journalists.[8] As in China, journalists working in or on topics that are sensitive to the Russian government are at high risk of targeted surveillance and must therefore operate in an environment where mass surveillance of digital media is the norm.

In the wake of the Snowden disclosures, it is likely that China- and Russia-based surveillance and targeted digital attacks will escalate. Prior to the disclosures, the U.S. government was applying pressure, specifically on China, to de-escalate their cyberespionage campaigns. As the disclosures have cast the United States and its allies in a hypocritical light around these and other "Internet Freedom" issues, both China and Russia face fewer obstacles to their ambitious surveillance practices and, indeed, more incentive to ramp them up.

While Russia and China are exceptional in terms of the resources they expend on information controls and the autocratic nature of governance, they are not unique. Numerous countries are quickly developing advanced surveillance systems typically as a component of broader national cybersecurity development. For example, India's version of PRISM, the Central Monitoring System (CMS), gives India's SIGINT agencies a one-stop access point for mobile, landline, satellite, VOIP, e-mail SMS, and geolocation traffic. All telecommunications companies must comply with the CMS in order to get an operating license in India.[9] In 2013, Nigeria explored the purchase of a $40 million national surveillance system from the Israeli company Elbit Systems.[10] In Kenya, the government passed a law in 2014 giving the security services unrestricted access to Internet and cellular communications after the Westgate terrorist attack, and contracted a private company to install a centralized street-level video-surveillance system modeled after London's expansive network.[11] In 2014, the U.K.'s Privacy International report on surveillance in the Central Asian region found governments implementing comprehensive communications-surveillance systems at the backbone of their telecommunications networks, borrowing Russian intelligence expertise and using products and services developed in the West. Also in 2014, Iran's telecommunications minister announced the development of a surveillance system that will monitor every user, saying "there will be no web surfer whose identity we do not know." Iranian authorities also perform routine spot checks at Internet cafés and shut down those that do not comply with user surveillance requirements.[12]

A troubling concern around mass surveillance involves the spread of technologies that facilitate precise monitoring of communications traffic at a national scale. Citizen Lab research has shown the global proliferation of the sale of deep-packet inspection technologies (DPI) to regimes with questionable human rights record (DPI is a network monitoring technology used to engage in fine-grained monitoring of Internet traffic). While DPI technologies can be used for benign purposes, they can also be powerful tools in the arsenal of repressive regimes, employed to isolate certain types of communications with precision. Citizen Lab's global scan found evidence of the presence of Blue Coat's DPI systems on the public networks of dozens of countries with questionable human rights records, including Thailand, Indonesia, China, Saudi Arabia, Colombia, Singapore, India, Nigeria, Kuwait, Guatemala, Democratic Republic of the Congo, Uganda, and Qatar.[13] In situations where democratic oversight is lacking, these systems can be turned on and against journalists and other civil society organizations, and should be factored into any risk analysis carried out by journalists operating in or undertaking investigations regarding events in the country and activities of its people.

The Snowden disclosures will likely accelerate developments around mass surveillance of communications infrastructure. Governments now have the model of the NSA to compare themselves to, and agencies within those governments responsible for cybersecurity have added both pressure and incentive to develop comprehensive approaches to cyberwarfare and surveillance. In many cases, these new assets will turn into tangible risks for journalists, dissidents, and others.

TARGETED SURVEILLANCE

Mass surveillance is an omnipresent risk, but there are other types of surveillance that are more concentrated and focused. Targeted digital attacks are defined by Citizen Lab "as persistent attempts to compromise and infiltrate the networked devices and infrastructure of specific individuals, groups, organizations, and communities."[14] These types of attacks are becoming a more common threat across the civil society landscape, especially for journalists. It is important for every journalist to be aware of the character of targeted digital threats and how to equip him- or herself for safe and secure digital communications.

We know that targeted digital attacks are undertaken by all major state powers, but public reports on those originating in China date back at least ten years and are the most notorious. In the past five years, the number of reports on these activities has exploded with documentation of high-profile compromises against government and industry around the world, including major media corporations such as the *Washington Post* and the *New York Times*. Journalists working on China-related issues are also routinely targeted for surveillance. In 2009, Citizen Lab uncovered a major China-based cyberespionage campaign called Ghostnet, which affected numerous high-profile targets including the e-mail servers of the Associated Press.[15] Later that year, Citizen Lab documented a digital attack that compromised the computers of the Foreign Correspondents' Club of China.[16] In 2014, Citizen Lab published the results of a four-year study involving ten participating NGOs—including several independent media groups—that were persistently targeted by digital attacks during the course of the study. Attacks like these typically involve malicious software embedded in e-mail attachments. For example, the e-mail messages are drafted as "lures" to entice the recipient to click on the link. Other types of malware are delivered via hyperlinks that are clicked on or through compromised websites that are visited using web browsers that are not updated with security patches. Once a target is compromised, attackers typically install remote-access trojans (RATs) that exfiltrate data from target machines; some RATs even give the attackers the ability to turn on webcams, microphones, and record keystrokes.

A major concern around targeted digital attacks is the growing sophistication of the tools and methods used to undertake them. Citizen Lab researchers have conducted extensive investigation into the global proliferation of so-called lawful interception malware sold exclusively to governments, which ends up in fact being employed against civil society organizations, including journalists. Products such as Hacking Team's Remote Control System and Gamma Group's FinFisher allow governmental purchasers the ability to remotely and secretly access and monitor the computers and phones of their targets. Research published by Citizen Lab as well as other investigative groups has demonstrated that some governments and security services abuse these tools by hacking political opponents, human rights groups, and journalists both within their own jurisdictions and abroad. For example, in the United States, journalists working at an independent Ethiopian news organization were compromised with Hacking Team's Remote Control System spyware. At the time of writing, the government of Ethiopia is facing a lawsuit brought by the Electronic Frontier Foundation on behalf of the Maryland-based victim.[17] Meanwhile, Privacy International has asked the U.K. National Cyber Crime Unit (NCCU) to investigate the Bahrain government's targeting of victims on U.K. soil, with the knowledge of Gamma Group, the manufacturer of the lawful intercept product FinFisher. Despite the potential for abuse, the market for these tools is very difficult to regulate, which has helped the governmental customer base grow and has likely led to substantial profits for developers.

Even in zones of conflict, where basic Internet connectivity is sparse, targeted digital threats are becoming a major concern. Since at least January 2012, Syrian opposition groups and independent media have experienced a growing volume of suspicious messages and social-media postings directed at them to download documents and programs purporting to contain useful information for the opposition.[18] Troublingly, some of the files were sent from the accounts of individuals currently detained by the regime. In one documented case, an activist was arrested by the regime, and during interrogation he was told that the security services had been watching his activities on his laptop. Shortly after his arrest, his account began sending suspicious files to his contacts, including a foreign-aid worker who was later infected. Early analysis of these files within the opposition led to the conclusion that they were being targeted by malware attacks. Researchers and journalists began investigating these cases and were eventually able to develop compelling evidence linking the attacks to the Assad regime.

While physical risks to journalists working in war zones may be the most immediate and palpable concern, digital risks are an increasing threat. Markets for digital-attack techniques, and even more homegrown solutions to digital attacks, are becoming larger and more widely available. This suggests that the risks around this area are going to expand in the near future. For journalists working in sensitive topic areas or zones of conflict, this is likely to be a growing risk area. Unfortunately, many journalists are not equipped to understand the risks and can easily be putting themselves, their colleagues, and/or their sources at risk.

LAWS, POLICIES, PRACTICES

Laws, policies, and practices set the context within which digital media can be employed and how journalism can be undertaken. These can include rulings or conventions that restrict access to information and freedom of speech. Over the past decade, research by Citizen Lab and others has documented a growing range of these types of information controls, many of which are directed at or impact journalism and journalists. In general, legal and regulatory information controls are becoming more stringent, creating more risks for journalists and journalism while stifling critical voices. Another type of information control seeks to restrict what defines a "journalist." With the widespread availability of social media and blogs, many individuals and groups are undertaking journalistic reporting that in ways would be considered legitimate journalism. However, these individuals and groups lack institutional affiliation and hence the protections that are typically afforded by those connections. Independent journalists present a challenge for authorities because they are less contained, therefore less controllable, than institutionalized media. For example, the latter may require licensing to operate or have other connections to the government that can be leveraged by government to apply pressures. To rectify this problem, governments are now implementing laws and regulations that pertain to social media, blogs, and bloggers, in addition to conventional media.

Although a comprehensive review of cases is out of the scope for this chapter, a cursory glance at particular cases indicates a troubling trend worldwide:

- In 2014, the Hungarian government introduced new laws that require media agencies to release in-depth data about their employees and contracts to the government; the government has also been helping "friendly" media companies with advertising purchases at the same time they are withdrawing support from other critical media outlets. Observers note that the government is intending to extend such restrictions to Internet publications.[19] In September 2015, the OSCE representative on Freedom of the Media Dunja Mijatović called out Hungary's authorities for harassment of journalists covering refugees, saying that "Hungarian police beat reporters with batons, forced journalists to delete heir footage, broke their equipment, and threw teargas."[20]

- The Vietnamese government has introduced a decree that restricts online anonymity, prevents the use of pseudonyms, and requires journalists to reveal their sources. According to Reporters Without Borders, "This decree is trying to apply the censorship already in force for traditional media to blogs."[21]

- In a speech at Malaysian Journalists Night on June 12, 2013, Malaysian prime minister Najib Razak pronounced that freedom of speech "must be suited and match Malaysian norms which are synonymous with good manners and noble values."[22] To that end, he called for the public to submit proposals for a new "form of monitoring and control to ensure what is written in the social media do not breach the laws." The Malaysian communications and multimedia ministry then announced that it "will review all aspects of the law, control and education, pertaining to the abuse of social media." As an indication of a growing trend, the Malaysian communications minister also mentioned that his department will work closely with the Malaysian cybersecurity offices to monitor posts to Twitter, Facebook, and other social media to ensure they are "accurate." In April 2015, Malaysia's parliament approved sweeping new powers to censor online media in what some observers see as pressure to control journalists' and independent bloggers' coverage of a growing financial scandal sweeping the government.[23]

- In 2013, the Singaporean government proposed a news-licensing plan that would require certain news websites to obtain licenses to operate, and may oblige them to remove content.[24] The new rules affect websites that attract more than fifty thousand visitors a month. Owners of these websites are required to obtain a license and to remove posts, within twenty-four hours, that are deemed by the government to be infringements of its policies. Singaporean activists denounced the regulations as a justification of state censorship of online media in a rare public protest (organized through social media) against the government. In 2016, an Australia-based editor of a popular (but subsequently shuttered) website, The Real Singapore, was sentenced to ten months in prison for "sedition" related to posts made on the website.[25]

- In Russia, Internet access was previously more or less unrestricted, However, in 2012, anti-Putin demonstrations prompted the government to become more aggressive. An Internet control agency, Roskomnadzor, quickly took action on information controls, including developing a blacklist of websites to be censored by ISPs, and eventually requiring foreign web-service companies to host their data in Russia,[26] where the companies and their data can be more easily controlled.[27]

At the same time that standard regulations around journalist practices are being tightened and extended to independent web-based media, governments are also applying pressures around content. There are an increasing number of cases of journalists being arrested for content they post online, or website editors being arrested for what they allow to be posted. The latter is particularly noxious for the liabilities that are passed on to website editors or blog-platform hosts.

- In 2014, a Thailand magazine editor, Thanapol Eawsakul, was arrested for posting comments critical of the Thai military on his Facebook website. He was released on July 9 on the basis that he sign a written agreement to cease all political activities.[28] Also in 2014, a web editor named Nut Rungwong was sentenced to four and a half years in jail for allowing an article to be published on his website in 2009 that was judged to be defamatory to the king of Thailand.[29]

- Vietnamese authorities have arrested an increasing number of bloggers for posts critical of the regime.[30] On May 26, 2013, Truong Duy Nhat was detained in Da Nang and taken to Hanoi for "abusing democratic freedoms in order to infringe upon the interests of the state, the legitimate rights and interests of organizations and/or citizens." His blog was disabled for a short time following his arrest.[31] Upon reactivation, the blog was booby-trapped to download malware onto the PCs of its visitors.[32] On June 13, 2013, Pham Viet Dao was arrested in Hanoi under similar accusations.[33] Dao used his blog to criticize Vietnam's single-party government. Dinh Nhat Uy was arrested on June 15, 2013, for using his blog to "distort the truth and defame state organizations."[34] These concerted attempts to stifle online expression by the Vietnamese government have continued into the time of writing.[35] Numerous journalists and bloggers have subsequently been jailed in Vietnam, including, in 2016, Nguyen Quang Lap and Hong Le Tho under article 258 of Vietnam's penal code for "abusing democratic freedoms" for writings posted on their blogs.[36]

- In India, a computer engineer who police claimed ran a Twitter account glorifying the Islamic State terrorist organization was arrested in December 2014, and charged with violating Internet regulations and attempting to "wage war against Asiatic powers."

- In Sudan, the government has voiced intentions to enact legal measures to restrict content regarded as "a threat to national and social security" and employs a "Cyber Jihadist Unit" that actively monitors social media and infiltrates online forums, even going so far as reportedly hacking into dissident journalist websites and e-mail accounts.[37]

- Iran is one of the world's most prolific jailers of writers and female journalists, according to Reporters Without Borders, including many web-based and social-media writers.[38] As of July, at least sixty-five journalists, bloggers, and social-media activists were in prison on various charges related to their speech or writings. In August 2014, Soheil Arabi,

a blogger, was sentenced to death by hanging for Facebook posts he allegedly made "insulting the Prophet."[39] In 2015, the Iranian tech reporter and
blogger Arash Zad was arrested, even though he did not routinely comment on political issues, in what one observer saw as "a strong signal from
the Revolutionary Guards," of a growing threat to online freedom.[40]

- In Kenya, a new national security law proposes heavy criminal
penalties for journalists who publish information that authorities deem
undermining to "investigations or security operations relating to
terrorism" and for Internet users who "post updates that praise, advocate
or incite acts of terrorism."[41]

Growing information controls on content include Internet censorship
at the ISP and national levels, and government requests to websites to
remove content. Dozens of countries now routinely filter access to websites
online. Some do so in a limited sense and on the basis of access to content,
content related to child abuse, pornography, or that which is considered
"hate speech." Many other countries, however, take a broad view of content targeted for censorship—including that which criticizes the regime in
power—and block social and political content, including media.

Restricting the type of content that appears online extends to government requests to the private social-media companies themselves. Numerous countries have requested that social media remove information or
turn over information about users, which are reflected in transparency
reports of the companies. For example, in the period from January to June
2014 (the most recent data available), Google reports that Brazil requested
to remove content from 342 requests for 1,244 items.[42] In the same period,
Turkey made 487 requests for the removal of 2,284 items.

———— ∞∞∞ ————

Digital media have empowered journalists and journalism in unprecedented ways, and have contributed to a remarkable transformation in the
journalism profession. These changes have not gone unnoticed by those
for which they present the most risk: autocratic and authoritarian regimes
and others caught in the crosshairs of independent reporting are taking
stock and developing sophisticated countermeasures. While the Snowden
disclosures have opened a window into the phenomenal extent to which

all digital communications are at risk of surveillance to governments, and journalists and others are developing safeguards, there are unintended impacts of the disclosures that muddy the waters. The disclosures have alleviated pressures on governments such as those of China and Russia, and have provided a model of how to undertake advanced computer espionage for countries just starting to develop such programs, and thus created a convenient excuse to put in place more expansive domestic-level information controls. Therefore, the risks around digital media for journalists are likely to expand in the short term.

Addressing these challenges is daunting, but there are steps that should be taken immediately:

• Media outlets can implement HTTPS encryption on their websites by default. While the costs are significant, such a basic step will do much to alleviate a certain class of risks and establish a norm for the industry.

• Journalism programs can include digital-security modules as foundational. There is a pressing need to educate entire communities as to best practices and instill a culture of security in the journalism profession from the schools to the newsrooms and beyond.

• Journalists and editors should evaluate the digital-security practices of their organizations in a comprehensive fashion. More independent and systematic research is required to evaluate existing practices and the risks to journalists around digital media in specific cases.

• Secure communications tools are necessary but not sufficient. Changes in communication practices are essential. No amount of sophisticated encryption will immunize a journalist from the full range of growing risks. Some of the growing information controls around digital media, such as laws, regulations, and practices, cannot be counteracted with tools and software. Even while some technological proficiency can help guard against targeted digital threats, behavioral changes are equally as important.

NOTES

1. Ryan Gallagher, "British Spies Are Free to Target Lawyers and Journalists," *Intercept*, November 6, 2014, https://theintercept.com/2014/11/06/uk-surveillance-of-lawyers-journalists-gchq/.

2. Mark Sherman, "Gov't Obtains Wide AP Phone Records in Probe," May 14, 2013, AP: The Big Story, http://bigstory.ap.org/article/govt-obtains-wide-ap-phone-records-probe.

3. Tom Lowenthal, "Simple Steps to Protect Journalists and Sources from Eavesdroppers," October 16, 2016, Committee to Protect Journalists, https://cpj.org/blog/2014/10/simple -steps-to-protect-journalists-and-sources-fr.php.

4. Christopher Soghoian, "When Secrets Aren't Safe with Journalists," New York Times, October 26, 2011, http://www.nytimes.com/2011/10/27/opinion/without-computer -security-sources-secrets-arent-safe-with-journalists.html?_r=3.

5. "The Citizen Lab—University of Toronto," Citizen Lab, https://citizenlab.org/.

6. "China Chats: Tracking Surveillance and Censorship in TOM-Skype and Sina UC," July 2, 2013, Citizen Lab comments, https://citizenlab.org/2013/07/china-chats/.

7. "WUP! There It Is: Privacy and Security Issues in QQ Browser," March 28, 2016, Citizen Lab, https://citizenlab.org/2016/03/privacy-security-issues-qq-browser/.

8. Andrei Soldatov, "FSB's Olympic Spying," Moscow Times, November 21, 2013, http:// www.themoscowtimes.com/opinion/article/fsbs-olympic-spying/489998.html.

9. Indu Nandakumar, "Government Can Now Snoop on Your SMSs, Online Chats," Times of India, May 7, 2013.

10. Ogala Emmanuel, "EXCLUSIVE: Elbit Systems Officials Arrive; Begin Installation of $40 Million Internet Spy Facility for Nigeria," Premium Times Nigeria," November 26, 2013, http://www.premiumtimesng.com/news/150333-exclusive-elbit-systems-officials -arrive-begin-installation-40-million-internet-spy-facility-nigeria.html.

11. "Kenya Police to Deploy Safaricom's Surveillance System to Boost Security," May 16, 2014, Homeland Security Technology, http://www.homelandsecurity-technology.com/news /newskenya-police-to-deploy-safaricoms-surveillance-system-to-boost-security-4269752.

12. "Iranian Regime Intensifies Crackdown on Internet Freedom," December 8, 2014, NCRI: National Council of Resistance of Iran, http://www.ncr-iran.org/en/news/human -rights/17648-iranian-regime-intensifies-crackdown-on-internet-freedom.

13. Morgan Maquis-Boire, Collin Anderson, Jakub Dalek, Sarah McKune, and John Scott -Railton, "Some Devices Wander by Mistake: Planet Blue Coat Redux," July 9, 2013, Citizen Lab comments, https://citizenlab.org/2013/07/planet-blue-coat-redux/.

14. Citizen Lab, "Communities @ Risk: Targeted Digital Threats Against Civil Society," https://targetedthreats.net/.

15. John Markoff, "Vast Spy System Loots Computers in 103 Countries," New York Times, March 28, 2009, http://www.nytimes.com/2009/03/29/technology/29spy.html?pagewanted=all.

16. Sophie Beach, "Targeted Malware Attack on Foreign Correspondents Based in China," China Digital Times, September 28, 2009, http://chinadigitaltimes.net/2009/09/targeted -malware-attack-on-foreign-correspondents-based-in-china/.

17. "Ethiopian Journalists Targeted with Hacking Team Spyware," February 13, 2014, Citizen Lab comments, https://citizenlab.org/2014/02/ethiopian-journalist-group-targeted-hacking -team-spyware/; "Hacking Team and the Targeting of Ethiopian Journalists," February 12, 2014, Citizen Lab comments, https://citizenlab.org/2014/02/hacking-team-targeting-ethiopian -journalists/.

18. "A Call to Harm: New Malware Attacks Target the Syrian Opposition," June 21, 2013, Citizen Lab comments, https://citizenlab.org/2013/06/a-call-to-harm/; Dave Maass, "Social Engineering and Malware in Syria: EFF and Citizen Lab's Latest Report on the Digital Battlefield," December 23, 2013, Electronic Frontier Foundation, https://www.eff.org/deeplinks/2013/12/social-engineering-and-malware-syria-eff-and-citizen-labs-latest-report-digital.

19. Philip N. Howard, "Hungary's Crackdown on the Press," New York Times, September 8, 2014, http://www.nytimes.com/2014/09/09/opinion/hungarys-crackdown-on-the-press.html?smid=tw-share.

20. "OSCE Representative Calls on Authorities in Hungary to Ensure the Safety of Journalists Covering the Refugee Crisis," September 17, 2015, Organisation for Security and Co-operation in Europe, http://www.osce.org/fom/182646.

21. "Journalists Arrested, Relatives Held Hostage in New Crackdown," February 17, 2011, Reporters Without Borders, https://rsf.org/en/news/journalists-arrested-relatives-held-hostage-new-crackdown.

22. "Practice Freedom of Speech Within Malaysian Norms," June 12, 2013, Office of the Prime Minister, http://www.pmo.gov.my/home.php?menu=newslist&news_id=11560&news_cat=13&cl=1&page=1731&sort_year=2013&sort_month=.

23. "Amid Financial Scandal, Malaysia Increases Pressure on Media," February 2016, Committee to Protect Journalists, https://cpj.org/blog/2016/02/amid-financial-scandal-malaysia-increases-pressure.php.

24. "1,000 Singaporeans Rally Against New Website Rules," Jakarta Post, June 8, 2013, http://www.thejakartapost.com/news/2013/06/08/1000-singaporeans-rally-against-new-website-rules.html.

25. Meredith Griffiths, "Singapore Jails Australian Journalist Ai Takagi for Ten Months for Sedition," March 24, 2016, ABC News, http://www.abc.net.au/news/2016-03-24/journalist-ai-takagi-sentenced-to-10-months-prison/7275938.

26. Paul Sonne, "Russia Steps Up New Law to Control Foreign Internet Companies," Wall Street Journal, September 24, 2014, http://www.wsj.com/articles/russia-steps-up-new-law-to-control-foreign-internet-companies-1411574920.

27. Robert McMillan, "Russia's Creeping Descent into Internet Censorship," Wired, December 10, 1014, http://www.wired.com/2014/12/rospotrebnadzor/.

28. Thanpol Eawsakul, "Thailand: Editor Arrested for Facebook Comments," July 8, 2014, Human Rights Watch, https://www.hrw.org/news/2014/07/08/thailand-editor-arrested-facebook-comments.

29. Todd Pittman, "Journalist Jailed 4½ Years for Posting Criticism of Thailand's King," Toronto Star, November 24, 2014," http://www.thestar.com/news.html.

30. "Southeast Asia CyberWatch," April 2, 2013, Citizen Lab comments, https://citizenlab.org/2013/04/southeast-asia-cyberwatch-march-2013/#vietnam.

31. "Newly-detained Blogger Insisted He Was 'Neither Criminal nor Reactionary,'" May 29, 2013, Reporters Without Borders, www.slyck.com/forums/viewtopic.php?f=46&t=61495&sid.

32. Casey Johnston, "Vietnamese Blogger Arrested, Blog Becomes Booby-trapped with Malware," *Arstechnica*, May 29, 2013, http://arstechnica.com/tech-policy/2013/05/vietnamese-blogger-arrested-blog-becomes-booby-trapped-with-malware/.

33. Robert Birsel, "Vietnamese Police Arrest Anti-government Blogger," June 14, 2013, Reuters, http://www.reuters.com/article/2013/06/14/us-vietnam-arrest-blogger-idUSBRE95D06P20130614.

34. "Third Blogger Arrested in Less Than a Month," June 17, 2013, Reporters Without Borders, http://en.rsf.org/vietnam-blogger-and-former-party-official-17–06–2013,44801.html.

35. Rosalind Russell, "Vietnam Detains Blogger for 'Bad' Content," November 30, 2014, Yahoo News, https://ca.news.yahoo.com/vietnam-detains-blogger-bad-content-124544090.html.

36. "Vietnamese Bloggers Imprisoned for 'Abusing Democratic Freedoms,' " March 23, 2016, Committee to Protect Journalists, https://cpj.org/2016/03/vietnamese-bloggers-imprisoned-for-abusing-democra.php.

37. "Cyber Jihadist Unit Monitors Sudan's Online Communication," December 10, 2014, Radio Dabanga, https://www.dabangasudan.org/en/all-news/article/cyber-jihadist-unit-monitors-sudan-s-online-communication.

38. "Iran Is World's Leading Jailer of Female Journalists and Netizens," July 28, 2014, Reporters Without Borders, http://en.rsf.org/iran-iran-is-world-s-leading-jailer-of-28–07–2014, 46712.html.

39. "Iran: Death Sentence for Facebook Posts," December 2, 2014, Human Rights Watch, https://www.hrw.org/news/2014/12/02/iran-death-sentence-facebook-posts.

40. Mahsa Alimardani, "In Iran, Even Bloggers Who Stay Away from Politics Can Be Arrested," *Slate*, October 2, 2015 http://www.slate.com/blogs/future_tense/2015/10/02/iranian_blogger_arash_zad_arrested_even_though_he_stayed_away_from_politics.html.

41. "Iran: Death Sentence for Facebook Posts"; Ellery Robert Biddle et al., "Netizen Report: Draft Security Law in Kenya Could Bring Surveillance, Stiff Penalties," December 10, 2014, Global Voices, http://advocacy.globalvoicesonline.org/2014/12/10/netizen-report-draft-security-law-in-kenya-could-bring-surveillance-stiff-penalties/.

42. "Brazil—Government Removal Requests," Google Transparency Report, https://www.google.com/transparencyreport/removals/government/BR/?hl=en.

18

FIBER AND OPEN COMMUNICATIONS NETWORKS

SUSAN CRAWFORD

In the fall of 2014, I taught a seminar in the Law of Surveillance at Harvard Law School and spoke and wrote about subjects stemming from my first two books, *Captive Audience* (about Comcast's power in America) and *The Responsive City* (about city use of data to improve the effectiveness of local government and the quality of life in cities).[1] I've been steeped in Snowden, surrounded by the politics of Internet access in America, and stunned by the possibilities of improved democratic processes in a high-capacity digital era. I've also spent a lot of time talking to depressed and lonely journalists as well as optimistic mayors.

So I feel uniquely qualified to assert that the ground beneath all these changing worlds—journalism, local governance, and surveillance—is about to shift in a major way. This will be a phase change, a moment of punctuated equilibrium, a difference in kind rather than one of degree. All you have to do is connect the dots.

———— ∞ ————

Today, fiber-optic networks reaching homes and businesses are ubiquitous in many countries, including South Korea, Japan, Sweden, and Norway. These networks, once installed, are "future proof": the ducts in which they're laid will last for fifty years and the fiber itself for thirty. The United States, though, for the first time in its history, has no national plan to upgrade its basic communications grid—and only 14 percent of Americans have access to a fiber Internet access product (FiOS, sold by Verizon). FiOS, in turn, is five or six times as expensive as access in other countries, and Verizon is throttling its upload capacity so as to keep users' focus on consumption of pay television—downloading. The United States is in the middle of the pack of the thirty-four OECD (Organisation for Economic Co-operation and Development) countries when it comes to fiber subscriptions as a percentage of the overall high-speed Internet access market. Even Turkey, Portugal, and Hungary are ahead of us.

In fact, the digital divide in U.S. cities remains extraordinary.[2] Fully 40 percent of houses in Detroit have no Internet access at all, whether over a mobile device or a wire. And an astonishing 56.9 percent of houses in Detroit don't have what the FCC calls "fixed broadband subscriptions" (meaning anything other than dial-up or access over mobile devices). More than 33 percent of Cleveland residents have no Internet access at all. Miami, New York City, Los Angeles, Boston, Washington, D.C., and Chicago are all on the list of radically underserved communities.[3]

Americans, by and large, haven't had much experience with fiber connections and may not know how they work. Fiber-optic networks are made up of hundreds of thin, flexible strands of pure glass. Each strand is less than one-tenth as thick as a human hair and can carry 10 million different phone calls—or any other form of information—around the world at the speed of light. The information making up those voices or online sessions or videos is carried by pulses of light coming from lasers. The particles of light, or photons, stay within each thin glass strand (within the "core" of the fiber) as they zip along. They don't leak because every strand is surrounded by cladding made up of a different form of glass that has properties that encourage the light to stay within the pure, transparent core: light travels more slowly inside that cladding, so signals inside the core tend to stay there.

Compared with radio waves, light carries tens of thousands of times more information because it is vibrating at such high frequencies. (More wobbles per second, more opportunities to add data to more wobbles.) And scientists discovered in the 1960s that if a glass-fiber core was extraordinarily pure and transparent, it could carry a million times more information in the form of light than radio waves had been able to just fifty years earlier. Photonics (the science of light) is advancing at such an extraordinary rate that engineers have not found a limit to the amount of information each glass thread can carry. As science marches on, the electronics that trigger lasers to shoot out encoded light can be swapped out when improved versions are developed; the pure glass strands, meanwhile, can stay in place for decades once installed.

It's hard for humans to imagine infinity. It's scary to do so. But think of what is happening when you are in the presence of another human being. What you're getting is full-bandwidth communication: a complete sense that you are in the same room with someone else. Fiber, similarly, is a window of glass that can provide the sight and sound of any environment in as real a way as we can experience. (Smell, taste, and feel are informational as well, and will someday be synthesized elements of online experiences.) The pixels fall away; you are there. And you aren't just passively watching. You are part of the meeting, part of the class, part of the appointment with your doctor, part of the jam session, part of whatever is making news in a community you care about, fully participating with no lag or fuzziness—as long as there is fiber running all the way between you and them. Engineers say that fiber can provide unlimited-capacity, symmetrical (equal upload to download) high-speed Internet access. Humans don't care about the buzzwords. They just feel, using fiber connections, that they can see others and be authentically seen in turn.

<hr />

Meet the most optimistic millennial around: a Swedish college student named Daniel, majoring in virtual-reality design. He's shaggy-haired and stocky, and he's holding large black goggles in his hands. He straps them carefully on my head and leads me by the elbow to sit me in a chair. We're in a classroom in a university building in Kista City, an innovation center made up of tall buildings and located just outside Stockholm. Daniel stays by my side, but I can't see him. What I'm seeing, from a great height as I look from side to side, are the rooftops and spires of a colorized town on a bright sunny day. In front of me are the tracks of a roller coaster, and I'm being gradually, creakily, pulled forward and up. From 360 degrees around me, as I turn my head, this seems real: I'm in this animated scene; I'm present. As the car reaches the top of the track, Daniel tells me to be sure to look down for the next bit. The roller coaster plunges into free fall, and my stomach is totally convinced that I'm doing the same. Daniel giggles at my alarmed reaction.

Daniel is supremely confident that he will get a very good job that involves high-resolution environments for human activities. He strikes me as a fully grounded young person, even though his calling will be virtual. He's also full of energy—he loves the Internet, he loves how much he shares with his friends and colleagues online, and he sees no difference between online and offline life. It's all the same thing to him; just different layers of existence. Daniel's confidence about his future (together with his perception that having unlimited cheap high-capacity Internet access is just like having access to clean water) is possible only because Stockholm installed fiber decades ago. He takes it for granted; he can't imagine another way of living.

Today we'd call the environments that Daniel will be building "games"—tomorrow, they could be anything from an international meeting to a band rehearsal, all taking place in different physical locations.

I was stunned by the virtual-reality experience that Daniel arranged. For me, it was like the very first time I saw a website in 1995. I distinctly remember clicking on a link to a Santa Monica beach house peopled by twenty-somethings. The site was called The Spot, and it had arresting, bold graphics. There were pictures of the housemates on the front page of this site reading, invitingly, "Click Here If You Want To Talk To Us." And I clicked. That moment in 1995 felt like the *Lion, the Witch, and the Wardrobe* to me. The back of the computer fell away. And my life was changed: I could interact.

Someday, with flexible screens that you will be able to wrap around your head, very very high resolution, and ample bandwidth stemming from ubiquitous fiber, humans won't really notice they aren't "there." Facebook's purchase of Oculus, the manufacturer of the goggles I strapped on my head that day in Stockholm, signals that they know where the world is going—in countries other than the United States that can count on cheap fiber connectivity.

———— ✿ ————

So what's the phase change I'm touting? I am talking about the process by which America finally makes the upgrade to fiber-optic Internet access. It's happening at the city level. Although public trust in the institutions of the federal government is at record low levels these days,[4] trust in local government remains strong. Mayors from either party have to shovel the streets and take care of business, and by and large they do. These days, mayors are getting fed up with the terrible state of Internet access in their cities. And—here's the final straw from a mayor's perspective—polls show that world-class Internet access is becoming a voting issue in America.[5]

So mayors are going to be working on installing alternative fiber networks. These networks will serve their interests in many ways. Only fiber has the symmetric (both upload and download) capacity they'll need to handle floods of data, and once it's in, it's good for decades; to upgrade, all they'll need to do is swap out the electronics at the ends. (Many mayors have recently joined Next Century Cities[6] to learn more about municipal fiber, and they're banding together through the Coalition for Local Internet Choice[7] to oppose state-level barriers to local networks—barriers that already exist in twenty states and need to be lifted.) And only cities have the public-interest incentives and mandate needed to ensure that everyone gets the dignity of a world-class high-capacity Internet connection. Fiber networks are like functioning street grids—they're essential to everything else the city and its citizens do, and they would never be provided at a fair price to everyone by any rational profit-seeking company unconstrained by competition or oversight.[8] I'm confident that fear of fiber will be stoked by the movie industry, which is worried about piracy;[9] the existing telecommunications incumbents, which like the private electrical trusts of a century ago have every interest in resisting competition stemming from any source; and oldsters who worry that younger generations are plagued by short attention spans, decreased ability to empathize, passive acceptance of total surveillance, and lowest-common-denominator sensationalism and "over-sharing." But someday soon, we'll be using fiber networks.

Right now, an increasing number of Americans are starting to recognize that our failure to upgrade our communications networks to fiber poses a problem for the country's future and its ability to compete on the world stage. In 2015, the merger of AT&T with DirecTV, taken together with media reports about mass protests focused on Washington over net neutrality, a symptom of consolidation in the infrastructure industry, has prompted new audiences to care about how lousy and expensive Internet access is in America. I predict that this issue will soon be at the level of presidential politics—just as the electrification of America was a central policy question in 1930s presidential campaigns.

Why do I say that this development will cause the ground to shift under journalism, governance, and surveillance? Imagine the fibered American city or town of the future. (Rural areas need to be part of this vision too.) Any piece of street furniture could become a repository of useful local information and a locus for neighborhood interaction. Any screen—on any device, wall, or statue—could be an interactive surface. Reporters could become truly local: combine fiber with the local, social instincts of Reported.ly and an easy-to-use browser-based streaming app like Rhinobird.tv (which will make it possible for a thousand witnesses to stream an event by using a common hashtag, and allow anyone to be a VJ on his or her own channel). Essentially, you'll be able to be present for anything you care about. A tweet is a snapshot; presence is different. With fiber in place, the beauty and density of life's events could be enhanced by visible electronic layering. When needed, as needed. (The business model of journalism will remain a challenge; I do think nonprofit status is not to be sneezed at.) Local ecosystems of news can spring up. If the *New York Times* is smart, it will morph into a contextual platform for these efforts as well as continue to have an authoritative voice of its own.

When it comes to governance, the fibered city and neighborhood could become much more responsive to the needs of their people. With fiber-optic lines connecting municipal buildings and the pulsing infrastructure of the city—transport, energy, water, sewage, public safety, you name it—city managers will be finally able to gather, aggregate, visualize, collaborate over, ship around among agencies, report on, and use the data they have. This will allow cities to meet the increasingly real-time expectations of their smartphone-toting citizens.

Which brings us, smoothly, to surveillance. If Edward Snowden's June 2013 disclosure that the NSA was capturing data about phone calls (but not the calls themselves) was enough to get people (temporarily) up in arms, imagine how much data-content-lifestreaming-whatever-it-will-be-called will be available when fiber is everywhere. Using its existing interpretation of its legal authorities, the NSA can gather any communication that has one foot in another country (or travels over a satellite). That's going to be a lot of data.

Not only will the NSA have to expand its real-estate holdings near Bluffdale, Utah, where it is already soaking up enormous (and secret) amounts of water to cool its existing computing facilities,[10] but we as a country will need to finally decide how much surveillance is enough. My view is that we cannot stop the collection of information and should not waste time trying. Rather, we will need to establish policies covering data access, retention, security, and transparency. Forensic capacity—to look back and see who had access to what for what reason—should be a top priority for future policy development. So, too, should clear consequences for data misuse by government employees. If we get this right, the payoffs for journalism and democracy could be enormous.

NOTES

1. Susan Crawford, *Captive Audience: The Telecom Industry and Monopoly Power in the New Gilded Age* (New Haven, Conn.: Yale University Press, 2013); Stephen Goldsmith and Susan Crawford, *The Responsive City: Engaging Communities Through Data-Smart Governance* (San Francisco: Jossey-Bass, 2014).

2. John Brodkin, "In Detroit and Other Cities, Nearly 40 Percent Go Without Internet," *Arstechnica*, November 4, 2014, http://arstechnica.com/business/2014/11/in-detroit-and -other-cities-nearly-40-percent-go-internet-free/.

3. Bill Callahan, "Redistributing the Future: America's Worst-Connected Big Cities: The Whole List," November 5, 2014, BlogSpot, http://redistributingthefuture.blogspot.com /2014/11/americas-worst-connected-big-cities_5.html.

4. Gallup, "Trust in Government," http://www.gallup.com/poll/5392/trust-government. aspx; Pew Research Center, "Public Trust in Government: 1958–2014," November 13, 2014, http://www.people-press.org/2014/11/13/public-trust-in-government/.

5. Tom Freedman, Alan Davidson, and Alexander C. Hart, "Voters Agree: A Free and Open Internet Is Crucial to Our Economic Future," *San Jose Mercury News*, December 29, 2014, http://www.mercurynews.com/opinion/ci_27222562/voters-agree-free-and-open-internet -is-crucial.

6. "Member Cities," Next Century Cities: Connecting Communities, http://nextcenturycities .org/member-cities/.

7. "Mission Statement" and "Principles," CLIC: Coalition for Local Internet Choice, http:// www.localnetchoice.org/.

8. Crawford, *Captive Audience*.

9. Joe Wolverton, "Utah Rep. Introduces Bill to Cut Off Water to the NSA Data Center," *New American*, November 23, 2014, http://www.thenewamerican.com/usnews/constitution /item/19589-utah-rep-introduces-bill-to-cut-off-water-to-the-nsa-data-center.

10. Sarah Zhang, "Leaked Slides Reveal Hollywood's Blind Google Fiber Fears," December 29, 2014, Gizmodo, http://gizmodo.com/leaked-slides-reveal-hollywoods-blind-google-fiber -fear-1676100540.

19

FREE THOUGHT, FREE MEDIA

EBEN MOGLEN

This text has been adapted from a lecture that Eben Moglen delivered at re:publica in Berlin in May 2012.

For the last thousand years, we, our mothers, and our fathers, have been struggling for freedom of thought. The basic concern was for the right to read in private and to think and speak and act on the basis of a free and uncensored will. Now we are less than two generations from the moment at which every human being will be connected to a single network in which all thoughts, plans, dreams, and actions will flow as electrical impulses in the species-wide nervous system of our hive-mind. Our generation, unique in the history of the human race, will decide how that network is organized. The fate of freedom of thought, indeed the fate of human freedom altogether, depends on how we make those decisions.

Unfortunately, we are beginning badly.

Here's the problem: we grew up to be consumers of media. That's what they taught us. Now media is consuming us. The things we read watch us read them. We are tracked, we are monitored, we are predicted by the media

Verbatim copying is allowed in any medium as long as this notice is preserved. Translations to languages other than English are allowed under the terms of CC BY-SA 4.0.

we use. The architecture of the network institutionalizes basic principles of information flow. It determines whether there is such a thing as anonymous reading. And it is determining against anonymous reading.

The right to read and the right to publish were the central subjects of our struggle for freedom of thought for most of the last half millennium. From the adoption of printing by Europeans in the fifteenth century, we began to be concerned primarily with access to printed material. The basic concern was for the right to read in private and to think and speak and act on the basis of a free and uncensored will. The primary antagonist for freedom of thought in the beginning of our struggle was the Roman Catholic Church, an institution directed at the control of thought in the European world. Its power was based in regular surveillance of the conduct and thoughts of every human being, around the censorship of all reading material, and, in the end, upon the ability to predict and to punish unorthodox thought.

The tools available for thought control in early modern Europe were poor, even by twentieth-century standards, but they worked. And for hundreds of years, our struggle primarily centered around that increasingly important first mass-manufactured article in western culture: the book. We struggled over whether we could print them, possess them, traffic in them, read them, teach from them without the permission or control of an entity empowered to punish thought.

By the end of the seventeenth century, censorship of written material in Europe had begun to break down. First in the Netherlands, then in the UK, then afterwards in waves throughout the European world. The book became an article of subversive commerce and began eating away at the control of thought. By the late eighteenth century, that struggle for the freedom of reading had begun to attack the substance of Christianity itself and the European world trembled on the brink of the first great revolution of the mind. It spoke of "Liberté, Égalité, Fraternité," but actually it meant freedom to think differently. The Ancien Régime tried unsuccessfully to initiate a war against thinking, and we moved into the next phase of the for freedom of thought, which presumed the possibility of unorthodox thinking and revolutionary action. For 200 years we struggled with the consequences of those changes.

That was then and this is now.

Now we are in a new phase in the history of the human race. We are building a single nervous system which will embrace every human mind. And we have abandoned the anonymity of reading. We didn't build the net with anonymity built in. Our network assumes that you can be tracked everywhere. And we've taken the web and we've made Facebook out of it. We put a few profit-motivated men and women in the middle of everything. That was a mistake. Now we're paying for it. We live our social lives, our private lives, in the web and we share everything with our friends, and also with our super-friend, the one who reports to anybody who makes him, who pays him, who helps him or who gives him the 100 billion dollars he desires. We are creating media that consume us, and media loves it.

The primary purpose of twenty-first-century commerce is to predict how we can be made to buy. And the thing that people most want us to buy is debt. So we are going into debt. We're getting heavier, heavier with debt, heavier with doubt, heavier with all we need we didn't know we needed until they told us we were thinking about it. Because they own the search box and we put our dreams in it. Everything we want, everything we hope, everything we'd like, everything we wish we knew about is in the search box, and they own it. We are reported everywhere, all the time.

In the twentieth century you had to build Lubyanka, you had to torture people, you had to threaten people, you had to press people to inform on their friends. In the twenty-first century, why bother? You just build social networking and everybody informs on everybody else for you. Why waste time and money having buildings full of little men who check who is in which photographs? Just tell everybody to tag their friends and Bing, you're done.

They figure us out, the machines do. Every time you make a link, you're teaching the machine. Every time you make a link about someone else, you're teaching the machine about someone else. Facebook wants to be a media company. It wants to own the web. It wants you to punch "like" buttons. "Like" buttons are terrific because they show Facebook every other webpage that you touch that has a "like" button on it. Whether you punch it or you don't, they still get a record. The record is that you read a page which had a "like" button on it and either you said yes or you said no, and either way you made data, you taught the machine.

So media want to know you better than you know yourself and we shouldn't let anybody do that. We fought for a thousand years for the internal space, the space where we read, think, reflect, and become unorthodox, inside our own minds. That's the space that everybody wants to take away.

> Tell us your dreams.
> Tell us your thoughts.
> Tell us what you hope.
> Tell us what you fear.

This is not weekly auricular confession; this is confession 24 by 7.

All thanks to the mobile robot that you carry around with you, the one that knows where you are all the time and listens to all your conversations. The one that you hope isn't reporting in at headquarters but whose behavior you can only guess about? The one that runs all that software you can't read, can't study, can't see, can't modify, and can't understand? That one. That one is taking your confession all the time. When you hold it up to your face from now on it is going to know your heartbeat. That's an Android app right now. Micro changes in the color of your face reveal your heart rate.

That's a little lie detector you're carrying around with you. Pretty soon I'll be able to sit in a classroom and watch the blood pressure of my students go up and down. In a law school classroom in the United States, that is really important information. But it is not just me of course, it's everybody, right? Because it's just data and people will have access to it. The inside of your head becomes the outside of your face, becomes the inside of your smartphone, becomes the inside of the network, becomes the front of the file at headquarters. So we need free media or we lose freedom of thought. It's that simple.

What is free media?

Media that you can read, that you can think about, that you can add to, that you can participate in without being monitored. Without being surveilled, without being reported in on. That's free media. If we don't have it, we lose freedom of thought, possibly forever.

Having free media means having a network that behaves according to the needs of the people at the edge, not according to the needs of the servers in the middle. Making free media requires a network of peers, not a network of masters and servants, not a network of clients and servers, not a network where network operators control all the packets they move. This is not simple, but it is still possible.

We need free software. That means software you can read, copy, modify, and redistribute. We need that because we need the software that runs the network to be modifiable by the people the network embraces. The tablets that you use that the late Mr. Jobs designed are made to control you. You can't change the software. It's hard even to do ordinary programming. It doesn't really matter, they're just tablets, we just use them, we're just consuming the glories of what they give us. But they're consuming you too.

We live, as the science fiction we read when we were children suggested we would, among robots. We live commensally with robots. But they don't have hands and feet, we're their hands and feet. We carry the robots around with us; they know everywhere we go, they see everything we see; everything we say they listen to and there is no first law of robotics. They hurt us every day and there is no programming to prevent it. So we need free software. Unless we control the software in the network, the network will, in the end, control us.

We need free hardware. What that means is that when we buy an electronic something, it should be ours, not someone else's. We should be free to change it, to use it our way, to assure that it is not working for anyone other than ourselves. Of course most of us will never change anything. But the fact that we can change it will keep us safe. Of course we will never be the people that they most want to surveil.

The man who will not be president of France, for sure, but who thought he would, now says that he was trapped and his political career was destroyed, not because he was accused of attempting to rape a hotel housekeeper, but because he was set up by spying inside his smartphone. Maybe he's telling the truth and maybe he isn't. But he's not wrong about the smartphone. Maybe it happened, maybe it didn't, but it will. We carry dangerous stuff around with us everywhere we go. It doesn't work for us, it works for someone else. We put up with it, we have to stop.

We need free bandwidth. That means we need network operators who are common carriers, whose only job is to move the packet from A to B. They're merely pipes, they're not allowed to get involved. It used to be that when you shipped a thing from point A to point B, if the guy in the middle opened it up and looked inside it, he was committing a crime. Not any more.

In the United States, a 2012 law gives network operators legal immunity for cooperating with illegal government spying so long as they do it "in good faith." And capitalism means never having to say you're sorry; you're always doing it in good faith. In good faith all we wanted to do was make money, your honor, let us out. Ok, you're gone.

We must have free bandwidth. We still own the electromagnetic spectrum; it still belongs to all of us. Government is a trustee, not an owner. We have to have spectrum we control, equal for everybody. Nobody's allowed to listen to anybody else, no inspecting, no checking, no record keeping. Those have to be the rules. Those have to be the rules in the same way that censorship had to go. If we don't have rules for free communication, we are re-introducing censorship, whether we know it or not.

We have very little choice now, our space has gotten smaller, our opportunity for change has gotten less. We have to have free software. We have to have free hardware. We have to have free bandwidth. Only from them can we make free media. But we have to work on media too, directly. Not intermittently, not off-hand.

We need to demand of media organizations that they obey primary ethics, a first law of media robotics: do no harm. The first rule is: "do not surveil the reader." We can't live in a world where every book reports every reader. If we are, we're living in libraries operated by the KGB. Well, amazon.com or Google Books. Or the KGB, or both, you'll never know.

The book, that wonderful printed article, that first commodity of mass capitalism, the book is dying. It's a shame, but it's dying. And the replacement is a box which either surveils the reader or it doesn't. You will remember that amazon.com decided that a book by George Orwell could not be distributed in the United States for copyright reasons. They went and erased it out of all the little amazon book reading devices where customers had "purchased" copies of the book 1984. Oh, you may have bought it, but that doesn't mean that you're allowed to read it.

That's censorship. That's book burning. That's what we all lived through in the twentieth century. We fought. We killed tens of millions of people to bring an end to a world in which the state would burn books. And then we watched as it was done again and again. And now we are preparing to allow it to be done without matches. Everywhere, any time.

We must have media ethics, and we have the power to enforce those ethics because we're still the people who pay the freight. We should not deal with people who sell surveilled books. We should not deal with people who sell surveilled music. We should not deal with movie companies that sell surveilled movies. We are going to have to refuse to buy surveillance, even as we work to free the technology from hidden surveillance, because otherwise capitalism will move as fast as possible to make our efforts at freedom irrelevant and there are children growing up who will never know what freedom means.

We must make a point of this. It will cost us a little bit. Not much, but a little bit. We will have to forgo some "experiences," and make a few sacrifices in our lives to enforce ethics on media. But that's our role. Along with making free technology, that's our role. We are the last generation capable of understanding directly what the changes are because we have lived on both sides of them and we know. We have a responsibility.

If we forget, no other forgetting will ever happen. Everything will be remembered. Everything you read, all through life, everything you listened to, everything you watched, everything you searched for. Surely we can pass along to the next generation a world freer than that. Surely we must.

What if we don't?

What will they say when they realize that we lived at the end of a thousand years of struggling for freedom of thought—at the end. When we had almost everything and we gave it away. For convenience. For social networking. Because Mr. Zuckerberg asked us to. Because we couldn't find a better way to talk to our friends. Because we loved the beautiful pretty things that felt so warm in the hand. Because we didn't really care about the future of freedom of thought. Because we considered that to be someone else's business. Because we thought it was over. Because we believed we were free. Because we didn't think there was any struggling left to do. That's why we gave it all away. Is that what we're going to tell them?

Is that really what we're going to tell our grandchildren?

Free thought requires free media. Free media requires free technology.

We require ethical treatment when we go to read, to write, to listen, and to watch. Those are the hallmarks of our politics. We need to keep those politics until we die. Because, if we don't, something else will die, something so precious that many many many of our fathers and mothers gave their lives for it. Something so precious that we understood it to define what it meant to be human. It will die if we don't keep those politics for the rest of our lives. But if we do, then all the things we struggled for, we'll get.

Because everywhere on earth, everybody will be able to read freely. Because all the Einsteins in the street will be allowed to learn. Because all the Stravinskys will become composers. Because all the Salks will become research physicians. Because humanity will be connected and every brain will be allowed to learn and no brain will be crushed for thinking wrong.

We're at the moment where we get to choose.

Whether we carry through that great revolution we've been making bit by bloody bit for a thousand years, or whether we give it away for convenience, for simplicity of talking to our friends, for speed in search, and other really important stuff.

We can win. We can be the generation of people who completed the work of building freedom of thought. We are also the generation that can lose. We can slip back into an inquisition worse than any inquisition that ever existed. It may not use as much torture, it may not be as bloody, but it will be more effective. And we mustn't mustn't let that happen. Too many people fought for us. Too many people died for us. Too many people hoped and dreamed for what we can still make possible.

We must not fail.

20

SHOULD JOURNALISM BE A
SURVEILLANCE-SAFE SPACE?

ETHAN ZUCKERMAN

It has rapidly become conventional wisdom that the documents about NSA surveillance released by Edward Snowden constitute a turning point in public dialogue about rights and privacy in a digital age. The Snowden revelations may also represent a turning point in journalism, illuminating the need for investigative journalism to be supported by robust legal protections, while also suggesting that most contemporary newsrooms are not ready to defend against sustained, aggressive, well-resourced surveillance. Journalism post-Snowden will need to become more technically savvy, more sensitive to risks to sources, and more aware of surveillance and privacy as a beat that readers wish to read about.

But in civic and political senses, it is less clear that Snowden's revelations and the accompanying reporting have been as pivotal as the former security consultant had hoped. Passage of the USA Freedom Act, which has reined in bulk collection of communications metadata and brought some much-needed transparency to the FISA (Foreign Intelligence Surveillance Act) courts is excellent news, though the reforms do little to address the NSA's massive collection of intelligence on people outside the United States and people in the United States in touch with them. And while activists and legislators have made this significant change, a major, sustained public movement against surveillance has yet to emerge. The public reaction to widespread surveillance has been, in many quarters, a resigned shrug, an acceptance that this is simply how things are on the Internet. This chapter explores the manufacture of the apathy toward normalized surveillance, and the small but significant role major journalistic outlets have played in cultivating this apathy, in the hopes of persuading journalistic leaders to take up the protection of reader privacy as part of their civic mission.

THE LEAST SURPRISING SURPRISE

Unpacking the mixed responses to the Snowden revelations might start from a simple, if somewhat contrary, observation: the government and private surveillance that Snowden and collaborators revealed was one of the world's least surprising surprises. For many years, scholars of Internet security have been split into roughly two camps regarding online surveillance: (1) those who believed that a select set of governments were practicing mass data collection online and investing significant resources in compromising specific targets; and (2) a more paranoid set, who believed that the United States was likely to be one of these governments. The most paranoid in this community consistently warned that the United States could and would use massive computational power and unclear legal frameworks to put millions of Americans and users of American Internet services under surveillance. Apparently, paranoid security professionals like Jacob Appelbaum, who saw the United States as a likely adversary even before he began working with WikiLeaks, got it right, and the rest of us got it wrong.[1]

It wasn't a surprise that governments were capable of extremely sophisticated electronic surveillance. Research conducted by groups like Citizen Lab had extensively documented the capabilities of software like FinFisher, designed to allow law-enforcement officials to target the communications of criminal suspects, but widely speculated to be used by repressive governments to surveil dissidents and political activists.[2] Widespread, sweeping surveillance of social media is a technique scholars had seen as well, with Tunisian intelligence officials intercepting user logins to Facebook so they could read the messages of thousands of users of those systems. What was surprising about the Snowden revelations was that widespread electronic surveillance was taking place in a democracy where we would expect more oversight and scrutiny. For some, the most surprising aspect was not that U.S. intelligence agencies were surveilling users of U.S. services, but that American corporations were providing those agencies with access to their systems. Again, the most paranoid had long observed that these platforms were vulnerable to discovery through subpoena or other means—those who were surprised expected that the owners of these platforms would have put up more of a fight.

In the wake of Snowden's revelations and the accompanying reporting, a set of diverse commentaries appeared with variants on the same head-line: "Why is anyone surprised?" Some were knowing pieces from intelli-gence insiders and security experts who made clear that they were aware of the government's capabilities.[3] Other commenters argued that anyone who had been watching the expansion of U.S. government security pow-ers under the Patriot Act should have anticipated precisely this sort of overreach.[4] A cynical and worldly undertone in these stories suggests that anyone who did find massive metadata collection surprising, simply hadn't been paying close enough attention or was a naïf.

The Snowden revelations were also unsurprising in a structural way. They followed an established model of how a whistleblower story unfolds in the press. As with the WikiLeaks documents revealed by Chelsea Manning, a massive collection of apparently important documents was released by a whistleblower whose character, personality, and motiva-tions became a story line in themselves. The documents themselves were intriguing but near incomprehensible, a stew of code words and acronyms that demanded deep investigation by experts, and careful interpretation and storytelling from skilled journalists. (While the Pentagon Papers as revealed by Daniel Ellsberg were an easier read than the WikiLeaks or NSA document caches, the emergence of Ellsberg as a story in and of himself and the use of the Pentagon Papers as a jumping-off point for journalistic analysis of the U.S. role in Southeast Asia suggest this model of journalistic response goes back at least forty years.)

Because the revelations were deeply uncomfortable for the U.S. and U.K. governments, these journalistic interpreters needed one of the most powerful features of the professional newsroom: a strong legal team to ensure they would be allowed to publish what they discovered. The *Guardian* documented a set of actions and threats made by the U.K. government—the detention of David Miranda, Glenn Greenwald's partner and document courier; threats of police raids and invocation of the Official Secrets Act, which led the newspaper to destroy the files containing the Snowden documents rather than give the hard drives that contained them to U.K. authorities.[5] The heavy-handed U.K. government response was a reminder that we need strong, independent journalism in a digital age, where organizations have not only the fiscal resources to invest in significant investigation but also the legal backing to make publication possible.

This reminder of the importance of the newspaper's civic role as a principled opponent of the government, when necessary, might be seen as a reassurance to the otherwise uncomfortable reminder that Snowden sought out an activist filmmaker and a highly opinionated advocacy journalist to offer his revelations, out of concern that traditional newsrooms might not pursue the story and might not have the technical chops to pursue the story carefully. While the *Guardian* and the *Washington Post* surely deserve the Pulitzer Prize for public service for their brave, careful reporting, it is also possible to see the award as the industry reassuring itself of its continued importance, and of the continued validity of a model of journalism that interprets complex stories to the general public.

For some, the biggest surprise of the Snowden revelations is that they have not led to a broad public movement against surveillance in the United States. Instead, surveillance has become an issue on which the American population seems neatly split and not on conventional party lines.[6] The neo-Libertarian Rand Paul has been a vocal advocate against surveillance,[7] while democratic leaders like Nancy Pelosi have been sharply critical of Snowden's actions.[8] It is perhaps unsurprising that a mainstream protest movement has not emerged given that neither party has embraced it as a campaign issue. The significant reforms of the USA Freedom Act, which fall far short of eliminating the cozy relationship between the intelligence and tech communities, at least as concerns non-Americans, may be as much political change as emerges from the Snowden revelations.

This slow and partial governmental response may point to the structural limits of whistle-blowing as a force for change. When whistle-blowing leads to reporting that leads to congressional investigation and pressure, or embarrasses the executive branch into action, it is a powerful tool for individuals and the press to seek change. But without strong reactions within the executive and legislative branches, substantial change may not happen without a sustained popular movement. Newspapers in the United States and the United Kingdom are traditionally more comfortable pressuring elected representatives than serving as organizers of citizen movements. It is possible that Edward Snowden had hoped that Laura Poitras and Greenwald could take a less conventional role and serve as heads of this movement, and Poitras's documentary *Citizenfour* may become the rallying point for that movement. But thus far, readers of these stories who experienced a sense of outrage have had few obvious channels for their rage. Given the paralysis of the U.S. government at legislative and executive levels, and resulting closure of paths toward citizen pressure and engagement, a recurrent twenty-first-century pattern, the legislative outcomes of the Snowden revelations are a positive surprise.

THE MODEL THAT MAKES US EXPECT SURVEILLANCE

Another possible explanation for the fact that Snowden revelations haven't generated a broad public movement is that we may simply expect to be surveilled when we interact online.[9] The dominant online business model to support content and services is one in which we trade our attention (and our data?) for content and services. This model is the response to the fact that in the mid-1990s, it was difficult to charge users for subscriptions and impossible to charge for micropayments. The advent of web banner ads as an easily implemented revenue source for pioneering web firms created a culture where advertising, rather than subscription revenue, was the default.[10] The popularity of this model trained early adopters of the web to assume that content and services would be free, subsidized by advertising.

Unfortunately, this has turned out to be fiscally challenging for publishers, as a user's attention appears to be worth significantly less online than offline. Felix Stadler used a set of back-of-the-envelope calculations to determine that Facebook captured twenty hours a month of users' attention, but that Facebook was able to yield only twenty cents per month for marketing that attention to advertisers.[11] By contrast, Don Marti calculates (using similar methods) that print newspapers capture seven hours of user attention per month, but that this attention is worth four times as much to advertisers.[12] An "attention minute" is worth ten times more on a paper publication than online, despite the fact that ads in a newspaper can't lead a viewer directly to more information or to a transaction. At present, advertisers are treating print and digital advertisements as different products: they appear willing to pay for the "brand-building" aspects of advertising offline but not online.

This "paper dollars, digital dimes" problem has led to a wave of businesses working to improve the dismal performance of online ads, most often by collecting additional information about the viewer of a particular page. Advertising networks set "cross-site cookies," which track a user's movements between websites, hoping to generate psychographic data about the viewer based on what sites she visits. Other techniques like a browser fingerprinting attempt to overcome the web's structural anonymity and identify each web browser with a unique signature determined from information that the browser leaks to the website it interacts with (screen size, fonts installed, version numbers, plug-ins, and other apparently innocuous data are combined into a profile that is difficult to disguise and highly likely to be unique).[13] Social networks like Facebook collect a wealth of personal data on users, and then complement these rich profiles with behavioral data (who we interact with, what we post about) to offer yet richer targeting data. Even with this data, Facebook ads are worth less than print ads, leading start-up companies to promise yet more invasive forms of surveillance and targeting, leading Jeff Hammerbacher, an early Facebook employee (and early defector from the company) to observe "The best minds of my generation are thinking about how to make people click ads."[14]

It is extremely difficult for most citizens to avoid this sort of surveillance. The kinds of techniques Snowden used to contact Poitras and pass documents to her is powerful enough to defeat a technique like browser fingerprinting, but is well outside the skill set of most Internet users. (Another positive outcome from the Snowden revelations is that Facebook has built changes to make its service usable by Tor users. Many other social-media sites are unusable with Tor or other strong privacy servers.) A savvy and determined user might use ad-filtering software like AdBlock

Plus (which advertises a user base of 21 million per day)[15] and an additional tool like Privacy Badger (which boasts only 150,000 installs)[16] to block third-party cookies, but these users are a tiny minority of online users. (Ghostery, a popular service to block third-party cookies, claims 20 million users,[17] while Tor has approximately 2 million daily users.)[18] Helen Nissenbaum, a philosopher of technology and privacy, suggests that this problem may be best solved by flooding sites and ad networks with bogus data, obscuring a user's searches in a wave of algorithmically generated cover traffic. (Nissenbaum's tool, Ad Nauseum, confronts the absurdities of Internet advertising head-on, blocking all ads on a web page from a user's view, while registering a click on each ad, attempting to bankrupt advertisers, who pay per click.)[19]

If we assume that users of tools like Ghostery are also blocking ads with Ad Blocker Plus, roughly 0.7 percent of Internet users are taking significant steps to protect their online privacy.

Since the vast majority of web users do not take these unusual steps to frustrate commercial surveillance, we might conclude that they either are unaware that surveillance takes place or do not feel like such surveillance is avoidable. Pew Research's Privacy Panel Survey, conducted in January 2014, suggests that the latter is much more likely than the former, as 50 percent of people who said they did not know much about government surveillance programs, and 61 percent of those who were well informed about surveillance did not see their social-network communications as secure.[20] But another dynamic may be at play as well. A leading researcher on youth behavior online, danah boyd, reports that the young people she interviews tell her they prefer ad-supported tools because they know those tools will remain free for them to use.[21] Consciously or not, these users have accepted the bargain that "if you're not paying for something, you're the product, not the customer."

This dynamic may be changing. When the nascent social network Ello advertised that it planned on building a Facebook competitor that was not based on targeted advertising, it was swamped by requests for accounts.[22] That an absence of targeting was the network's chief selling point makes clear how firmly surveillance has been established as the default. That there's not massive pressure on Facebook to offer a nonsurveillant version might suggest that although many users long for an unsurveilled Internet, they've been taught that such a thing is not possible.

WHAT DOES SURVEILLANCE DO TO US?

What's the significance of pervasive surveillance on us as individuals and citizens? This is not a new topic. Thousands of commentators have reminded us that George Orwell's *1984* anticipated a society in which a government attempted to police thought by subjecting elite citizens to continual surveillance via telescreens, which both watched and recorded citizens' behavior and broadcast images designed to combat thought-crime.[23] While Orwell's imagery resonates well almost seventy years after it was authored, the analogy is inexact at best: Orwellian surveillance is visible, confrontational, and deeply human—Winston Smith lives in constant fear of individuals who may be watching and waiting to inform on him. The surveillance that Snowden helped reveal is invisible, secret, and algorithmic. (It's also less targeted; one small consolation of surveillance in Orwell's Oceania is that it was targeted at educated elites, while the proletariat lived a life largely unobserved.)

Jeremy Bentham's design for the panopticon, as analyzed by Michel Foucault in *Discipline and Punish*, is a more apt metaphor.[24] Bentham's proposed prison design featured a central tower from which guards could look into any cell at any time.

Foucault argues that Bentham's proposed design cannot be understood as purely architectural but as part of a larger system of practices designed to transform prisoners into self-disciplining actors, a model as applicable to the factory as it was to the prison. As with prisoners watched via panopticon, Internet users are not aware whether they are being watched at any given moment, or not, and that perpetual possibility of scrutiny likely shapes how we use this tool. Consider the invention of the "private mode" offered by most Internet browsers—the implication is that the rest of our time online is anything but private, and that we'd need to choose to hide from scrutiny. (Of course, all the private mode does on most browsers is keeps sites from your browser history, helpful in avoiding scrutiny from your spouse or children, but not from advertisers tracking your movements online.) If private browsing is a special mode, the default is public mode, an interesting inversion in that what we choose to read and watch has traditionally been a carefully protected aspect of personal privacy.

Two reasons the panopticon falls short as an analogy for surveillance after Snowden: One, the builders of the Internet panopticon hadn't wanted to discipline those whom they were watching. Government surveillance becomes useless if it trains terrorists to act as if they're always being observed; commercial surveillance becomes less useful if we're aware that our online actions create a saleable profile, as we're more likely to take action to obscure or shape it. Two, the panopticon implies a single actor watching our behavior—subsequent scholars have suggested "the superpanopticon" or "the electronic panopticon" as broader terms. But the most helpful term for understanding how contemporary surveillance works is "the surveillant assemblage," a term coined by Kevin Haggerty and Richard Ericson,[25] building on the work of Gilles Deleuze and Felix Guattari.

The surveillant assemblage isn't a single system and isn't controlled by a single actor—it's what happens at the intersection of hundreds of commercial and government systems, and its power comes from collating and correlating these different pieces of information. Considering any form of surveillance in isolation gives an incomplete and inaccurate picture, because the ever-spreading, rhizomal nature of the assemblage means it's always incorporating new systems and new information.

The PRISM system, as explained in the documents released by Snowden, is a near-perfect exemplar of this rhizomal structure; systems that allowed corporations to monitor chat, e-mail, and other forms of communication became parts of the larger assemblage. It's here that the line between commercial and government surveillance blurs to the point of indistinguishability. Google had an incentive to store e-mail as plaintext due to a commercial model where it supports free e-mail by algorithmically surveilling text and targeting ads based on keywords in user e-mails; when Google came under pressure to share that information with the NSA, the systems architected to permit commercial surveillance were easily converted into the broader surveillant assemblage. Avoiding the surveillant assemblage is impractical if not functionally impossible, as Haggerty and Ericson noted: "Privacy advocates bring this point home in their facetious advice that individuals who are intent on staying anonymous should not use credit, work, vote or use the Internet." Add to that a prohibition on phone use and, given the rise of CCTV, a strict avoidance of public spaces, and then the challenge of following this advice becomes clearer. If the effect of Big Brother is to make you watch your speech carefully and plot revolution in a clandestine diary, and the effect of the panopticon is to turn you from a rebellious prisoner into a self-monitoring factory worker, the effect of the surveillant assemblage is to make you give up. Haggerty and Ericson call this "the disappearance of disappearance," the loss of the ability to be anonymous in public space.

The Internet has a long and uncomfortable history with anonymity. Early Internet boosters celebrated the idea that the Internet's anonymity would allow users to experiment with different identities,[26] or to seek out information they might be uncomfortable searching for in the physical world—think of the gay teen in a small town looking for information and support. At the same time, we've blamed the Internet's often corrosive culture on anonymity and the idea that people behave badly online because anonymous actions are consequence free. Facebook's insistence that people identify themselves by their real names online, and an attempt by Google to enforce similar rules on its Google+ social network, has led to a wave of online protest called Nymwars but has also established real-name identity as a norm for the majority of Internet users. For longtime users, the Internet has never been a wholly anonymous and private space—as early as 1992, there have been cases on apparently anonymous online speech leading to real-world legal consequences.[27] But for many of us, the possibility of searching for information anonymously was a core Internet value that has eroded in the face of Snowden's revelations.

AVOIDING (BEING PART OF) SURVEILLANCE

Instead of asking if we can avoid being surveilled, we might ask if we can avoid becoming part of the surveillant assemblage. It's a question we might ask of the newspapers responsible for publishing the Snowden revelations. Ghostery is a browser plug-in that detects "web bugs," small pieces of code that detect when a user visits a website and transmits that information to web-marketing firms that develop detailed user profiles that include information on the sites you visit. Basically, when you're loading a web page from a server, you're also loading snippets of content from other servers all around the web; an ad on a web page probably comes from a web server run by an ad network. Some of these snippets are invisible—many web pages incorporate web bugs that help Google track how many people visit your web page. Other bugs communicate information to third parties, aggregators, and brokers of information. Uncomfortably, a good place to find some of these bugs is on the websites of the *Guardian* and the *Washington Post*, on the stories where they reveal NSA revelations.[28]

Bob Sesca, who analyzed the *Guardian*'s use of web bugs on its surveillance coverage, writes at some length about a particular technology: Omniture, Adobe's web-analytics platform. Omniture has advertised that it is capable of collecting not only a user's IP address, her hardware and software configuration, and her use of other sites that have the Omniture bug but also her search history and behavior on social media. The presence of a web bug like Omniture's on the *Guardian*'s site is not an unwitting inclusion. These bugs take time to load and slow down page speed, which means that a sane webmaster would include them only because you're paid to or because you have to. In the *Guardian*'s case, their presence is likely because the publishers need detailed information on their readers to make their ads more saleable; allowing the presence of the Omniture bug on their site allows them to track where *Guardian* readers go after visiting the site, which then becomes data they can sell to their advertisers.

There's a distinction between tracking a user's path through the Internet and intercepting a person's personal communications, and here I don't mean to construct a false equivalency. I also want to recognize that newspapers face a particularly fearsome problem when it comes to paying for their investigative reporting. Newspapers want to have a widespread civic impact, which means they want, if possible, to be accessible to as many readers as possible. Approaches to revenue that reduce reach—making content accessible only by paid subscription—reduce the reach and civic impact, which means that newspapers have a particular incentive to generate revenue through targeted ads.

That said, the similarities between the systems of surveillance that enable targeted advertising and those used by intelligence officials go beyond analogy; instead, those systems have merged. An internal NSA slide-presentation deck reveals that the NSA and GHCQ use Google's "PREF" cookie, used by Google to track preferences of users of their services, to identify an individual's web-surfing behavior in large sets of data.

Google is so effective in identifying individual users in the crowd of the web that the NSA simply piggybacks on its technology. The NSA uses another Google cookie, set by the Doubleclick ad network, to "decloak" users who use Tor to disguise their IP address, determining that a Tor user with a given Doubleclick cookie is the same uncloaked user with the same cookie.[29] The very technologies used to deliver ads on newspaper stories about NSA surveillance are part of the NSA's surveillance apparatus.

If we accept that newspapers have a civic responsibility beyond their commercial responsibility, we might ask whether the *Guardian* and the *Washington Post* have a responsibility to help their readers understand commercial surveillance and its potentially corrosive effects. Given the pervasiveness of surveillance in our contemporary world, understanding surveillance should be a beat.

We could imagine the *Guardian* publishing a user guide to safely reading the *Guardian*'s coverage of NSA surveillance as a form of public service. (I've included a brief version of such a guide as an addendum to this chapter.)

SURVEILLANCE-FREE ZONES?

In a world of pervasive surveillance, it's both encouraging and strangely sad to see the emergence of spaces that are explicitly privacy respecting— the need for these spaces is almost as uncomfortable as the Orwellian "free speech zones" that have been built to accommodate the right to protest at public events. Libraries are probably the most visible of these privacy zones, as American librarians have been zealous defenders of the privacy rights of their patrons. Four Connecticut librarians fought a gag order associated with a National Security Letter demanding access to the logs of their Internet-connected computers and have become some of the most visible opponents of these gag orders.[30] The American Library Association now advises librarians on best policies for protecting user privacy, including destroying circulation records as soon as possible to keep them subpoena proof.[31] The Massachusetts ACLU is working with local libraries to install Tor on their computers to provide patrons with a surveillance-resistant ability to access the Internet.[32]

The emergence of libraries as surveillance-resistant spaces is important in both practical and symbolic terms. Even if we don't feel the need to use a Tor-enabled browser to search for health information, the commitment that librarians have made to protect privacy, even when it's expensive and inconvenient, is a reminder that civic responsibility can trump expediency. The existence of a surveillance-free space reminds us how rare these spaces are, and how much work is necessary to create and protect them.

The *Guardian*, the *Washington Post*, and journalism as a whole should be proud of the important role they have played in prompting a national debate about surveillance, privacy, and government overreach. But it is fair to ask whether these critical civic institutions, critical to make sure that we can take action as informed citizens, should find a way to escape their role as part of the surveillant assemblage and become another one of the rare, precious surveillance-resistant public spaces.

ADDENDUM: ON SAFELY READING NEWSPAPER COVERAGE OF SURVEILLANCE

It is deeply ironic that reading coverage of NSA and GCHQ surveillance on the *Washington Post* and the *Guardian* websites subjects readers to surveillance by the newspapers, by advertising networks, and perhaps by the NSA itself. It is possible to reduce the information shared with third parties while reading these stories, though technologies used to escape surveillance tend to lead to less rich user-experiences on these sites. This brief guide suggests a number of methods, in order of increasing discomfort, that one could take to preserve one's privacy while reading the fine surveillance coverage the *Washington Post* and the *Guardian* have produced.

• Don't log on. Most newspapers offer customized content for subscribers, and readers tend to remain logged into these websites to avoid reentering passwords when reading a website. This makes it very easy for a website to associate your personally identifiable subscriber information with your online behavior. Read these websites as a guest user, not one logged into the site.

- Block third-party cookies. Even if you're comfortable with a website knowing your reading behavior, you may not wish to share that behavior with the advertising companies that the website has allowed to inject third-party cookies into the web pages you access. Apple's Safari browser allows users to block third-party cookies explicitly (as well as blocking cookies entirely, which may lead to unpredictable behavior on sites that attempt to customize to your reading behavior). Firefox users can use the Privacy Badger plug-in to block third-party cookies. Clear all cookies when you finish any web-browsing session.

- Block ads. Even if you're blocking third-party cookies, you are leaving traces in the logfiles of advertisers by loading ads from their web servers. AdBlock Plus is an effective and free tool for ad blocking.

- Don't read using mobile devices. These devices are far harder to anonymize than web browsers on conventional computers, as mobile phones transmit a unique identifier to their networks when in use. This information is tracked by mobile Internet service providers and is susceptible both to subpoena requests and to NSA data aggregation. Furthermore, many mobile devices "leak" geolocation information to web servers. Ads are more valuable to advertisers if they can be targeted to a user's location, so there is an incentive for developers of apps to leak this information.

- Use Tor. Even if you aren't logged into a website and blocking cookies, you are identifying yourself through your IP address, which can sometimes be used to uniquely identify a computer and more often can be used to identify your rough geographic location. Tor routes your traffic through a set of intermediary computers using a clever scheme that makes it extremely difficult for websites to know the actual IP address of your computer. (Even more cleverly, Tor knows that you're using the system but not which sites you're visiting.) Using Tor will slow down your Internet connection, and using it in ways that successfully disguises your IP address requires you to turn off significant functionality in your web browser. (It is wise to turn off JavaScript, which will likely break many features on most modern websites.) For those more concerned about security (this is probably overkill for reading a newspaper website safely), a portable operating system called Tails allows you to reboot a computer into a configuration that is highly secured and runs all communications through Tor.

- Use public computers. If your concern is ensuring that advertisers and publishers cannot connect your online behavior and your real-world identity, one solution is to use computers that cannot be traced to your identity. Many public libraries offer computers that allow you to access the Internet without producing an ID. Your surfing behavior becomes indistinguishable from that of other users, as long as you avoid using services associated with your identity, like webmail, personalized search, and the like.

• Read the physical newspaper, preferably purchased at a newsstand where you can make your purchase, in cash, out of the view of surveillance cameras.

NOTES

1. Jacob Applebaum, "We Don't Live in a Free Country" [interview], April 20, 2012, Democracy Now, http://www.democracynow.org/2012/4/20/we_do_not_live_in_a.

2. Morgan Marquis-Boire, Bill Marczak, Claudio Guarnieri, and John Scott-Railton, "For Their Eyes Only: The Commercialization of Digital Spying," April 30, 2013, Citizen Lab, https://citizenlab.org/2013/04/for-their-eyes-only-2/.

3. Sean M. Kenner, "NSA, Snowden Revelations Not Surprising: RSA Panel," *eWeek*, February 25, 2014, http://www.eweek.com/security/nsa-snowden-revelations-not-surprising -rsa-panel.html#sthash.I5bpDxWE.dpuf.

4. Lou Kilzer, "Snowden's 'Secrets' Should Not Surprise," *Pittsburgh Tribune-Review*, August 3, 2013, https://www.highbeam.com/doc/1P2-34976317.html; Adam C. Estes, "Why Is Anyone Surprised That the Government Spies on Us?" July 6, 2013, Gizmodo, http:// gizmodo.com/why-is-anyone-surprised-that-the-government-spies-on-us-511923095; Barin Kayaoğlu, "Washington, Snowden, NSA: Learning the Right Lessons," June 27, 2013, http://www.barinkayaoglu.com/tag/nsa/.

5. Julian Borger, "NSA Files: Why the *Guardian* in London Destroyed Hard Drives of Leaked Files," *Guardian*, August 20, 2013, http://www.theguardian.com/world/2013/aug /20/nsa-snowden-files-drives-destroyed-london.

6. Pew Research Center, "Public Sees U.S. Power Declining as Support for Global Engagement Slips," December 3, 2103, http://www.people-press.org/2013/12/03/public -sees-u-s-power-declining-as-support-for-global-engagement-slips/.

7. "Rand Paul's Snowden Apologia" [editorial], *Wall Street Journal*, January 8, 2014, http:// www.wsj.com/articles/SB10001424052702303433304579304791043726948.

8. Ginger Gibson, "Pelosi: Snowden No Hero," June 30, 2013, Politico, http://www.politico .com/blogs/politico-now/2013/06/pelosi-snowden-no-hero-167385.

9. "The Public Feels Most Secure Using Landline Phones, Least Secure on Social Media," in Mary Madden et al., *Public Perceptions of Privacy and Security in the Post-Snowden Era*, November 11, 2014, Pew Research Center, http://www.pewinternet.org/2014/11/12 /public-privacy-perceptions/pi_2014-11-12_privacy-perceptions_02/.

10. Ethan Zuckerman, "The Internet's Original Sin," *Atlantic*, August 14, 2014, http://www .theatlantic.com/technology/archive/2014/08/advertising-is-the-internets-original -sin/376041/; Maceij Ceglowski, "The Internet with a Human Face" (talk delivered at "Beyond Tellerrand" Conference, May 20, 2014, Düsseldorf), idlewords.com/talks/internet _with_a_human_face.htm.

11. Felix Stalder, "Paying Users for Their Data," July 24, 2014, The Mail Archive, https://www .mail-archive.com/nettime-l@mail.kein.org/msg02721.html.

12. Don Marti, "Newspaper Dollars, Facebook Dimes," July 26, 2014, http://zgp.org/~dmarti /business/newspaper-dollars-facebook-dimes/#.V4XB25MrLeQ.

13. Ibid.

14. Ashlee Vance, "This Tech Bubble Is Different," *Bloomberg Business Week*, April 14, 2011, http://www.bloomberg.com/news/articles/2011-04-14/this-tech-bubble-is-different.

15. "Adblock Plus Usage Statistics," Adblock Plus, https://addons.mozilla.org/en-US/firefox /addon/adblock-plus/statistics/?last=30.

16. Zach Miners, "EFF's Snoop-stopping, Ad-smashing Privacy Badger Plugin Hits Beta," *PCWorld*, July 21, 2014, http://www.pcworld.com/article/2456500/eff-releases-chrome -firefox-plugin-to-block-thirdparty-tracking.html.

17. Ibid.

18. "Tor Metrics—Users," Tor Project, December 2014, https://metrics.torproject.org/users .html.

19. Ethan Zuckerman, "Helen Nissenbaum on Ad Nauseum, Resistance Through Obfusca- tion, and Weapons of the Weak," October 6, 2014, . . . My Heart's in Accra, http://www .ethanzuckerman.com/blog/2014/10/06/helen-nissenbaum-on-ad-nauseum-resistance -through-obfuscation-and-weapons-of-the-weak/.

20. Madden et al., *Public Perceptions of Privacy and Security in the Post-Snowden Era*, Pew Research Center, http://www.pewinternet.org/files/2014/11/PI_PublicPerceptionsofPrivacy _111214.pdf.

21. danah boyd, "Why Youth (Heart) Social Network Sites: The Role of Networked Publics in Teenage Social Life," in *MacArthur Foundation Series on Digital Learning: Youth, Identity, and Digital Media*, ed. David Buckingham (Cambridge, Mass.: MIT Press, 2007), 119–42.

22. Mike Isaac, "For Some Tech Start-Ups Like Ello, Exclusivity Draws Demand," *New York Times*, September 26, 2014, http://bits.blogs.nytimes.com/2014/09/26/for-some-tech-start -ups-like-ello-exclusivity-draws-demand/?_r=0.

23. George Orwell, *Animal Farm and 1984* (New York: Houghton Mifflin Harcourt, 2003).

24. Michel Foucault, *Discipline and Punish: The Birth of the Prison*, trans. Alan Sheridan (New York: Random House, 1977).

25. Kevin D. Haggerty and Richard V. Ericson, "The Surveillant Assemblage," *British Journal of Sociology* 51, no. 4 (2000): 605–22.

26. Sherry Turkle, *Life on the Screen: Identity in the Age of the Internet* (New York: Simon and Schuster, 2011).

27. "Campus Journal; an Anarchist, a Threat to Bush and the Spotlight," *New York Times*, June 9, 1992, http://www.nytimes.com/1992/06/10/news/campus-journal-an-anarchist -a-threat-to-bush-and-the-spotlight.html.

28. Bob Cesca, "How the *Guardian* Is Quietly and Repeatedly Spying on You," *Daily Banter*, September 9, 2013, http://thedailybanter.com/2013/09/how-the-guardian-is-quietly -and-repeatedly-spying-on-you/.

29. Ashkan Soltani, Andrea Peterson, and Barton Gellman, "NSA Uses Google Cookies to Pinpoint Targets for Hacking," *Washington Post*, December 10, 2013, https://www .washingtonpost.com/news/the-switch/wp/2013/12/10/nsa-uses-google-cookies-to -pinpoint-targets-for-hacking/.

30. Andrea Peterson, "Librarians Won't Stay Quiet About Government Surveillance," *Washington Post*, October 3, 2014, https://www.washingtonpost.com/news/the-switch /wp/2014/10/03/librarians-wont-stay-quiet-about-government-surveillance/.

31. Cory Doctorow, "How to Foil NSA Sabotage: Use a Dead Man's Swith," *Guardian*, September 9, 2013.

32. Jessamyn West, "The FBI, and Whether They've Been Here or Not," September 9, 2013, librarian.net, http://www.librarian.net/stax/4182/the-fbi-and-whether-theyve-been-here -or-not/.

POSTSCRIPT

Journalism After Snowden

JONATHAN ZITTRAIN

n many countries journalists report independently at their peril: speaking truth about power runs the risk of retaliation from criminals or state officials—and at times it can be hard to distinguish between the two.

In countries with a commitment to the rule of law, journalists have much less to fear over their livelihoods or physical safety, notwithstanding the astonishing specter of three senior staff members of the *Guardian* who were compelled to smash their own computers containing leaked documents under the watchful eyes of officials from one of the United Kingdom's intelligence agencies. That theater illustrates more the futility of government intervention than its effectiveness—the documents had already been replicated to ProPublica and the *New York Times*. In the years since, the *Guardian* editors have been publicly venerated—not jailed.

There has been a more insidious, less lurid threat to independent journalism in such countries: a withering away of public respect for professional journalists and traditional media, which in its best moments aspired to values other than simply what garnered the most clicks. Of course, we should not rue the disappearance of consolidated mass media

Verbatim copying is allowed in any medium as long as this notice is preserved. Translations to languages other than English are allowed under the terms of CC BY-SA 4.0.

and its oracular voice. And if anything, such consolidation may be returning: companies like Facebook are playing to become the new global newsstands, not only hosting others' material but indexing and directing traffic to it—when they feel so moved.

In the lead-up to the computer-smashing incident, the *Guardian* had offered to work with the British government to help secure the files that Edward Snowden leaked against further compromise, while its editors reviewed them for journalistic value in the public interest. The government should have taken up the offer. And it is not too late for some of the inevitable leaks to come. Post-Snowden, governments should be ready to deal with leaks and leakers in ways currently off-limits, drawn from how they negotiate with mainstream newspapers when stories grounded in classified information were slated for publication. Imagine if the U.S. government had offered Edward Snowden a secure server on which to place his files, with a genuine promise to maintain access for some agreed-upon journalists, despite the government's straightforward view that the files were illegally compromised. In turn, Snowden would endeavor to delete all other copies, and the journalists would agree to a process for listening to and evaluating the government's case for why particular draft stories drawn from the documents would unduly hurt public safety. Ultimately the journalists would bear responsibility for deciding what to do.

Such an arrangement recognizes that role assignment is one of the best ways for a system to self-balance. It's why a person who is a successful prosecutor or defense attorney may act quite differently once becoming a judge, or an elected official, or the head of an agency. When we ask people to inhabit too many roles at once, to perform balancing within their own minds or as part of small groups with common incentives, sensitive decisions will not be made well. Meaningful participation by elected legislators in surveillance policy is important, along with searching judicial review. But perhaps it is not enough without also having a responsible, independent media in the frame.

In a democracy, a government program that cannot be successfully publicly defended—whether because it is ethically wrong, or contrary to the rule of law, or simply because it is out of step with what an informed citizenry would want—should not persist simply thanks to secrecy. The longer the truth takes to get out, the greater the likelihood of haphazard and ill-contextualized leaks about it, and the higher the cost of accounting for it, once people do know. Policies and practices in the earnest pursuit of security, which understandably begin in urgency after an attack or a compromise, should be disclosed by governments in general terms soon after—indeed, not even waiting for a freedom of information request. The specter of an elected representative taking to the well of the Senate to say, "If you only knew what I did, you would disapprove greatly," while unable ethically to begin a discussion with his colleagues at large or the general public about what troubled him, is a strong signal that the system before Snowden had become too insular, with no escape valve for when prudential and ethical, if not legal, lines had been crossed.

We urgently need to buttress our independent media around the world, including those outlets and individuals not affiliated with large news organizations but who embrace journalistic values. These organizations and people must be able to work without intimidation, and without blanket surveillance. Surely some of the tactics described in this book for operational security by the media are helpful. But they are also actions that over time generate reactions of more intensive and intrusive surveillance. Ultimately, technological maneuvers are no substitute for strong (if arm's-length) respect and understanding between governments and journalists of their respective roles. The enemies of freedom and security shared by journalists and democratic governments alike are those regimes that do not even aspire to cultivate the rule of law, and that may end up inheriting or reinventing the tools and practices of surveillance honed and defended elsewhere. In any event, intense secrecy punctuated by indiscriminate *Exxon Valdez*-size leaks is the worst of both worlds.

Any postscript to this thoughtful volume is, given how quickly circumstances are changing, really a foreword to what will come next. These essays show how reasonable people, inhabiting their roles across the spectrum, will disagree on the specifics while agreeing through the fact of their contributions that the right to express oneself through speech, writing, and journalism is essential. Discourse—persuasion based on facts and rigorous back-and-forth, rather than the raw exercise of power—remains civilization's most precious, if at times elusive, coin.

CONTRIBUTORS

Jill Abramson is a journalist who spent seventeen years in the most senior editorial positions at the *New York Times*, where she was the first woman to serve as Washington bureau chief, managing editor, and executive editor. In those positions, she was responsible for national security and intelligence stories, and dealt with senior government officials on various issues concerning news coverage.

Before joining the *Times*, she was deputy Washington bureau chief and an investigative reporter covering money and politics at the *Wall Street Journal* for nine years. She was the editor of *Legal Times* in Washington, D.C. She is the author of three books, including *Strange Justice: The Selling of Clarence Thomas* (Houghton Mifflin, 1994), which she wrote with Jane Mayer. She is currently working on a book about news and writing a political column for the *Guardian*.

Before joining Harvard's English department as a lecturer teaching nonfiction narrative writing and journalism in 2014, she taught undergraduate writing seminars at Yale for five years and at Princeton. Abramson is a member of the American Academy of Arts and Sciences and the American Philosophical Society. She is on the advisory boards of the Columbia University School of Journalism, ProPublica, and the Knight-Wallace Foundation. She is a 1976 graduate of Harvard. She grew up in New York City, is married, and has two children.

———— ∞∞∞ ————

Julia Angwin is a senior reporter at ProPublica. From 2000 to 2013, she was a reporter at the *Wall Street Journal*, where she led a privacy investigative team that was a finalist for a Pulitzer Prize in Explanatory Reporting in 2011 and won a Gerald Loeb Award in 2010. Her book *Dragnet Nation: A Quest for Privacy, Security and Freedom in a World of Relentless Surveillance* (Times Books, 2014) was shortlisted for Best Business Book of the Year by the *Financial Times*.

Also in 2014, Angwin was named reporter of the year by the Newswomen's Club of New York. In 2003, she was on a team of reporters at the *Wall Street Journal* that was awarded the Pulitzer Prize in Explanatory Reporting for coverage of corporate corruption. She is also the author of *Stealing MySpace: The Battle to Control the Most Popular Website in America* (Random House, 2009). She earned a B.A. in mathematics from the University of Chicago and an M.B.A. from the Graduate School of Business at Columbia University.

———— ∞∞∞ ————

Valerie Belair-Gagnon is assistant professor of journalism studies at the School of Journalism and Mass Communication at the University of Minnesota. She is also an affiliated fellow at the Yale Information Society Project. Her work intersects media sociology, news production, and emerging media. Her first monograph, *Social Media at BBC News: The Re-Making of Crisis Reporting*, Routledge Research in Journalism (Routledge, 2015), looks at how the BBC covered a series of international crises and how a major global media organization integrated social media into its international news reporting. Before joining the University of Minnesota, Belair-Gagnon was executive director and research scholar at the Yale Information Society Project and research fellow at the Tow Center for Digital Journalism.

———— ∞∞∞ ————

Steven G. Bradbury is a litigation partner at a Washington law firm. During the George W. Bush administration, he was the head of the Office of

Legal Counsel in the Department of Justice, where he served from 2004 until 2009. While at OLC, Bradbury advised the White House, the attorney general, and the heads of executive departments and agencies on a full range of matters involving the exercise of the president's constitutional and statutory authorities, including appointment authorities, statutory enforcement discretion, war powers, and issues arising in the areas of national security and foreign affairs, among other issues. Bradbury served as a law clerk to Justice Clarence Thomas on the Supreme Court and to Judge James Buckley on the D.C. Circuit. He is a graduate of the University of Michigan Law School and Stanford University.

Steve Coll, dean of the Graduate School of Journalism at Columbia University, is a staff writer at the *New Yorker*, the author of seven books of nonfiction, and a two-time winner of the Pulitzer Prize. Between 1985 and 2005, he was a reporter, foreign correspondent, and senior editor at the *Washington Post*. There he covered Wall Street, served as the paper's South Asia correspondent, and was the *Post*'s first international investigative correspondent, based in London. Over the years, he has won the Gerald R. Loeb Award for his business coverage, the Livingston Award for his work from India and Pakistan, and the Robert F. Kennedy Award for his coverage of the civil war in Sierra Leone. He served as managing editor of the *Post* between 1998 and 2004. The following year, he joined the *New Yorker*, where he has written on international politics, American politics and national security, intelligence controversies, and the media.

Susan Crawford is a professor at Harvard Law School and a co-director of the Berkman Klein Center. She is the author of *Captive Audience: The Telecom Industry and Monopoly Power in the New Gilded Age* (Yale University Press, 2013), a coauthor of *The Responsive City: Engaging Communities Through Data-Smart Governance* (Jossey-Bass, 2014), and a contributor to Medium.com's Backchannel. She served as Special Assistant to the President for Science, Technology, and Innovation Policy (2009) and co-led the FCC transition team between the Bush and Obama administrations.

She also served as a member of Mayor Michael Bloomberg's Advisory Council on Technology and Innovation and is now a member of Mayor Bill de Blasio's Broadband Task Force. Crawford was formerly a (Visiting) Stanton Professor of the First Amendment at Harvard's Kennedy School, a visiting professor at Harvard Law School, and a professor at the University of Michigan Law School (2008–2010). As an academic, she teaches Internet law and communications law. She was a member of the board of directors of the Internet Corporation for Assigned Names and Numbers (ICANN) from 2005 to 2008 and is the founder of OneWebDay, a global Earth Day for the Internet that takes place each September 22. Crawford received her B.A. and J.D. from Yale University. She served as a clerk for Judge Raymond J. Dearie of the U.S. District Court for the Eastern District of New York, and was a partner at Wilmer, Cutler & Pickering (now WilmerHale), in Washington, D.C., until the end of 2002, when she left that firm to enter the legal academy.

Ron Deibert is professor of political science and director of the Citizen Lab at the Munk School of Global Affairs, University of Toronto. The Citizen Lab undertakes interdisciplinary research at the intersection of global security, information and communications technologies (ICTs), and human rights. He is a founder and former principal investigator of the OpenNet Initiative (2003–2014) and a founder of Psiphon, a world leader in providing open access to the Internet. Deibert is the author of *Black Code: Surveillance, Privacy, and the Dark Side of the Internet* (Random House, 2013), as well as numerous books, chapters, and articles on Internet censorship, surveillance, and cyber security. He was one of the authors of the landmark reports "Tracking Ghostnet: Investigating a Cyber Espionage Network" (2009) and "Great Cannon" (2015), and co-editor of three major volumes with MIT Press on information controls (the Access series). He is on the steering committee for the World Movement for Democracy; on the board of advisers for Pen Canada, Access, and Privacy International; and in the technical advisory groups for Amnesty International and Human Rights Watch. He is co-chair of the University of Toronto's Information Security Council. In 2013, he was appointed to the Order of Ontario and awarded the Queen Elizabeth II Diamond Jubilee

Medal, for being "among the first to recognize and take measures to mitigate growing threats to communications rights, openness and security worldwide."

———⊶⊷———

Siobhan Gorman is a director in the Washington, D.C., office of the Brunswick Group, where she focuses on the Cybersecurity and Privacy Practice. She specializes in breach preparedness, breach crisis response, and thought leadership initiatives in the cybersecurity arena. She has worked on confidential cybersecurity breaches, as well as preparedness projects in the airline, automotive, and retail sectors. She has also worked on public affairs and reputational projects in the financial sector. Prior to joining Brunswick, she spent seventeen years as a reporter, most recently at the *Wall Street Journal*, where she covered surveillance, cybersecurity, data and privacy issues, terrorism, counterterrorism, and intelligence issues spanning across the seventeen spy agencies. Before joining the *Wall Street Journal* in 2007, Gorman was a Washington correspondent for the *Baltimore Sun*, covering intelligence and security. From 1998 to 2005, she was a staff correspondent for *National Journal*, covering similar issues. Gorman won the 2006 Sigma Delta Chi Award for Washington Correspondence for her coverage of the National Security Agency and in 2000 received a special citation in national magazine writing from the Education Writers Association. She is a graduate of Dartmouth College.

———⊶⊷———

Glenn Greenwald is the author of several best sellers, including *How Would a Patriot Act? Defending American Values from a President Run Amok* (Working Assets, 2006) and *With Liberty and Justice for Some: How the Law Is Used to Destroy Equality and Protect the Powerful* (Holt, 2011). His most recent book is *No Place to Hide: Edward Snowden, the NSA, and the U.S. Surveillance State* (Holt, 2014). Acclaimed as one of the twenty-five most influential political commentators by the *Atlantic*, one of America's top-ten opinion writers by *Newsweek*, and one of the Top 100 Global Thinkers for 2013 *by Foreign Policy*, Greenwald is a former constitutional law and civil rights litigator. He was a columnist for the *Guardian* until October 2013 and is now a founding editor of a new media outlet, the *Intercept*. He is a frequent guest on CNN, MSNBC, and various other television and radio outlets. He has won numerous awards for his NSA reporting, including the 2013 George Polk Award for national security reporting, the top 2013 investigative journalism award from the Online News Association, the Esso Award for Excellence in Reporting (the Brazilian equivalent of the Pulitzer Prize), and the 2013 Pioneer Award from the Electronic Frontier Foundation. He also received the first annual I. F. Stone Award for Independent Journalism in 2009, and a 2010 Online Journalism Award for his investigative work on the arrest and detention of Chelsea Manning. In 2013, Greenwald led the *Guardian* reporting that was awarded the Pulitzer Prize for public service.

Eben Moglen began building software as a professional programmer at age thirteen. He worked as a designer of advanced computer-programming languages at IBM from 1979 to 1985. In 1991, he represented Philip Zimmerman, the developer of PGP (Pretty Good Privacy), threatened with prosecution by the U.S. government for having made strong encryption-free software that everyone could use. In 1993, he joined forces with Richard M. Stallman to provide world-class legal representation and expertise to the free-software movement. With Stallman, he conceived, wrote, and created a public process for discussion and adoption of GPLv3, the current version of the world's most widely used free-software license.

In addition to his work with free-software developers, Moglen has advised major IT companies and national governments around the world. In 2010, he testified before the European Commission on the FOSS consequences of Oracle Corporation's acquisition of Sun Microsystems, and before the U.S. Congress on Internet privacy and consumer protection. He has appeared numerous times on software- and privacy-related issues as amicus curiae before the U.S. Supreme Court.

Moglen earned his Ph.D. in history and his J.D. at Yale University. After law school, he clerked for Judge Edward Weinfeld of the U.S. District Court for the Southern District of New York and for Justice Thurgood Marshall of the U.S. Supreme Court. He has taught at Columbia Law School since 1987 and has held visiting appointments at Harvard University, Tel Aviv

University, and the University of Virginia. In 2003, he was given the Electronic Frontier Foundation's Pioneer Award for efforts on behalf of freedom in the electronic society. Moglen is admitted to practice in the state of New York and before the U.S. Supreme Court.

Alan Rusbridger was editor of the *Guardian* for more than twenty years. He was editor in chief of Guardian News and Media, a member of the GNM and Guardian Media Group boards, and a member of the Scott Trust, which owns the *Guardian* and the *Observer*. He stepped down as editor in the summer of 2015. In October 2015, he became principal of Lady Margaret Hall, at the University of Oxford.

Rusbridger's career began on the *Cambridge Evening News*, where he trained as a reporter before first joining the *Guardian* in 1979. He worked as a general reporter, feature writer, and diary columnist before leaving to succeed Clive James and Julian Barnes as the *Observer*'s television critic.

Born in Zambia, he graduated from Cambridge University with a degree in English in 1976. He has been a visiting fellow at Nuffield College, Oxford, and is a visiting professor of history at Queen Mary's College, London, and at Cardiff University. He has honorary doctorates from Lincoln, Oslo, and Kingston Universities.

David E. Sanger is chief Washington correspondent of the *New York Times*. He has reported from New York, Tokyo, and Washington, covering a wide variety of issues surrounding foreign policy, globalization, nuclear proliferation, and Asian affairs. Twice he has been a member of *Times* reporting teams that won the Pulitzer Prize. In 2011, Sanger was part of a team that was a Pulitzer Prize finalist for International Reporting for its coverage of the tsunami and nuclear disaster in Japan.

Before covering the White House, Sanger specialized in the confluence of economic and foreign policy, and wrote extensively on how issues of national wealth and competitiveness have come to redefine the relationships between the United States and its major allies. As a correspondent and then bureau chief in Tokyo for six years, he covered Japan's rise as the world's second largest economic power, and then its humbling recession. He also filed frequently from Southeast Asia and wrote many of the first stories about North Korea's secret nuclear weapons program in the 1990s. He continues to cover proliferation issues from Washington, D.C.

⎯⎯⎯ ✪ ⎯⎯⎯

David A. Schulz is a clinical lecturer, senior research fellow, and codirector of the Media Freedom and Information Access Clinic at Yale Law School, and a partner in Levine Sullivan Koch & Schulz, where he represents journalists and news organizations in their newsgathering and content-related litigation. Among other significant matters, Schulz has argued precedent-setting cases establishing the constitutional right of access to jury-selection procedures, pretrial motions, and court dockets; has defended journalists' right to protect their confidential sources in federal leak investigations; and has advised on publication of classified documents leaked by Edward Snowden. Schulz was an adjunct several years at Columbia law School and regularly writes and speaks on First Amendment and media law issues. For many years, he chaired the biennial conference "Newsgathering and Libel Litigation," sponsored by the Practising Law Institute, and served as a charter member of the Sedona Conference Working Group on Protective Orders, Confidentiality, and Public Access. Schulz is a public member of the New York Committee on Open Government.

⎯⎯⎯ ✪ ⎯⎯⎯

Clay Shirky holds a joint appointment at New York University, as an associate arts professor in the Interactive Telecommunications Program (ITP) and as an associate professor in the Arthur L. Carter Journalism Institute. He is also a fellow at the Berkman Klein Center for Internet and Society, and was the Edward R. Murrow Visiting Lecturer at Harvard's Joan Shorenstein Center on the Press, Politics, and Public Policy in 2010.

⎯⎯⎯ ✪ ⎯⎯⎯

Edward Snowden is a former intelligence officer who served the CIA, NSA, and DIA for nearly a decade as a subject-matter expert on technology and cybersecurity. In 2013, he revealed the scope of NSA surveillance globally by providing classified NSA documents to journalists Glenn Greenwald, Laura Poitras, Barton Gellman, and Ewen MacAskill. He has been exiled in Russia since July 2013.

———— ∞ ————

Cass R. Sunstein is the Robert Walmsley University Professor at Harvard Law School. He clerked for Justice Benjamin Kaplan of the Massachusetts Supreme Judicial Court and Justice Thurgood Marshall of the U.S. Supreme Court. He worked as an attorney-adviser in the Office of the Legal Counsel of the U.S. Department of Justice and was a faculty member at the University of Chicago Law School from 1981 to 2008. From 2009 to 2012, he served as administrator of the White House Office of Information and Regulatory Affairs. From 2013 to 2014, he served on the President's Review Group on Intelligence and Communications Technologies.

Sunstein is the author of hundreds of articles and dozens of books, including *Republic.com* (Princeton University Press, 2001) and *Simpler: The Future of Government* (Simon & Schuster, 2013), and the coauthor, with Richard H. Thaler, of *Nudge: Improving Decisions About Health, Wealth, and Happiness* (Yale University Press, 2008). His latest books are *The World According to Star Wars* (Dey Street, 2016) and *The Ethics of Influence: Government in the Age of Behavioral Science* (Cambridge University Press, 2016).

Sunstein received his B.A. from Harvard College in 1975 and his J.D. from Harvard Law School in 1978

———— ∞ ————

Nabiha Syed is the assistant general counsel at BuzzFeed in New York. Prior to BuzzFeed, Syed helped launch the emerging technology practice at Levine Sullivan Koch & Schulz, a leading First Amendment law firm, and was named the First Amendment Fellow at the *New York Times*. She has worked on legal access issues at Guantanamo Bay, Cuba; advocated for women's rights in Pakistan; counseled on the publication of hacked and leaked materials; and advised documentary filmmakers through the Sundance Institute Documentary Film Program. She is the cofounder of

Drone U and the Media Freedom and Information Access legal clinic at Yale Law School. Syed is a graduate of Johns Hopkins University, Yale Law School, and Oxford University, which she attended as a Marshall Scholar. She serves as a nonresident fellow at both Stanford Law School and Yale Law School.

⸻ ⟨∞⟩ ⸻

Trevor Timm is a cofounder and the executive director of the Freedom of the Press Foundation. He is a journalist, an activist, and a lawyer who writes a twice-weekly column for the *Guardian* on privacy, free speech, and national security. He has contributed to the *Atlantic*, Al Jazeera, *Foreign Policy*, *Harvard Law and Policy Review*, and Politico. He formerly worked at the Electronic Frontier Foundation.

In 2013, he received the Hugh Hefner First Amendment Award for journalism. In 2016, he was named a TED Fellow.

⸻ ⟨∞⟩ ⸻

Patrick Weil is a visiting professor of law, Oscar M. Ruebhausen Distinguished Senior Fellow, and a senior research scholar in law at Yale Law School, and a senior research fellow at the French National Research Center in the University of Paris 1, Panthéon-Sorbonne. His work focuses on comparative citizenship, immigration, and church–state law and policy. His most recent book in English is *The Sovereign Citizen: Denaturalization and the Origins of the American Republic* (Penn Press, 2013). Among his other recent publications are "Can a Citizen Be Sovereign?" *Humanity Journal* 8, no. 1 (2016), http://humanityjournal.org/blog/can-a-citizen-be-sovereign/; "Citizenship, Passports, and the Legal Identity of Americans: Edward Snowden and Others Have a Case in the Courts," *Yale Law Journal Forum* 123 (2014): 565; "Headscarf versus Burqa: Two French Bans with Different Meanings," in *Constitutional Secularism in an Age of Religious Revival*, ed. Susanna Mancini and Michel Rosenfeld (Oxford University Press, 2014); and "From Conditional to Secured and Sovereign: The New Strategic Link Between the Citizen and the Nation-State in a Globalized World," *International Journal of Constitutional Law* 9, nos. 3–4 (2011): 615–35.

Jonathan Zittrain is the George Bemis Professor of International Law at Harvard Law School and the Kennedy School of Government at Harvard, professor of computer science at the Harvard School of Engineering and Applied Sciences, and cofounder and faculty director of the Berkman Klein Center for Internet and Society. He is a member of the board of directors of the Electronic Frontier Foundation and contributes to the advisory board of the National Security Agency. His book *The Future of the Internet and How to Stop It* (Yale University Press, 2008) predicted the end of general-purpose client computing and the corresponding rise of new gatekeepers. That and other works may be found at http://www.jz.org.

Ethan Zuckerman is director of the Center for Civic Media at MIT and a principal research scientist at MIT's Media Lab. He is the author of *Rewire: Digital Cosmopolitans in the Age of Connection* (Norton, 2013). With Rebecca MacKinnon, Zuckerman cofounded the international blogging community Global Voices. Global Voices showcases news and opinions from citizen media in over 150 nations and 30 languages. His research focuses on issues of Internet freedom, civic engagement through digital tools, and international connections through media. He blogs at http://ethanzuckerman.com/blog and lives in the Berkshire Mountains of western Massachusetts.

EDITORS

Emily Bell is founding director of the Tow Center for Digital Journalism at Columbia's Graduate School of Journalism and a leading thinker, commentator, and strategist on digital journalism. Established in 2010, the Tow Center has rapidly built an international reputation for research into the intersection of technology and journalism. The majority of Bell's career was spent at Guardian News and Media in London, working as an award-winning writer and editor both in print and online.

As editor-in-chief across *Guardian* websites and director of digital content for Guardian News and Media, Bell led the web team in pioneering live blogging, multimedia formats, data, and social media, making the *Guardian* a recognized pioneer in the field. She is a coauthor, with C. W. Anderson and Clay Shirky, of "Post Industrial Journalism: Adapting to the Present" (2012). Bell is a trustee on the board of the Scott Trust, the owner of the *Guardian*; a member of the *Columbia Journalism Review*'s board of overseers; and an adviser to Tamedia Group in Switzerland. She has served as chair of the World Economic Forum's Global Advisory Council on social media and as a member of Poynter's National Advisory Board. She delivered the Reuters Memorial Lecture in 2014 and the Hugh Cudlipp Lecture in 2015, and was the 2016 Humanitas Visiting Professor in Media at the University of Cambridge. She lives in New York City with her husband and children.

—⊗⊗⊗—

Taylor Owen is assistant professor of digital media and global affairs at the University of British Columbia, a senior fellow at the Columbia Journalism School, and the founder and editor of OpenCanada.org. He was previously the research director of the Tow Center for Digital Journalism at Columbia University, where he led a research program studying the impact of digital technology on the practice of journalism, and has held research positions at Yale University, The London School of Economics, and the International Peace Research Institute, Oslo where his work focused on the intersection between information technology and international affairs. His doctorate is from the University of Oxford, where he was a Trudeau Scholar. He has held Banting Postdoctoral and Action Canada fellowships and currently serves on the board of directors of the Center for International Governance Innovation (CIGI). He is the author, most recently, of *Disruptive Power: The Crisis of the State in the Digital Age* (Oxford University Press, 2015) and, with Roland Paris, of *The World Won't Wait: Why Canada Needs to Rethink Its Foreign Policies* (University of Toronto Press, 2015). His work can be found at www.taylorowen.com and @taylor_owen.

—⊗⊗⊗—

Smitha Khorana is a journalist and fellow at the Tow Center for Digital Journalism at Columbia Journalism School, where she works on research at the intersection of journalism and technology. She has contributed to the *Guardian*, the *Intercept*, BuzzFeed, and *Columbia Journalism Review*. She was a Fulbright Scholar to India, where she conducted research on Indian Muslim youth, human rights, and democratic participation. She briefly attended the Mount Sinai School of Medicine, where she was an M.D. candidate. Khorana is a graduate of Brown University.

Jennifer R. Henrichsen joined the Reporters Committee for Freedom of the Press in January 2015 as the organization's' first technology fellow. The fellowship is supported by a grant from First Look Media to assist the Reporters Committee in developing a strategic approach to addressing technology issues related to press freedom. As the First Look Media Technology Fellow, Henrichsen serves as an adviser and a researcher on issues including digital security, government surveillance, and the future of media.

Prior to joining the Reporters Committee, Henrichsen was research and program coordinator for Journalism After Snowden and a research fellow at Columbia University's Tow Center for Digital Journalism. She has been a consultant to UNESCO, where she carried out a research project about digital-security issues facing journalists, and has worked as a strategic-communications consultant at Hattaway Communications in Washington, D.C., and as a research assistant at the Open Society Foundations.

A Fulbright Research Scholar, Henrichsen was awarded a B.A. with honors from Pacific Lutheran University and a master of advanced studies in international and European security with honors from the University of Geneva and the Geneva Center for Security Policy. She is a coauthor of *War on Words: Who Should Protect Journalists?* (Praeger, 2011).

INDEX